The Land of Lost Content

The Land of
Lost Content

*Children and Childhood
in Nineteenth-Century
French Literature*

ROSEMARY LLOYD

CLARENDON PRESS · OXFORD
1992

Oxford University Press, Walton Street OX2 6DP
Oxford New York Toronto
Delhi Bombay Calcutta Madras Karachi
Petaling Jaya Singapore Hong Kong Tokyo
Nairobi Dar es Salaam Cape Town
Melbourne Auckland
and associated companies in
Berlin Ibadan

Oxford is a trade mark of Oxford University Press

Published in the United States
by Oxford University Press, New York

British Library Cataloguing in Publication Data
Data available

Library of Congress Cataloging in Publication Data
Lloyd, Rosemary.
The land of lost content: children and childhood in nineteenth-
century French literature / Rosemary Lloyd.
Includes bibliographical references (p.) and index.
1. French literature—19th century—History and criticism.
2. Authors, French—Biography—Youth—History and criticism.
3. Children in literature. 4. Self in literature.
5. Autobiography. I. Title.
PQ283.L58 1992
840.9'352054—dc20 91–38741
ISBN 0–19–815173–X

Typeset by Pentacor PLC, High Wycombe, Bucks
Printed and bound in
Great Britain by Biddles Ltd.
Guildford and King's Lynn

For Margaret, Lindsay, and Marianne,

in loving memory of our mother,
Elwyn Lindsay Furness (1923–1991),
who gave us all such a happy childhood.

Preface

> Where are the children?
> Où sont les enfants?
>
> (Colette, *La Maison de Claudine*)

To readers of nineteenth-century English and French literature it often appears that while the former is rich in images of children and childhood—one thinks of Blake, Wordsworth, Charlotte Brontë, Dickens, George Eliot, to name only these few—in French literature of the same period they are far less common and more scantily treated. What my study sets out to do is to examine this premiss, asking whether it is indeed valid and if so why such a situation should prevail. Is it because the French literary canon for the nineteenth century privileges male over female and rational over imaginative? Is it because the views of women were largely repressed and suppressed throughout the century?[1] Does a shift in the parameters of the traditional canon reveal very different concerns? What images of children and of childhood are depicted in works generally, and not always justifiably, omitted from university programmes? Is the apparent lack of children connected with ways in which French writers presented the self? Does the autobiographical record reveal a similar embarrassment about childhood, or were writers able to find in such precursors as Rousseau's *Confessions* sufficient justification for the detailed exploration of their early years? If there is a scarcity of children, is it caused by linguistic problems or those of narrative focus, or are there problems more connected with sociological factors? How far do historical conditions play a role? How much did changes in literary fashion, developments in educational theory, the encroachment of the State into private life, and the progress in printing techniques affect what children read and what they later came to present in their adult creations? To what extent do the visual arts, which for

[1] Added to the problem of silenced voices, moreover, are the ways in which not only literary and social conventions, but also the forms of language itself, can force a writer or speaker into expressions that are inadequate to the emotion or experience they wish to convey.

centuries had explored the Madonna and child theme, influence this aspect of literature? Is there any link with the fact that there are so few good books for children written in French, when England, the United States, and Australia have produced so many?

Questions, of course, may be of value less in leading to specific answers than in generating further questions. While I have, in what follows, attempted to suggest various hypotheses, I have found that these initial questions are most interesting in the way in which they lead to an exploration of a particularly rich and frequently overlooked section of nineteenth-century literature, that which deals with the presentation of children and the evocation of childhood. Because social attitudes to children, and the laws providing for their well-being, altered through the century, this study is both diachronic and synchronic, attempting to indicate changes in perspective as the century progresses, but also adopting as a constant point of reference the kinds of narratological and stylistic problems that the evocation of childhood must inevitably pose.

In this book I adopt three working hypotheses: first, that autobiography is not a genre in itself but, as de Man suggests, a mode of reading; secondly, that while symbol, metaphor, and irony dominate literature in such a way as to render problematic its transformation of history, we in turn distort literature by disregarding historical and social co-ordinates; and, thirdly, that certain states of being pose difficulties of expression that may be linguistic or psychological or both in origin, but where the type of resolution attempted (first person or third person, prose or poetry, etc.) has to be taken into account if we are to reach a true assessment of literary encodings of childhood.

I have kept my definition of 'child' flexible, although I do not include the extension of the term that we find in, for instance, Musset's *Confession d'un enfant du siècle*. While there is ample evidence of a growing interest in adolescence, many nineteenth-century writers do not explicitly separate it out from childhood, but portray both as part of the preparation for adulthood. In this study I have, therefore, left largely aside such texts as Fromentin's *Dominique* and Lautréamont's *Les Chants de Maldoror* whose primary focus is on the awakening of the sexual personality, but included works where the writer designates the central character as a child, even if his or her age may appear to us to be that of adolescence.

The potential material for such a study is immense: I have limited myself, with a few exceptions, to works written in French during the course of the nineteenth century, leaving out such twentieth-century novels and autobiographies as Proust's *A la recherche du temps perdu*, Alain-Fournier's *Le Grand Meaulnes*, and Gide's *Si le grain ne meurt*, although they evoke nineteenth-century child-hoods, mainly because the focus through which those childhoods are perceived has already shifted from the positions generally adopted in the nineteenth century. Works written for children, for purposes of both pedagogy and entertainment, also cast an important, if indirect, light on the topic. I have been able to explore only a very small proportion of these, attempting to concentrate on those works most frequently mentioned by the autobiographers or novelists themselves. I am well aware that the vastness of my subject condemns me to omit writers and aspects other critics will see, or have seen, as important; all I can offer is what I perceive as a representative sample, in the hope that others will enter into further aspects of a topic that still deserves, and would certainly reward, more study.

R.L.

Acknowledgements

It is a pleasure to thank the University of Cambridge and my college, New Hall, for the two terms' sabbatical leave I devoted to writing this book; the Leverhulme Foundation for its generous financial aid; Jeannot and Lloyd Austin, who allowed us to spend the golden autumn of 1989 in their house in Île de France; and the Camargo Foundation, Cassis, which provided an apartment, a library, and companionship in idyllic surroundings for the azure spring of 1990. Numerous people suggested works I should read, and I am grateful to all of them. Audiences at the Camargo Foundation, at the French Studies Conference held in Glasgow, and at the universities of Cambridge, Adelaide, Melbourne, and Bloomington asked stimulating questions and suggested further possibilities. A version of the section entitled 'Food' in Chapter 4 appeared in *Romance Studies*, 13 (Winter 1988), 81–8. I am grateful to the editors for permission to reproduce it here. The following galleries kindly gave permission for the reproduction of the illustrations: the Burrell Collection, Glasgow; the Louvre, Paris; the Musée des Beaux Arts, Chartres; the National Gallery, Washington; the Metropolitan Museum of Art, New York. In particular, I would like to acknowledge the advice and assistance of Catherine Clarke, Alan Spitzer, Sonya Stephens, Emma Wilson, Penny Wilson, Nigel Wilkins, and Paul Lloyd.

Note

Footnote references give the title and page references only, except where this would lead to confusion. Full publication details are provided in the bibliography. Except where indicated, translations are my own.

Contents

List of Plates

Introduction

> Childhood is neither nostalgia, nor terror, nor paradise lost, nor the Golden Fleece, but perhaps a horizon, a point of departure, co-ordinates from which the axes of my life may find their direction.

> L'enfant n'est ni nostalgie, ni terreur, ni paradis perdu, ni Toison d'Or, mais peut-être horizon, point de départ, co-ordonnées à partir desquelles les axes de ma vie pourront trouver leur sens.

> (G. Perec, W: *Ou souvenirs d'enfance*)

> All the cards have been dealt before we turn 12 years old.

> Tout est joué avant que nous ayons douze ans.

> (C. Péguy, 'L'Argent')

WHEN Ellen Key proclaimed in 1910 that the new age would be the century of the child, she was both registering a change in relationships between adult and child, and reflecting a shift in the ways in which the West envisaged both the individual and the future. It can certainly be argued that this sense of transformation stems partly from changing conceptions of place, time,[1] and class. Yet throughout the nineteenth century there had been writers who, inspired by Rousseau and eighteenth-century emotionalism or by the Romantics' privileging of the imaginative and the irrational, had proclaimed the value and importance of childhood. It almost seems that each generation of adults, in order to recover its own experience of childhood, needs the goading conviction that previous generations failed to comprehend the meaning of youth. However troubled the relationship between experience and the literary transformation of that experience, the nineteenth century does undoubtedly offer a rich range of responses to the theme of childhood, even if these responses are not necessarily to be found in works inscribed in a literary canon wedded to Balzac's affirmation that the dominant forces of the age were those adult preoccupations of 'money and pleasure' (*l'or et le plaisir*).

---

[1] As F. Kermode suggests in his series of lectures, *The Sense of an Ending*, the discovery of infinite time becomes central to the sciences in the 19th century and gradually permeates the general consciousness.

Since one of the central problems of conveying the world of the child in literature lies with the restrictions imposed by a vision that is prelinguistic or that at best seeks expression through a limited control of language, it may be helpful to enter the topic by a brief exploration of the ways in which contemporary visual arts[2] responded to the theme of childhood. If the child had for centuries been an all but banal part of painting—primarily, of course, as a result of the Madonna and child theme—it was with the rise of family portraits in the seventeenth century and particularly with the increase in sentimentalism in the eighteenth century that children began to play a major role in the visual arts. Certainly the paintings of such eighteenth-century artists as Greuze and Chardin (Plates 1 and 2) reflect the growing sensitivity of the age in their tender scenes of childhood. Yet it is indisputable that many of their studies of children have an ulterior moral, or immoral, purpose—depicting the vanity of human activity in Chardin's case, or offering erotic stimulation in Greuze's—and all presuppose an adult onlooker whose gaze is above that of the child's. Here, in other words, there is less exploration than exploitation of the image of the child. There does, however, seem to be a perceptible change between these paintings and, say, Delacroix's *Orphan Girl* (Plate 3) or Daumier's *The Burden* (Plate 4). In both, the central questions of who looks and who sees—which is clearly also crucial to a study of the presentation of childhood in literary texts or autobiographies, where the writer is almost always an adult—lead to radically different answers from the earlier paintings, where the onlooker is the adult looking back on childhood from a position of alterity and almost always of superiority. In Delacroix's depiction of the orphan girl there is certainly no suggestion that the child's grief is less intense than an adult's, no indication of a lack of emotional depth, and the gaze she projects on the sky which gazes back with such tender indifference is in no way banalized or sentimentalized, as it might be, say, in a painting by Greuze. Equally, in Daumier's *The Burden*, which exists in many versions, engravings, paintings, and small statues, and which depicts a washerwoman weighed down both by the burden of the washing she is carrying and by the child

[2] P. Ariès, in *L'Enfant et la vie familiale*, provides a close reading of the artistic portrayal of childhood, but without recognizing the specificity of painting as compared to written documents. His interpretations depend on a conviction that painting presents, rather than represents, the world.

clinging to her hand, the child's presence—its independence, its future already determined both physically and socially by the figure of its mother—means that the work's title fragments, opens up in meaning to encompass not merely the mother's load of washing but the existence of the child, both in the sense of its future development, and in the sense that Baudelaire has in mind when he asks which is the widow to be most pitied, the one who is all alone or the one who has a child. Moreover, if we turn to Goya, whose influence on French painters and writers was immense, we can find portraits of children that convey childhood as a time of intensely threatened fragility. In his portrait of Don Manuel Osorio de Zuñiga (Plate 5) our gaze is constantly drawn back to the child, who is imprisoned in his pretentious clothes as the birds behind him are imprisoned in their cage, and whose existence is just as threatened as that of his pet magpie on whom the cats cast such penetrating stares. A painting like this, or Préault's terrifying carving *Killing (Tuerie)* (Plate 6), where the child is the still, fragile centre of a world disintegrating into barbarism, force us to admit— to return to my earlier question of who looks and who sees—not just that '*je le regarde*', I look at it, but also that '*ça me regarde*', I am involved in it. Moreover, many of the Impressionists, particularly Renoir and Mary Cassatt, reflect that change of direction by forcing the viewer to adopt the child's point of view. Renoir's *Little Girl with Watering Can* (1876) or *Mme Charpentier and her Children* (Plate 7), like Mary Cassatt's[3] painting, *Little Girl in a Blue Armchair* (1878) (Plate 8), illustrates perfectly how far the angle of vision had changed. Just as Impressionism in general had raised the horizon to reduce the space allotted to the sky and thereby to increase the emphasis placed on material values, so here the cropped perspectives, the refusal to suggest a benevolent or sentimental adult viewer by opening up a view from on high, all indicate that we are forced to see the child as children, to admit not only that we are there as inquisitive or bored child, but that we look on with the eyes of childhood.

A comparable shift seems to have taken place in fiction, although it did so somewhat later. Certainly, literary critics began drawing attention from the last decade of the nineteenth century to what appeared to be an alteration in attitudes towards the theme of childhood and adolescence in French literature. As early as 1889,

[3] Born in America, Mary Cassatt spent most of her adult life in France.

H. Durand proclaimed the reign of the child, and signalled a shift in sensibility, asserting, as he puts it, that almost all contemporary writers unite to form a superb choir chanting, in honour of childhood, a song of happiness and love.[4] Highly sentimental and with little critical acumen, Durand's pioneering work nevertheless offers a significant contribution in its wide-ranging bibliographical references and in its basic premiss that 'it is no longer the fashion to be a bad husband and an uncaring father: we know only too well what we have lost in that stupid game' (*la mode n'est plus d'être mauvais mari et père indifférent: on sait trop ce qu'on a perdu à ce jeu stupide*).[5] M. Braunschvig in 1903 and H. Bordeaux in the following year both focused on the increased interest in the child reflected by French literature, and in 1925, C. S. Parker, in his study, *The Defense of the Child by French Novelists*, postulates a direct relationship between literature and political change when he argues not only that 'an examination of the dates of the laws [concerning children] leads one to the conclusion that the child would legally be in a bad way in France, were it not for the Third Republic'[6] but also that the changes that were instituted by the Third Republic were largely a response to the depictions of childhood in the literature of the time.

Nevertheless, it was not until the 1930s that the topos attracted more general critical attention. In 1930 J. Calvet set out, as he puts it, to follow the luminous path of childhood through French literature,[7] in a study predicated on the questionable and limiting conviction that the kind of art that glorifies the child is a Christian art. Although primarily concerned, through long quotations and paraphrase, to reveal the presence of the child as a theme rather than subject it to critical appraisal, Calvet's investigation was instrumental in suggesting the richness of the topic. A. Dupuy, in a work significantly entitled *Un personnage nouveau du roman français: L'Enfant* (*A New Character in the French Novel: The Child*), which appeared in 1931, insists that while Romanticism introduced children into French literature it is only after 1870 that we find 'the Child affirming itself, in a definitive way, as a *new character in the French novel*' (*l'Enfant s'affirmer, d'une manière définitive, comme* un personnage nouveau du roman français).[8]

---

[4] *Le Règne de l'enfant*, 103.   [5] Ibid., 10.
[6] *The Defense of the Child*, 134.
[7] *L'Enfant dans la littérature française*, i. p. ix.
[8] *Un personnage nouveau*, 11.

Dupuy's work is above all a catalogue of his reactions and responses rather than an analysis of the works as literature, since his aim is to produce 'a *psychological and sociological Study* of the Child as seen in the French Novel' (*une* Étude psychologique et sociologique *de l'Enfant à travers le Roman français*).[9] One might justifiably question whether it is valid to extrapolate psychological and social facts from these findings in the way Dupuy suggests, or whether the '*enfant*' thus revealed is merely a product of the literature studied, with little direct psychological or sociological applicability beyond that literature. Equally questionable, in my view, is the conviction underlying his decision to deal only with those works for which the intended reader is adult. While he may affirm that such a decision requires no justification, it is at least arguable that books written for children are equally rich in suggestions and assumptions about the nature of childhood. V. Toursch, in *L'Enfant français à la fin du xixᵉ siècle d'après ses principaux romanciers*, published in 1939, follows a very similar pattern, in analysing from a psychological and social point of view five novels published after 1876, beginning, as does Dupuy, with Alphonse Daudet's *Jack*. Although this exploration is not without interest, one could again query not merely the assumption that literary materials directly reflect social structures and conditions,[10] but also the decision to choose as his prime texts only those written by men. J. O'Brien's sensitive and influential exploration, *The Novel of Adolescence in France*, appearing in 1937, is more concerned with questions of a literary order, and, as its title suggests, deals with the passage between childhood and adulthood. It, too, is resolutely male-oriented, on the curious and untenable supposition that 'it appears that the advent of puberty, whose physiological repercussions are so marked in girls, influences them intellectually and spiritually far less than it does boys'.[11]

Inspired less by literary concerns than by the anthropological studies of Lévy-Bruhl, and the psychological investigations of Piaget, Jean Schlumberger points to the association between lyricism and childhood, and asks of the former:

If it was so deficient in our literature at certain periods, is that not the result of the kind of hatred which, until the time of Romanticism, all our literary

---

[9] Ibid., 23. Original emphasis.
[10] Cp. Laslett, 'The Wrong Way through the Telescope', 340.
[11] *The Novel of Adolescence*, 12–13.

works directed at the child, its personality and its feelings, as well as at all irrationality and all naïvity?

S'il fut si déficient chez nous à certaines époques, cela ne tient-il pas à l'espèce de haine que, jusqu'au romantisme, toute notre littérature a vouée à l'enfant, à sa personne, à ses sentiments, à toute irrationalité et toute naïveté?[12]

And he concludes, with double-edged belligerence:

It is a question of knowing what one values most, where one places one's self-esteem; and France has not the slightest hesitation in making her choice. She prefers her intelligence. This statement, which can, according to sympathies, be expressed either as praise or criticism, sums up and closes the entire debate.

Il faut savoir à quoi l'on tient le plus, où l'on met son amour-propre; et la France n'hésite aucunement dans son choix. Elle préfère son intelligence. Cette constatation qu'on peut formuler, selon les sympathies, d'une manière élogieuse ou désobligeante, résume et clôt le débat.[13]

Other reasons for such a state of affairs, if indeed it does exist, certainly suggest themselves, reasons that have less to do with a cut-and-dried choice and more to do with the problematics of style and narrative voice, and I shall be exploring these in the course of this study. Nevertheless, Schlumberger's dichotomy between rationality, clarity, and intelligence on the one hand, and the irrational, the marvellous, the sentimental, on the other, together with its implicit assumption of an unbreachable gap between childhood and adulthood, cannot be dismissed lightly, since it runs as a leitmotif through much of the critical response to nineteenth- and twentieth-century texts, at least until the value of the playful began to gain recognition.[14]

Schlumberger's assertions are shared by the work which, however broadly and universally contested its arguments were to be, has given most impetus to the theme of childhood in the last thirty years: P. Ariès's *L'Enfant et la vie familiale sous l'Ancien Régime*, whose title in the English translation, *Centuries of Childhood*, harks back to Ellen Key's work. Drawing on a wide variety of documentary sources, including the visual arts and the

---

[12] 'La France sévère à l'enfance'.
[13] Ibid. Compare T. Zeldin's affirmation that 'according to a public opinion poll, the French think of themselves as being, above all, intelligent' (*Ambition and Love*, 1).
[14] On this see Huizinga, *Homo ludens*.

diary kept by Hérouard during the infancy and childhood of Louis XIII, Ariès asserts that medieval society lacked a *concept* of childhood and that this concept developed only slowly over the centuries.[15] Roughly speaking, Ariès's argument is that there was no notion of childhood as a separate state in the Middle Ages, since adults in general at that time were too emotionally immature to perceive their children as individuals, that there arose a gradual awareness of children as playthings for adults as the centuries progressed, but that it was not until the mid-eighteenth century that the growing influence of sentimentality and feminine concepts of the world produced an image of childhood that begins to resemble that held in our own times. The thesis itself is not new: the nineteenth-century writer Laprade, to give just one example of earlier versions of this conviction, asserted that

it has to be recognized that caring about children is one of the virtues of our own age; a virtue which is still very new, fairly self-centred and unenlightened. We have to admit that such a sentiment was utterly non-existent before the eighteenth century.

la sollicitude pour l'enfance est, il faut le reconnaître, une des vertus de notre temps; sollicitude bien nouvelle encore, assez égoïste et peu éclairée. Elle était nulle, sachons le reconnaître, avant le dix-huitième siècle.[16]

Although Ariès himself asserts, but does not prove, that the nineteenth century is the age of the child,[17] if one adheres to his general argument, it would no doubt be more accurate to extrapolate that this notion of the child was to a large degree suppressed during the first seventy years or so of the nineteenth century, when the waves of revolution and repression, together with the all but hysterical fear of crime,[18] led to a greater sense of strictness and a greater tendency towards brutality directed against children, following the usual precept that those bullied and humiliated by their superiors will take out their resentment on those inferior to them, often women and children.

L'Enfant et la vie familiale sparked off considerable debate, which has been ably and energetically summarized by Linda Pollock in her own analysis of parent–child relations in England

[15] But see Kroll, 'The Concept of Childhood in the Middle Ages'.
[16] *L'Éducation homicide*, 19.
[17] *L'Enfant et la vie familiale*, 21.
[18] A theme explored by Chevalier in his *Classes laborieuses et classes dangereuses à Paris pendant la première moitié du dix-neuvième siècle*.

and America from 1500 to 1900. While numerous scholars, whether or not they support Ariès's contentions about concepts of childhood, seem all but sadistically concerned to confirm his view of the brutality to which children were subjected and the degree of physical, financial, and sexual abuse of them,[19] Le Roy Ladurie's study of the village of Montaillou, like Pollock's own findings, which are based on over 400 diaries and autobiographies, suggest that there was in fact far less abuse of children, far more parental tenderness, and indeed far more awareness of childhood as a separate state than had been believed by some previous writers. Indeed, Pollock rejects the usual argument that when the infant mortality rate was high it was not worth the adult's while investing affection in a child who might not survive.[20] Nevertheless, she does acknowledge that while diaries present this far rosier picture, the autobiographical evidence is somewhat bleaker, and she faces up, albeit briefly, to the prickly truth that whereas writers might well record brutality directed at themselves, the diary writers are unlikely to acknowledge their own brutal treatment of their children. Pollock's study not only provides a fascinating and humane exploration of English and American childhood, but also focuses sharply on the problems inherent in the topic, asserting with admirable clear-sightedness and brevity: 'despite all the recent work on the history of childhood, we still know little about actual childhood.'[21] In exploring the literary transformations of child-hood I hope to add, if only indirectly, to our knowledge of what it was like to be a child in nineteenth-century France.

Whether or not the recent spate of historical and sociological investigations of childhood has had a direct impact on literary criticism, it is certainly the case that since the publication of Ariès's work several studies of the child in French and English literature have been published. Four of these are of particular importance for the present study. M. J. Chambart de Lauwe, in a long, subtle, and sensitive study published in 1971, rejects the assertion that it is only after the fall of Napoleon III that the child becomes a literary theme: she, indeed, maintains that 'around 1850 the character of the child makes a massive entry into literature. . . . The child-life

[19] See e.g. Badinter, De Mause, Hunt, Shorter, and Stone.
[20] See also Knibielher and Fouquet, *Histoire des mères*.
[21] *Forgotten Children*, 203. For a more traditionally historical study of the working-class child in France see Heywood, *Childhood in Nineteenth-Century France*.

becomes the essence of life.' (*autour de 1850, le personnage de l'enfant entre massivement dans la littérature. . . . L'enfant-vie devient essence de vie.*)[22] She asserts, moreover, that adults need their former child-self, and are moved by the image of themselves as children.[23] Yet if that is indeed the case, one might legitimately ask why the written evocation of childhood is so tardy a phenomenon. Her inquiry enters with more sympathy and greater sophistication into the major texts than those of her predecessors, in an attempt to reveal the crucial themes that constitute the world of childhood: the role of the school, relationships with others, revolt, reverie, friendships, and the awakening of sexual impulses. Avoiding the dangers of that kind of facile sentimentality that blinds itself to the complexity of childhood experience, she emphasizes the presence of revolt and hatred in the children that literature bodies forth, and insists that

The ways in which childhood memories have been consciously or unconsciously transformed express the meaning and importance of the image of the child for the creating subject and for the receiving public . . . From the need each of us feels to live our childhoods retrospectively, to the need of our child-self within us, there is a direct link, as is revealed by the repetition of themes and the idealization of characters.

Les déformations volontaires ou non apportées au souvenirs d'enfance expriment la signification et l'importance de l'image de l'enfant pour le sujet qui la crée et pour le public qui la reçoit . . . Du besoin de l'enfance vécue rétrospectivement par chacun, au besoin de la présence de l'enfant en soi, le lien est direct, les mêmes thèmes, la même idéalisation des personnages en font foi.[24]

Yet one might argue that, since the experience of children is more uniform than that of adults, the repetition of themes is unremarkable and predictable. Primarily a thematic study, *Un monde autre* still leaves room for an exploration of childhood based on a wider body of material and focusing not merely on the constituents of the mythology of childhood but also on the ways and means by which that mythology is conveyed.

Following very much in the footsteps of Chambart de Lauwe, M. Bethlenfalvay offers, in 1979, a 'sketch of a typology' entitled *Les Visages de l'enfant dans la littérature française du XIXe siècle*. More

[22] *Un monde autre*, 18.
[23] Ibid., 222.
[24] Ibid., 232.

sentimental and less analytical than that of Chambart de Lauwe, this work nevertheless has the virtue of ranging somewhat more widely, bringing in, for example, the thinking of Fourier and drawing to some extent on the historical background, particularly in the assertion that:

Faced with the obvious scandal of the economic exploitation of children, writers seem to have become aware of other forms of exploitation, more hidden and devious but just as frequent and as old as the world: that which makes of them unknowing instruments in power struggles or that which abuses them for purposes of sadistic pleasure.

Face au scandale évident de l'exploitation économique des enfants, les écrivains semblent avoir pris conscience d'autres formes d'exploitation, plus cachées et retorses, mais tout aussi fréquentes et vieilles comme le monde: celle qui en fait des instruments inconscients dans les luttes de pouvoir ou celle qui en abuse à des fins de gratification sadique.[25]

Nevertheless, a certain lack of penetration in her critical appreciations—one can surely expect more than the bald affirmation that the poems of Desbordes-Valmore and Hugo are among the most beautiful to be found in the genre (and is the poetry of childhood a genre?)[26]—weakens what is otherwise a sensitive and enthusiastic study.

More ambitious in range is R. Kuhn's *Corruption in Paradise*, a study of the child-figure in Western literature that overthrows almost all barriers of time and place to provide a comparative approach in which the text is perceived as a purely fictional construct with no ties to the historical or social circumstances in which it was produced. Yet even works of pure fantasy are limited by the language available at the time, at the mercy of the powerful shaping control of contemporary cliché and conviction, and to ignore these is to warp the text in ways that may indeed be exciting and provocative, but where the critic should at least acknowledge that warping. However stimulating Kuhn's comparisons between different ages and societies, they pose three central problems: there is a sense of self-indulgence, of infectious enthusiasm, but at the same time of lack of rigour in the rapidity with which he moves from example to example; his comparisons depend on thematic content to the point of ignoring the distinct demands (both writerly

[25] *Les Visages de l'enfant*, 62.
[26] Ibid., 19.

and readerly) made by different genres; and his premiss that childhood is so different from adulthood as to be largely irrecoverable demands a leap of faith that seems to me both unjustifiable and unnecessary.[27]

What limits the findings of all these critics is a sense of embarrassment about ranging more widely than what is generally defined and sanctified as 'literature'. No such embarrassment hampers R. Coe in his exhilarating, if breathless, exploration of the theme through time and across the world. Coe focuses exclusively on the 'Childhood', which he defines as:

an extended piece of writing, a conscious, deliberately executed literary artefact, usually in prose but not excluding occasional experiments in verse, in which the most substantial portion of the material is directly autobiographical, and whose structure reflects step by step the development of the writer's self; beginning often, but not invariably, with the first light of consciousness and concluding, quite specifically, with the attainment of a precise degree of maturity.[28]

Coe suggests that the 1830s were key years in the development of this form of presentation of the self, the decade that saw the publication of Balzac's *Louis Lambert*, Goethe's *Dichtung und Wahrheit*, Nodier's *Mémoires de Maxime Odin*, and Töpffer's *Bibliothèque de mon oncle*. By stressing the comparative lateness of this development, he rejects the often repeated conviction that 'the Childhood is a direct product of the Romantic sensibility. In point of fact, the majority of the Romantic poets were unable to make the distinction between the reality of their child selves and the sentimentalized-idealized image of childhood innocence.'[29] Although Coe's range, both geographically and chronologically, is far wider than that which will be attempted here, one further point he makes is germane to this study. 'From Rousseau onward, virtually every serious author of a Childhood . . . has attempted, in one fashion or another, to justify his [sic] use of "trivia".'[30] What one defines as trivia, as indeed what one defines as great literature in

---

[27] Compare the priest whom Malraux recalls at the beginning of *Le Miroir des limbes* whose knowledge of the confessional had taught him that 'the heart of the matter is that *there are no grown-ups*' (*le fond de tout, c'est* qu'il n'y a pas de grandes personnes). (*Antimémoires*, 9.)

[28] *When the Grass was Taller*, 8–9.

[29] Ibid., 40.

[30] Ibid., 211.

comparison with the sound upper second or racy third, is always to some extent a question of fashion and taste. Nevertheless de Man surely has a point when he argues that 'compared to tragedy, or epic, or lyric poetry, autobiography always looks slightly disreputable and self-indulgent in a way that may be symptomatic of its incompatibility with the monumental dignity of aesthetic values'.[31] But monumentality and dignity are not the sole aesthetic virtues and it is one of the purposes of this book to explore the disreputable and the self-indulgent as well as the monumental.

None the less, the study of autobiography does pose problems and has, like the literary representation of childhood itself, attracted considerable critical attention, from those interested in exploring the relationships between truth and fiction, from those charting the boundaries of different genres, and from those concerned with its structural and narratological fabric. For Anglo-Saxon critics, R. Pascal's *Design and Truth in Autobiography*, first published in 1960, has proved a challenging, if frequently challenged, starting-point. Of central importance for the present study is his affirmation that 'the nineteenth-century novels that delve deep into childhood, from Dickens, and the Brontës onwards, are unimaginable without the great autobiographies and their importance lies not just in the discovery of the child's world, but in the recognition that the obscure urges and vivid impressions and affections of childhood are so decisive for the adult'.[32] Yet, as is the case with many of those who have followed him, Pascal's investigation illustrates the ease with which, in studies of autobiography, critical analysis can give way to the demand that the reader accept, through what is no less than a leap of faith, the assertion being made. As an example one might offer the following statement: 'The best autobiographies seem to suggest a certain power of the personality over circumstance, . . . in the sense that the individual can extract nurture out of disparate incidents and ultimately bind them together in his own way, disregarding all that was unusable.'[33] How can the reader know what was unusable as distinct from merely unused? And who does the binding: life, the writer, the text, or the reader? R. Butler, E. Bruss, J. Mehlman, and J. Olney have all, in differing ways, drawn inspiration from Pascal's

---

[31] 'Autobiography as De-facement', 919.
[32] *Design and Truth* 52.
[33] Ibid., 10–11.

study and have explored and extended his premisses, without necessarily always avoiding the pitfall outlined above.

In France, the autobiographical pinnacle has, for some twenty years, been energetically occupied by P. Lejeune, whose enthusiasm for the *Bibliothèque nationale*'s reference number Ln²⁷ (biographies) is both unbounded and infectious, but whose frequently repeated insistence on a *pact* between reader and writer that guarantees the identity of author and subject seems to me to demand yet another leap of faith and one, moreover, that is restrictive rather than productive. Equally questionable is his assertion that 'an overpolished or obvious style awakens in the reader of an autobiography a distrust he finds difficult to set aside, even if he knows it to be unfounded. When art is too visible it appears to be artifice.' (*une écriture trop soignée ou trop manifeste éveille chez le lecteur d'autobiographie une méfiance dont il saurait difficilement se défaire, même s'il comprend qu'elle est sans fondement. Quand l'art se voit trop, il paraît artifice.)*[34] But how does one judge that excess? How does one tease out style and writer? De Man provides a more fertile basis for exploration when he suggest that autobiography 'is not a genre or a mode, but a figure of reading or of understanding that occurs, to some degree, in all texts'.[35] This point of view is further clarified by B. J. Mandel's suggestion (even though he uses the word *genre*) that 'the kind of truth inherent in fiction and autobiography is released by a reader choosing one genre rather than the other. (I mean choosing in two senses: the literal choice of taking the book down from the shelf and the choice of opening up one's mind to the kind of book that presents itself.)'[36]

In exploring concepts of childhood and visions of the child in nineteenth-century France, there is little point in carefully differentiating between autobiography and fiction, and nothing to be gained by building sharp divisions between, for example, Balzac's novel *Louis Lambert*, Juliette Adam's fictionalized childhood *Le Roman de mon enfance*, Nadaud's socialist parable *Mémoires de*

---

[34] *Le Pacte autobiographique*, 189. This seems a belated echo of the accusations levelled at Camus by Jeanson and Sartre in the famous *Temps modernes* polemic which followed the publication of *L'Homme révolté* and *La Peste* and in which the stylistic attack masks a political attack.

[35] 'Autobiography as De-facement', 921.

[36] 'Full of Life Now', in Olney (ed.), *Autobiography: Essays Theoretical and Critical*, 55.

Léonard, and Chateaubriand's autobiography *Mémoires d'outre-tombe*. It is not merely that a certain fertile slippage always takes place between fact and fiction, but also that the interest of these texts lies more in the exploitation of certain tropes than in any particular speech act.

The proliferation of autobiographies by people of all social classes in the course of the nineteenth century raises questions of why the *moi* should have ceased to be regarded as *haïssable*, as it was in the age of classicism, and why, however much the question of trivia may have embarrassed them, as Coe rightly suggests, they nevertheless sought to create, in so public a way, a personal mythology. To some extent the historical context can provide certain clues. For the aristocrats, the Revolution of 1789, together with the uprisings, wars, and revolutions of the nineteenth century, swept aside many of the values that had allowed for self-definition in terms of name, family, and state, and forced a re-evaluation of the self along far more individual lines. The industrial revolution, together with a more general rise both in personal wealth and in literacy among the middle classes, led to an increasing bourgeois conviction of the practical worth of individual effort, and a desire to record that effort, much as individual features and dress were recorded by having one's portrait painted, or, later, one's photo taken. And both a growing sense of working-class power, and an interest in traditions that were on the point of disappearing altogether, created a climate that encouraged peasants, apprentices, and workers to record their own lives and customs.

Of course these lives and customs are to some extent transformed by the very act of relating them: as the critic A. Jollès remarks in a slightly different context: 'This Mussolini *in natura* is to the Mussolini of literature what wheat is to bread: language has refined, moulded, moistened and heated him; he is a poetic fabrication.' (*Ce Mussolini* in natura *est au Mussolini de la littérature ce que le blé est au pain: le language l'a bluté, moulu, mouillé, chauffé; c'est une fabrication poétique.*)[37] Yet, however problematic the relationship between literature and its historical context, however much it may seem that in looking at the past we are never able to select the lens that will pull details into sharp focus, it is nevertheless undeniable that writers exploring childhood did so in the context of social and legal factors that may shed light

[37] *Formes simples*, 23.

on their choice of topic and the ways in which they treated it, in particular the demography of the country, the laws concerning education, and the legislation controlling child labour. Unlike the rest of Europe, France during this period underwent a drop in the birth rate, for reasons that have not been satisfactorily explained.[38] Paris, it is true, all but doubled its population between 1820 and 1846, but at the expense of rural France rather than through any increase in the fertility of native-born Parisians. Throughout the century, moreover, the infant mortality rate remained high, as did the mortality rate for young people generally: indeed, Armengaud argues that at least in the first half of the century, one third of those born in any given year died before their twentieth birthday.[39] Yet, although he refers to the drop in the birth rate as the modern means of rejecting the child, he also acknowledges that 'it remains the case that the progress of this neo-Malthusianism went hand in hand, by and large, with greater attention being paid to the child' (*il reste que les progrès du néo-malthusianisme sont allés de pair dans l'ensemble, avec une plus grande attention portée à l'enfant*).[40] Flandrin argues that the Church itself, during this period, drew little inspiration from the biblical injunction to populate, placing its emphasis instead on chastity within marriage. He, too, however, points to strong Malthusian tendencies.[41] Nevertheless, Flandrin's opening remarks contain a salutary warning: 'The more one examines the behaviour of people who lived in the past, the more one feels that they were conforming to models that to us appear irrational.' (*Plus on examine le comportement des couples d'autre-fois, plus on a l'impression que leur conduite se conformait à des modèles, pour nous irrationnels.*)[42] It might perhaps be more accurate simply to refer to these models as 'unknown', for since so few women left any permanent record of their feelings about conception, pregnancy, and childbirth, we simply cannot know whether this drop in the birth rate was fortuitous or voluntary, and what, if anything, it had to do with attitudes to childhood and children. We can only record it as a factor affecting the theme.

[38] See Armengaud, 'L'Attitude de la société' and *La Population française*; Daumard, *Les Bourgeois de Paris*; Delzons, *La Famille française*; Shorter, *The Making of the Modern Family*; Zeldin, *France 1848–1945*.
[39] *La Population française*, 15.
[40] 'L'Attitude de la société', 311–12.
[41] 'L'Attitude à l'égard du petit enfant', 145.
[42] Ibid., 144.

Despite this drop in the birth rate a large number of children were nevertheless abandoned and left to the care of the state. While in England, even towards the end of the century, according to De Mause, dead infants were still to be found exposed in the streets of London,[43] in France, both the system of *tours*, which guaranteed parental anonymity, and the use to which the State could put foundlings as soldiers, colonists, or workers, encouraged a relatively large population of *enfants trouvés*.[44] This demographic fact fuses with certain psychological urges to produce the numerous stories of foundlings, orphans, and bastards in nineteenth-century French literature, and also feeds into the central topos of the child searching for its true identity.[45]

Whether it was because of this population of foundlings or for other reasons, connected with a shift in the power base, the State in the nineteenth century began to take an increasing interest in the family and to enter into a domain that had hitherto been regarded as private. Delzons, in a compelling early study of the French family, based largely on a philosophical reading of history and literature, asserts that

What was new in this nineteenth century was the fact that the general concern, not merely of parents but of public opinion and the State itself, focused with extraordinary intensity on the individual child and its fate.

La nouveauté de ce dix-neuvième siècle est que le souci général, non pas seulement celui des parents, mais de l'opinion publique et de l'État lui-même s'est porté d'une ardeur extraordinaire sur la personne et le sort de l'enfant.[46]

More recently, both Donzelot in *La Police des familles* and Foucault in *Surveiller et punir* have argued that the century saw the bourgeois family tightening its control of its children at the same time as the State, through such laws as those limiting the hours children could work and those enforcing universal education, increased its control of the family. Moreover, throughout the nineteenth century, parents were peppered with works advising them on their duties as physical and moral guardians of their children. Among the most forthright of these was P. Janet's *La*

---

[43] *The History of Childhood*, 29.
[44] On this theme see O. Haussonville, 'L'Enfance à Paris'; the writings of Terme and Monfalcon; and Turin, 'Enfants trouvés, colonisation et utopie'.
[45] See Robert, *Roman des origines*.
[46] *La Famille française et son évolution*, 110.

Famille, based on the unshakeable conviction that 'the most important duties are those of fatherhood and motherhood' (*les plus importants [des] devoirs, ce sont ceux de la paternité et de la maternité*).[47] Janet's sexual division of labour where the education of children was concerned was unrelentingly clear-cut: one imagines young parents thrown into despair at the demands imposed on them by, for instance, the following dictate: 'It is the father's role to form the child through his authority and passion, while that of the mother is to obtain the same results by encouragement and tenderness.' (*Le rôle du père est de former l'enfant par l'autorité et par la passion, le rôle de la mère est d'obtenir les mêmes effets par l'attrait et par la tendresse.*)[48] More humane, and far more emotional, is G. Droz's half-novel, half-treatise, *Monsieur, Madame et Bébé*, which is based on the belief that 'the baby is not an incomplete creature, an unfinished sketch—it is a man' (*le bébé n'est point un être incomplet, une ébauche inachevée—c'est un homme*),[49] and which pleads for relationships between parents and children based, not on fear and authority, but on love and mutual respect. Droz's most interesting passage, from our point of view, is that describing his narrator's feelings as he held his wife's hand while she gave birth, a passage that claims to record a significant shift in the ways in which children were perceived by adults:

I experienced a strange sensation: I was aware of a new emotion growing in my heart; it was as if something alien to me had entered my breast, and this delightful sensation was so new to me that it filled me with a kind of fear. I was aware of this little being who was present although he didn't yet exist, I felt him cling to me, his entire life belonged to me. I saw him at one and the same time a child and a full-grown adult; it seemed to me that my own life would be replayed in him.

Ce que j'éprouvais était quelque chose d'étrange: je sentais un sentiment nouveau me germer dans le cœur; j'avais comme un corps étranger dans la poitrine, et cette sensation si douce était pour moi si nouvelle que j'en étais comme effrayé. Je sentais ce petit être que était là sans être encore, je le sentais s'accrocher à moi, sa vie m'apparaissait tout entière. Je le voyais à la fois enfant et homme fait; il me semblait que ma propre vie allait se dédoubler en lui.[50]

---

[47] *La Famille*, 85–6.
[48] Ibid., 103–4.
[49] *Monsieur, Madame et Bébé*, 344.
[50] Ibid., 283.

While this passage may seem remarkable to readers of the numerous autobiographies, novels, and short stories in which father and child appear almost as different species, it has to be recorded that for some of Droz's contemporaries it represented far more a sugary glossing over of the truth than any real shift in relationships: the embittered Jules Renard, whose *Poil de carotte* and whose comment on Hugo's picture of domestic bliss—'When the child appears, I disappear' (*Lorsque l'enfant paraît je disparais*) —are far from Droz's image, jotted the following into his diary:

The child has been seen by Victor Hugo and many others as an angel. It ought to be seen as something ferocious and hellish. What is more, literature concerning children can find new impetus only if the writers accept such a point of view. It is essential to crush the sugar-plum child that up until now all the Drozes have given the public to suck. The child is in essence a little animal. A cat is more human. Not the child that comes out with precious sayings, but the child that sinks its claws into anything tender it encounters. The parent's continual preoccupation consists in making it retract those claws.

L'enfant, Victor Hugo et bien d'autres l'ont vu ange. C'est féroce et infernal qu'il faut le voir. D'ailleurs, la littérature sur l'enfant ne peut être renouvelée que si l'on se place à ce point de vue. Il faut casser l'enfant en sucre que tous les Droz ont donné jusqu'ici à sucer au public. L'enfant est un petit animal nécessaire. Un chat est plus humain. Non l'enfant qui fait des mots, mais celui qui enfonce ses griffes dans tout ce qu'il rencontre de tendre. La préoccupation du parent est continue, de les lui faire rentrer.[51]

That desire to keep the child's claws under control, and in particular to crush the potential for revolt in both the child and the proletariat, can also, indeed, be seen in laws that appear primarily concerned with preventing the abuse of the young, but which Foucault, in *Surveiller et punir*, sees as yet further interference by the State into the affairs of the family.

The relatively late introduction of industrialization in France and the largely rural nature of the country meant that a smaller percentage of children were employed in heavy industry than was the case in England.[52] Nevertheless, child labour was an issue in the political arena from the 1820s on, leading to a law of 22 March 1841 that banned children under 8 from working in factories that used machinery or in which a fire was kept burning continuously, and from all firms in which there were more than twenty

[51] Renard, *Journal*, 54.
[52] See Stearns, *Paths to Authority*, 37 and 61.

employees. No children under 13 could be employed for night work, and employers were supposed to ensure that children working for them were allowed time to attend school. Although this law was difficult to enforce, it was not entirely the dead letter it has sometimes been declared.[53] None the less, it was not until the fall of Napoleon III that France was to see a series of laws improving the situation of children, particularly with regard to work, education, and protection *vis à vis* their fathers, whose power was curbed by the laws of 1889 and 1898. It can, of course, also be argued more cynically that it was at about this time that technological changes meant that opportunities for children to work in industry decreased markedly, making any legislation more likely to succeed.

Clearly, whatever the dangers of greater state intervention in the decisions of the family, such laws opened more opportunities to the individual boy, if not girl. As R. D. Anderson argues, 'the really meritocratic feature of the French system was that it allowed a comparatively large number of young men to qualify to try their luck in middle-class careers, and to reach a point where their personal talent could become evident.'[54] Three important education laws were promulgated in the period concerning us here: Guizot's law of 1833, which obliged every commune to maintain a public school, although education was neither compulsory nor free, and no separate provision was made for girls, at a time when there were strong objections to mixed schooling; Falloux's law of 1850, which re-enacted the law of 1833 but forced communes of more than 800 inhabitants to provide separate schools for girls; and Ferry's law of 1882, which made schooling compulsory, free, and secular. Of course the nineteenth century was far from being the first to take an active interest in pedagogical questions, and writers concerned with the subject drew on such predecessors as Fénelon, Locke, Rousseau, and Jean-Paul Richter. Indeed, the education system, as it developed in the nineteenth century, was largely a product of the revolutionaries of 1789 and in particular of the thinking of Condorcet.[55] Yet, no doubt because schooling was now part of the lives of a far wider cross-section of the population than had previously been the case, this was an age of passionate polemics about the nature and content of education, much of which sheds

---

[53] See Heywood, *Childhood in Nineteenth-Century France*, 249.
[54] *Education in France*, 11.
[55] See Cacérès, *Histoire de l'éducation*, 15.

light on a certain conception of childhood without necessarily telling us much about what the experience of childhood was actually like. Nevertheless, the Jesuits' emphasis on eloquence, on continuity, on Greek and Latin, the Positivists' call for a more practical preparation, and the debate about the kind of education to be given to girls, makes for fascinating reading, and provides a further context in which to examine the autobiographical and fictional record.[56]

It was not, of course, only in the schools that children learnt to read. Geneviève Bollème, in studying the evolution and fortunes of the *bibliothèque bleue*, the small brochures sold from the seventeenth to the late nineteenth century by travelling salesmen, and likely to contain anything from lives of saints to fairy tales or moral tracts, hypothesizes that even at a time when most of France was illiterate people would buy these little booklets with the aim of having them read to them at some stage and in order to own something that would have the value of a talisman. But she also asserts that the very existence of the *bibliothèque bleue* seems to indicate a wider reading ability than had been thought.[57] Furet and Ozouf argue, moreover, that

> There is, indeed, a France that acquired literacy under the *ancien régime*, and a France that, on the contrary, owes its accession to written culture to the nineteenth century. Roughly speaking, north and north-east France could read and write by the end of the eighteenth century, at a time when the rest of France was only just beginning to try to catch up.

> Il y a bien, en effet, une France que a été alphabétisée sous l'Ancien Régime, et une France qui doit au contraire au dix-neuvième siècle son accession à la culture écrite. Grossièrement, la France du Nord et du Nord-Est sait lire et écrire à la fin du dix-huitième siècle, alors que l'autre France entreprend seulement de rattraper son retard.[58]

And Armengaud, exploring the records of conscripts through the nineteenth century, suggests that while over 30 per cent were illiterate at the beginning of the July Monarchy, only 25 per cent were so by the end of the Second Empire, a percentage that had fallen to less than five at the outbreak of the First World War.[59]

---

[56] Among the most stimulating studies one might cite Durkheim's *Évolution pédagogique en France*; Prost, *Histoire de l'enseignement en France*; Fénelon, *L'Éducation des filles*; Furet and Ozouf, *Lire et écrire*; Mayeur, *L'Éducation des jeunes filles en France*.
[57] Bollème, *La Bibliothèque bleue*.
[58] *Lire et écrire*, 56.
[59] *La Population française*, 120.

Although many factors would have played a role in this rise in literacy, two in particular are pertinent to this study: the sudden proliferation of periodical publications, and the development of a literature specifically produced for children. The increase in the number of newspapers resulted partly from the discovery of cheaper methods of paper production and printing techniques, partly from the use of advertisements to defray costs, and partly from the lifting, particularly between 1848 and 1851, and again towards the end of the Second Empire, of rigorous censorship laws.[60] One of the ways in which editors attempted to attract custom in an increasingly competitive market was through the publication of the *roman feuilleton*, a serialized novel specifically designed to encourage readers to buy the next number in order to follow the adventure or story. These tales may not have been written primarily for children, but they were certainly read by them. Moreover, this was also the beginning of a particularly fruitful age for publications written explicitly with children in mind. J. Glénisson, in an article published in Martin and Chartier's *Histoire de l'édition française*, argues that this golden age opens as early as the decade 1820–30, with over 500 different ABCs being produced during the First and Second Empires. While Mame was publishing books specifically chosen to be offered as prizes in schools, Hetzel, who himself wrote and translated books for children under the pseudonym of Stahl, commissioned tales from writers of the calibre of George Sand, Dumas, and Nodier for his *Nouveau Magasin des enfants*. So numerous did the periodical publications for children become that by 1920 A. Balsen was able to publish a full-length survey of them, handing out flowers and daggers with considerable energy. While periodicals for children are mainly a nineteenth- and twentieth-century phenomenon, books written specifically with them in mind did appear earlier, mainly in the form of the pedagogical or moralistic studies now associated above all with Mme de Genlis, Bouilly, and Berquin. Most students of children's literature, however, acknowledge that the real birth of books for children in France comes with the signing of the contract between Hachette and Mme de Ségur in 1855 and the associated development of the *bibliothèque rose*, the beautifully bound and illustrated works of which were to become so much a part of French childhood memories. That many of these were

[60] On these laws see *Histoire générale de la presse française*, edited by Bellenger.

translations from other languages is a point raised by most critics of children's literature, for which I. Jan proposes the following reasons:

Catholic and Protestant countries produce different books for children; there are differences also between countries like Britain and Scandinavia, for instance, where schools are not only institutions of learning but also of education and recreation, and countries like France, where children go to school to acquire knowledge; and the privileged position of children's literature in Britain and the U.S.A. is explained partly by the effective operation of the public library systems.[61]

But if children's literature is of relatively recent date, a fact that may bear on the concept and experience of childhood in the nineteenth century, it is, of course, also true that children of earlier ages were not totally deprived of reading matter, just as it is true that many nineteenth-century children preferred more adult fare: Baudelaire, for instance, claims that as a child he had the good or bad fortune to read only weighty adult tomes,[62] and much of the autobiographical record, as we shall see, reflects similar preferences for the universal classics.

It is, therefore, in the context both of the historical and social changes that marked the nineteenth century, and against the background of the visual arts, that this study will endeavour to explore the image of childhood as it is conveyed in the literature of the time. By setting aside preconceived notions concerning the nature of works that can be explored for this purpose, and focusing not merely on thematics but also on stylistics and narratology, we may be able to reach a more firmly grounded and more sharply etched image of childhood, and penetrate further into that deep horizon of remembrance.

[61] *On Children's Literature*, 13. See also Latzarus, *La Littérature enfantine en France*, and Escarpit, *The Portrayal of the Child*.
[62] *Œuvres complètes*, ii. 42.

I
Remembering Childhood

When we have gone beyond a certain age, the soul of the child
we used to be and the souls of the dead from whom we are
descended come and heap upon us handful after handful of
their riches and their evil spells.

Quand nous avons dépassé un certain âge, l'âme de l'enfant
que nous fûmes et l'âme des morts dont nous sommes sortis
viennent nous jeter à poignée leurs richesses et leurs mauvais
sorts.

(M. Proust: *La Prisonnière*)

He looked at his own Soul with a Telescope. What seemed all
irregular, he saw and showed to be beautiful Constellations:
and he added to the Consciousness hidden worlds within
worlds.

(S. T. Coleridge: *Notebooks*)

IN attempting to understand the image of childhood left by the
creative writing of the nineteenth century, there is much to be
gained by considering autobiographical and fictional works in
conjunction, since both combine, to different but incalculable
degrees, lived experience and the imaginary, the power of the
combining intellect and the apparent chance of memory. Nevertheless, there are areas, both thematic and stylistic, where the problems
of evoking childhood are more sharply revealed in memoirs than in
the novel or poetry, not necessarily through any inherent characteristic of autobiography, but simply because both the reasons for
writing and the range of writerly ability are so much greater. As
Q. Skinner points out, 'the nature and limits of the normative
vocabulary available at any given time will . . . help to determine
ways in which particular questions came to be singled out and
discussed',[1] and it is at least arguable that such normative
vocabulary is more in evidence in those who were not necessarily
professional writers and had not therefore developed the skills of
breaking free of readerly expectation. Moreover, it matters little for

[1] *Foundations of Modern Political Thought*, i. p. xi.

our purposes whether autobiographical and biographical records coincide: the critic Philarète Chasles's autobiography, to give just one example, is renowned for its economy with external truth, yet it is undeniable that it yields a different form of truth. By focusing first on certain aspects of autobiography, therefore, we can establish a firmer foothold for entering into the topic more generally.

FINDING A VOICE

Not all nineteenth-century autobiographies have much to say about childhood: many writers, indeed, claim to remember nothing of their early years, or pass over them with a rapidity suggestive of embarrassment or even suspicion. Those that do, however, while they gain in clarity from being set in their historical context, and while they have much in common, as we shall see, with those novels and poems in which children and childhood figure, nevertheless inscribe themselves within a different set of codes, regardless of whether they are presented as romanticized, or as 'true'. While one may not agree with Lejeune's insistence on a pact between writer and reader that guarantees the identity of writer and subject, de Man's evocation of a 'figure of reading' retains a degree of elasticity, which allows for the creation of a first-person fictional persona whom the writer seeks to make antipathetic (Marie-Claire Blais's Pierre, in her eponymous novel, or to a lesser extent Pip in *Great Expectations*, for instance), but renders unlikely (although not impossible) such willed antipathy in an autobiography. More simply, and perhaps especially in the age of high seriousness that was the Second Empire, writers of autobiographies seek to elicit from their readers a particular response, one of at least sympathetic understanding, based on a sense that childish errors have now been left behind. For this to operate, it is frequently felt necessary to introduce a sense of schism between narrator and subject, a suggestion that a mature narrator is looking back at a youthful self, with a combination of tender criticism and amused wonder. They encourage us to concentrate with particular sharpness on the central questions of 'who speaks?' and 'who sees?', even if they presume to answer those questions on our behalf.

It is, at least in part, this need for a mature voice implying, if not expressing, some degree of judgement in regard either to their youthful self or to the parents or guardians who shaped that self, that determines the nature of the narrative voice most of the autobiographies adopt. More centrally, perhaps, the fact that the narrative voice is almost invariably adult reflects less a philosophical choice than a stylistic difficulty. Nodier may well convey the conviction of many Romantics when he asserts: 'How happy children are, and how pitiable are adults when they no longer have sufficient wisdom to become children again' (*Que les enfants sont heureux, et que les hommes sont à plaindre, quand il ne leur reste pas assez de sagesse pour se refaire enfants*),[2] but Baudelaire's characteristic search both for intensity of experience and for the practicalities of expressing that intensity cuts through any mawkishness to insist: 'genius is merely *childhood rediscovered* at will, but a childhood now possessing, in order to express itself, adult organs and an analytical mind.' (*le génie n'est que* l'enfance retrouvée *à volonté, l'enfance douée maintenant, pour s'exprimer, d'organes virils et de l'esprit analytique.*)[3] For what kind of language can best transport one back to childhood? What degree of linguistic maturity can most adequately convey the child's intensity of experience, an intensity evoked with particular brilliance by Joyce Cary in the following passage:

The other day, in an inland town, I saw through an open window a branch of fuchsia waving stiffly up and down in the breeze; and at once I smelt the breeze salty, and had a picture of a bright curtain flapping inwards and, beyond the curtain, dazzling sunlight on miles of crinkling water. I felt too, expectancy so keen that it was like a physical tightening of the nerves: the very sense of childhood.[4]

How can one communicate in language that tightening of the nerves, particularly if we acknowledge the general validity of Bertrand Russell's affirmation that 'The grown-ups with whom [he] came in contact had a remarkable incapacity for understanding the intensity of childish emotions'?[5] And is the sense of childhood bound up with the limited range of expression possessed by most children? While one might feel that Henry James's experiment with

[2] *Souvenirs*, 15.
[4] *A House of Children*, 9.
[3] *Œuvres complètes*, ii. 690.
[5] *Autobiography*, 18.

presenting adult behaviour through the restricted vision of the child Maisie founders on the intricately wrought periods and sophistic-ated vocabulary foisted on her,[6] it is equally obvious that the vigour of sensual experience, as for that matter of emotional or intellectual experience, cannot be gauged merely by the power or complexity of the language in which they are recounted. Flaubert, choosing to convey the feelings of Emma and Charles through free indirect discourse rather than limit himself—and them—to the language of which they would have been capable, is, after all, responding to the same kind of difficulty. Moreover, while it can be argued that ordinary recall is intricately bound up with language and intellect, involuntary memory, which frequently puts us more directly in contact with our childhood than does willed recall, more often bypasses articulate language altogether, perhaps because it is triggered most strongly, as Proust suggests, by those senses for which we have the fewest words, those of smell and taste.

The problem of finding an adequate narrative voice is raised directly by Juliette Adam, whose *Roman de mon enfance* is one of the most endearing accounts of a nineteenth-century childhood: 'One wants to write about one's childhood in the childish words one said in those days' (*On voudrait écrire son enfance avec les mots enfants qu'on disait alors*), she affirms, 'it cannot be done' (*on ne peut pas*).[7] This is not, of course, a problem unique to nineteenth-century autobiographies: Nathalie Sarraute, to choose just one recent example, recounts her early life through the medium of a conversation with a second voice which frequently interrupts to object that an expression just used would not have been within the grasp of the child at the age concerned. Among the very few who do succeed is Laura Ingalls Wilder, whose series of 'Little House' books gradually acquires sophistication of vocabulary and syntax as the child grows up, although to achieve this feat Wilder transposes the narration to the third person. And for all their brilliance, the opening pages of Joyce's *Portrait of the Artist* indicate how quickly the evocation of childhood in the words of childhood would induce in the reader a sense of irritation or

[6] James, of course, made a conscious decision not to restrict himself to the language of childhood, arguing that 'small children have many more perceptions than they have terms to translate them' (*What Maisie Knew*, 9).

[7] *Le Roman de mon enfance*, 58. Although published in 1902, the work is situated in the years leading up to the fall of Louis-Philippe and the beginning of the Second Empire.

boredom, without thereby capturing the reality of the child's experience.

While it may seem to be straining after gnats to delve too deeply into questions concerning the adequacy of the narrative voice in evocations of childhood, to ignore those questions is to run the risk of rejecting certain recounted memories as falsified by over-mature or over-stylized expression. Lejeune's strictures about 'a style that is too polished or too obvious' (*une écriture trop soignée ou trop manifeste*), already discussed in my introduction,[8] certainly need to be tempered by a pragmatic awareness of the difficulties encountered by anyone seeking to express childhood memories. The few cases where a writer's childhood voice can be heard directly offer little help. The early letters of Baudelaire and Mallarmé provide few pointers to the poetic gifts that would appear later, and only rarely convey a sense of that intensity of experience with which it was part of Romanticism's credo to endow the child. A brief glimpse of the older Baudelaire's artistic sensitivity does, however, emerge in a letter written when he was only 10 years old:

As evening had fallen, I saw a beautiful sight, the setting sun; that reddish colour formed a curious contrast with the mountains which were as blue as the darkest pair of trousers. Having put on my little silk night cap, I let myself be carried along on the back of the carriage and it seemed to me that continual travel would be a life that would bring me much pleasure; I'd really like to tell you more but a *wretched translation* forces me to close my letter here.

Le jour étant tombé, je vis un beau spectacle, c'était le soleil couchant; cette couleur rougeâtre formait un contraste singulier avec les montagnes qui étaient bleues comme le pantalon le plus foncé. Ayant mis mon petit bonnet de soie, je me laissai aller sur le dos de la voiture et il me sembla que toujours voyager serait mener une vie qui me plairait beaucoup; je voudrais bien t'en écrire davantage, mais un *maudit thème* m'oblige de fermer ici ma lettre.[9]

Flaubert's early letters are more indicative both of writerly skills and of a strong sense of the mockery with which he already regarded social behaviour. At 9, for example, he was writing to his friend Ernest Chevalier:

you're right to say that New Year's Day is stupid, dear friend, they've just dismissed the bravest of the brave Lafayette of the snowy locks the freedom of two worlds. friend I'll send you my political and liberal constitutional

---

[8] See above, 13.
[9] *Correspondance*, i. 4.

speeches. . . . if you'd like the two of us to write something together, I could write comedies and you'll write your dreams. and as there is a lady who comes to Daddy's and who always tells us stupid things I could write them down.

tu as raison de dire que le jour de l'an est bête, mon ami on vient de renvoyer le brave des braves La Fayette aux cheveux blans la liberté des 2 mondes. ami je t'en veirait de mes discours politique et constitutionnel libéraux. . . . si tu veux nous associers pour écrire moi, j'écrirait des comédie et toi tu écriras tes rêves, et comme il y a une dame qui vient chez papa et qui nous contes toujours des bêtises je les écrirait.[10]

Whatever their charm, however, neither case offers a style that could be continued in an autobiography without undermining both the dignity of the child and the seriousness of the adult's purpose in recalling his or her childhood. Those children or adolescents whose precocity enabled them to write creative works seem, at least in the case of the works that have come down to us, to have been far less interested in conveying the essence of childhood than in commenting on the nature of adults. Jane Austen in her wickedly observant *Love and Freindship* (*sic*), Daisy Ashford in her delicious *The Young Visiters*, and Flaubert in his part tongue-in-cheek, part tormented, wholly adolescent juvenilia[11] set themselves exacting standards of sophistication, while Rimbaud's poem, 'Les Poètes de sept ans', for all it captures the child's gestures of defiance with the ellipticism of genius, is concerned above all, not with the childishness, but with the intelligence, of his protagonist:

> All day long he exuded obedience; very
> Intelligent; yet certain dark tics, certain characteristics
> Seemed to prove there were in him moments of bitter hypocrisy.
> In the shadow of the corridors with their mouldy hangings,
> He would stick out his tongue as he passed by, fists thrust
> Into his groin, and in his closed eyes he would see points of light.

> Tout le jour il suait d'obéissance; très
> Intelligent; pourtant des tics noirs, quelques traits
> Semblaient prouver en lui d'âcres hypocrisies.
> Dans l'ombre des couloirs aux tentures moisies,

---

[10] *Correspondance*, i. 4.
[11] With the exception of *Mémoires d'un fou*, which I examine in Chapter 3, 120–8.

En passant il tirait la langue, les deux poings
A l'aine, et dans ses yeux fermés voyait des points.[12]

Given the sheer intellectual and technical difficulties of inserting into the mind of the infant—etymologically, after all, the one who is incapable of speech—the linguistic awareness of the adult looking back, it is hardly surprising that most nineteenth-century autobiographies are written with the voice of maturity. Such a translation may indeed prompt questions of authenticity and sincerity. A case in point could well be Judith Gautier's evocation of her fears when her pet goat dies and is taken away on a cart which she remembers as being piled high with corpses:

Never has any poet's vision, no descent into Hell, no description of horrors or cataclysms ever again given me so intense an impression. I had the feeling of the inexorable; of the dangers of existence; of destiny striking suddenly, and of the terrifying unknown, to which travel cartloads of victims.

Jamais vision de poète, descente aux enfers, descriptions d'épouvantes et de cataclysmes ne m'ont redonné une impression aussi intense. J'eus le sentiment de l'inexorable; des dangers de vivre; du destin qui frappe soudainement, et de l'inconnu effrayant, où s'en vont des charretées de victimes.[13]

But while the highly, some might say excessively, adult tone and range of reference adopted here may be indicative of certain fears the writer might have had about ever being taken seriously, as a woman apparently inescapably defined as 'Théo's daughter', we allow our judgement to become distorted if we fail to set this highly polished style in its historical and literary context.

Only one writer, Jules Vallès, consistently attempts to capture the voice of childhood, through onomatopoeia, a relatively simplified syntax, and a selective vocabulary, even though he never pretends to be filtering that voice through anything but an adult perspective. The muscular slippage Vallès operates between the child's sensory awareness and the adult's range of metaphor, allusion, and expression frequently suggests the presence of three voices: that of the child, that of the educated adult recalling the experience, and

[12] *Œuvres complètes*, 43.
[13] *Le Collier des jours*, 38.

the received wisdom of the adult world that surrounded him, typified by his mother. The following passage, with its blend of classical allusion, its comparison between the child and a butchered calf, and its direct but unsignalled interpolation of the mother's voice, is typical of Vallès's experiment:

They used to clean me every week at home.

Every Sunday morning, I looked like a calf. They'd polished me on the Saturday; on the Sunday they used to put me through the dip; my Mother would throw buckets of water over me, pursuing me like Galatea—flee in order to be caught, my fine Jacques! I can still see myself in the wardrobe mirror, bashful in my immodesty, running over the tiles which were being washed at the same time, naked as a cupid, a light-weight putto, the guardian angel of the spotless.

All I needed was to have a lemon placed between my teeth and parsley put in my nostrils, as they do to calves' heads. I had a bluish tinge, I was pale and soft, but you couldn't deny I was clean! . . .

Cleanliness before everything, my lad!

Be clean and stand up straight, that's the alpha and omega.

On me nettoyait hebdomadairement à la maison.

Tous les dimanches matin, j'avais l'air d'un veau. On m'avait fourbi le samedi; le dimanche on me passait à la détrempe; ma mère me jetait des seaux d'eau, en me poursuivant comme Galatée—fuir pour être attrapé, mon beau Jacques! Je me vois encore dans le miroir de l'armoire, pudique dans mon impudeur, courant sur le carreau qu'on lavait du même coup, nu comme un amour, cul-de-lampe léger, ange du décrotté.

Il me manquait un citron entre les dents et du persil dans les narines, comme aux têtes de veau. J'avais leur reflet bleuâtre, fade et mollasse, mais j'étais propre, par exemple! . . .

La propreté avant tout, mon garçon!

Être propre et se tenir droit, tout est là.[14]

Despite the virulence of this attack on his mother's values and the indignities they inflict on the child's person, Vallès is not here indulging in the simplistic misogyny of Renard's *Poil de carotte* or Bazin's *Vipère au poing*, but rather, as I shall be exploring later, examining the means and experience of repression, in which the mother's treatment of the child mirrors her own treatment within contemporary society.

In an age of considerable linguistic and generic experimentation, therefore, finding a voice suitable for the narration of childhood

[14] *L'Enfant*, 132. See below, 145–58.

memories posed problems that few acknowledged and even fewer attempted to resolve, but that cannot simply be ignored.

THE SENSE OF A BEGINNING

Just as autobiographical texts raise the challenge of narrative voice, so they also offer a special case of the difficulties of the *entrée en matière* and of the closure. Where, after all, does knowledge of the self begin or end? E. Said, in his *Beginnings, Intention and Method*, argues that 'just as nature is a complex space in which events occur in temporal as well as spatial dimensions that are not uniformly linear or progressive, so man's knowledge of himself is (or ought to be considered) similarly complex'.[15] The desire to convey that complexity, as well as a longing to show what is unique to each individual behind an outward appearance of constant repetition of the human condition, the wish to reveal what is eternal within the temporal, can be detected even in the most banal of autobiographies. And whereas in a work of fiction the beginning frequently implicates the end, the writer of an autobiography can only seek a beginning that implicates a mid-point, since no one, despite the convention, writes from beyond the tomb. Many autobiographies, therefore, particularly the more consciously literary, search for an opening that carries with it echoes of the birth of great men and women, repetitions of other recounted lives, recognizable intertexts which also serve the function of creating in the reader a sense of familiarity. Whether or not the birth of the text coincides with the birth of the writer (in both senses of the term), the way in which the work begins is of central importance for what it conveys about childhood.

For the rumbustiously self-assured Cellini, producing an autobiography is both a duty and a delight, as his opening paragraph confirms:

All men, whatever be their condition, who have done anything of merit, if so be they are men of truth and good repute, should write the tale of their life with their own hand. Yet it were best they should not set out so fine an enterprise till they have passed their fortieth year. And now this very thing

---

[15] *Beginnings, Intention and Method*, 160.

occurs to me, when I am fifty-eight years old and more, here in Florence where I was born.[16]

Rousseau, for his part, insists neither that this is a universal duty nor that the enterprise is a particularly fine one: both in the prefatory paragraph and in the opening of the first book of his *Confessions*, he highlights the exceptional nature of his undertaking and promises an uncomfortable degree of sincerity which has little to do with Cellini's conception of the 'fine enterprise'. The nervous truculence of the preface—'Here is the only human portrait ever to have been painted exactly according to nature and in all its truth, and it is likely that it will remain the only one' (*Voici le seul portrait d'homme, peint exactement d'après nature et dans toute sa vérité, qui existe et qui probablement existera jamais*)— establishes the *Confessions* as the foundation piece for 'the study of mankind, a study that has certainly not yet been started' (*l'étude des hommes, qui certainement est encore à commencer*),[17] while the calmer tone of the first book presents the project as the specific delineation of a unique individual:

I am setting out on a venture that has never yet been attempted and that will never have any imitators. I wish to reveal to my fellows a man in all the truth of nature; and that man will be myself. I alone. I feel my heart and I know mankind. I am unlike any of those I have seen; I have the audacity to believe that I am unlike any of those who have ever lived. . . . I have shown myself as I was, despicable and vile when I have been so, good, generous, and sublime when I have been so.

Je forme une enterprise qui n'eut jamais d'exemple, et dont l'exécution n'aura point d'imitateur. Je veux montrer à mes semblables un homme dans toute la vérité de la nature; et cet homme, ce sera moi. Moi seul. Je sens mon cœur et je connais les hommes. Je ne suis fait comme aucun de ceux que j'ai vus; j'ose croire n'être fait comme aucun de ceux qui existent. . . . Je me suis montré tel que je fus, méprisable et vil quand je l'ai été, bon, généreux, sublime, quand je l'ai été.[18]

For Chateaubriand, the justification for a public self-analysis seems to lie more with the role he has played on the world's stage—'I have met almost all the men of my time who have played a role, large or small, abroad or in my homeland' (*J'ai rencontré presque tous les*

---

[16] *Autobiography*, 3.
[17] *Œuvres complètes*, i. 3.
[18] Ibid., i.5. On this question see Starobinski, *Jean-Jacques Rousseau*, esp. 216–39.

*hommes qui ont joué de mon temps un rôle grand ou petit à
l'étranger et dans ma patrie*)[19]—and with the nobility of his
ambitions:

In my three successive careers I have always set myself a great task: as a
traveller, I have sought to discover the polar regions; as a writer, I have
attempted to restore religion from its ruins; as a statesman, I have striven to
give the people the truly representative, monarchical system with its
various freedoms.

Dans mes trois carrières successives, je me suis toujours proposé une
grande tâche: voyageur, j'ai aspiré à la découverte du monde polaire;
littérateur, j'ai essayé de rétablir la religion sur ses ruines; homme d'état, je
me suis efforcé de donner au peuple le vrai système monarchique
représentatif avec ses diverses libertés.[20]

And what underpins Berlioz's decision to produce his swashbuck-
ling, often tongue-in-cheek, autobiography is a firmly based, if
amusingly conveyed, sense of personal worth:

In the months leading up to my birth, my mother, unlike that of Virgil, had
no dreams of giving birth to a sprig of laurel. However great a blow it may
be to my self-esteem I am obliged to add that neither did she believe, like
Olympias, the mother of Alexander, that she was carrying in her womb a
blazing coal. Now that is really extraordinary, I agree, but nevertheless it is
true. I came into the world quite simply, without any of the omens that
used to appear in poetic times to announce the arrival of one of those
predestined for glory.

Pendant les mois qui précédèrent ma naissance, ma mère ne rêva point,
comme celle de Virgile, qu'elle allait mettre au monde un rameau de
laurier. Quelque douloureux que soit cet aveu pour mon amour-propre, je
dois ajouter qu'elle ne crut pas non plus, comme Olympias, mère
d'Alexandre, porter dans son sein un tison ardent. Cela est fort
extraordinaire, j'en conviens, mais cela est vrai. Je vis le jour tout
simplement, sans aucun des signes précurseurs en usage dans les temps
poétiques, pour annoncer la venue des prédestinés de la gloire.[21]

Whatever the differences in their acknowledged reasons for writing
and publishing their memoirs, the dominant tone in all these
beginnings is one of certainty. Yet a significant proportion of
nineteenth-century autobiographies open on a note of doubt, a

---

[19] *Memoires d'outre-tombe*, i. 1.
[20] Ibid., i.3.
[21] *Mémoires*, i. 41.

sense of uncertainty about the value of such an enterprise, and in particular a hesitancy about introducing infant or childhood memories. Stendhal, in his *Vie de Henry Brulard*, is typical of many when a sudden realization of what he may have revealed leads him to the truculent assertion: 'my memory is merely a novel created for the purpose' (*mon souvenir n'est qu'un roman fabriqué à cette occasion*),[22] and Pierre Loti, writing towards the end of the century, expresses more intricately a similar point when he starts *Le Roman d'un enfant* with the following caveat:

It is with a kind of fear that I broach the riddle of my impressions concerning the beginning of my life, unsure whether I really experience them myself or whether they are not more accurately described as recollections that have been mysteriously transmitted to me . . . I feel a kind of religious hesitation in sounding that abyss . . .

C'est avec une sorte de crainte que je touche à l'énigme de mes impressions du commencement de la vie,—incertain si bien réellement je les éprouvais moi-même ou si plutôt elles n'étaient pas des ressouvenirs mystérieusement transmis . . . J'ai comme une hésitation religieuse à sonder cet abîme . . . [23]

The relationships linking memory, fantasy, imagination, and current mood are an explicit concern of many of those embarking on autobiographical writing. 'There is nothing more capricious than childhood memories. They go by leaps and bounds' (*Rien de plus capricieux que les souvenirs de l'enfance. Ils vont par bonds et par sauts*),[24] acknowledges Haussonville, while Marouzeau implicitly justifies his choice of evocation rather than narration with the following avowal:

No more than anyone else have I retained a complete image of my childhood. Often what is essential has been wiped away; a few details remain: sometimes they return with their colour, their relief, and even the sensation that accompanied them; most frequently, memory at first perceives in the dim past only a light, an indistinct shape; then, as one concentrates on it, the contours gradually appear and become more clear-cut.

Je n'ai pas plus que d'autres gardé de mon enfance une image totale. L'essentiel souvent est effacé; des détails demeurent: parfois ils se présentent avec leur couleur, leur relief, et la sensation même qui les

[22] *Vie de Henry Brulard*, 491.
[23] *Le Roman d'un enfant*, 43. Original ellipses.
[24] *Ma jeunesse*, 93.

accompagna; le plus souvent, la mémoire n'aperçoit d'abord dans l'obscur passé qu'une lueur, une forme indistincte; puis, à mesure qu'on s'y attache, les contours apparaissent et se précisent.[25]

And the Provençal novelist, Henri Bosco, in his significantly entitled autobiography *Un oubli moins profond* (*A Shallower Oblivion*) suggest that 'memory is merely a dream in which one is to a small extent what one was and to a much larger extent what the mind imagines' (*le souvenir n'est qu'un songe où l'on est un peu ce qu'on fut et beaucoup plus ce que l'esprit imagine*).[26]

Even those who express no disquiet about the reliability of early memories may have other reasons for passing over their childhood as rapidly as possible. The influential editor A. Houssaye, whose pomposity prevents him seeing childhood recollections as anything but *enfantillages*, nevertheless manages to have his cake and eat it too when he announces: 'Is it worth my while recalling my first childish pranks?' (*Est-ce la peine de me souvenir de mes premières gamineries?*) but adds immediately afterwards: 'One day I threw myself in complete despair into the Parmailles fountain. Why? The sorrow of life. I had read neither Werter [*sic*] nor Obermann: I was 5 years old!' (*Je me jetai un jour tout désespéré dans la fontaine de Parmailles. Pourquoi? Le mal de vivre. Je n'avais lu ni Werter* [sic] *ni Obermann: J'avais cinq ans!*)[27] Here, the desire to appear above and beyond any considerations of childhood, while still seeking to seize the reader's sympathy, together with the setting of the memory in the framework of a clichéd Romanticism, merely succeeds in conveying to us the image of a man for whom childhood memories are too disturbing and embarrassing either to be explored in any detail or to be left completely in silence. L. Véron, founder of the influential *Revue de Paris*, begins answering his initial question of 'who am I?' by defining himself as the young man who was named top hospital intern in the competitive examinations of 1821, when he was 23. It is not until the third volume of his memoirs that he finds the confidence to insert a few memories of his childhood. The attitude of the Provençal poet Mistral is more one of defiance, a shifting of any embarrassment that might be felt away from himself and on to the

---

[25] *Une enfance*, 10.
[26] *Un oubli moins profond*, 19.
[27] *Confessions*, i. 52.

reader, and a determined, if somewhat heavy-handed, refusal to share such doubts: 'it may perhaps be considered somewhat infantile to recount all these things' (*on trouvera peut-être tant soit peu enfantin de raconter toutes ces choses*),[28] he suggests, but goes on to record them apparently unabashed. Rémusat makes us more clearly aware of the historical context that produced an uncertainty which to post-Freudian minds seems distinctly curious. 'At the risk of being accused of opening these memoirs like a metaphysician, I shall begin with my first recollection, by that awakening of the distinct awareness of oneself in a specific environment.' (*Au risque d'être accusé de débuter en métaphysicien, j'ouvrirai ces mémoires par mon premier souvenir, par cet éveil d'une conscience de soi-même distincte dans un milieu déterminé.*)[29]

We should be careful, however, not to conflate embarrassment about talking of early memories with a failure to understand their importance for the subsequent development of the individual. Lamartine, for instance, might protest: 'I shall not imitate Jean-Jacques Rousseau in his *Confessions*. I shall not relate to you the puerile events of my early years. Manhood begins only with the awakening of sentiment and thought' (*Je n'imiterai pas Jean-Jacques Rousseau dans ses* Confessions. *Je ne vous raconterai pas les puérilités de ma première enfance. L'homme ne commence qu'avec le sentiment et la pensée!*),[30] but he is nevertheless convinced that 'The child's predestination is the house in which it is born; the soul consists above all of the impressions received there' (*La prédestination de l'enfant, c'est la maison où il est né; son âme se compose surtout des impressions qu'il y a reçues*). Among all the writers of autobiographies who acknowledge the general disquiet over including childhood memories, one, Hermant, stands out as offering a particularly ingenious rationalization:

I imagine you don't expect from me the sentence with which all confessions begin: 'I remember nothing of my childhood.' I, on the contrary, do remember; but I think I'm an exception. . . . You know that the changes undergone by the individual in the maternal womb imitate those of the race in the course of evolution. This principle also applies to moral existence. . . . Indeed, if men who have reached maturity have such difficulty in rediscovering the slightest memory of their childhood, it may well be quite

[28] *Mes origines*, 8.
[29] *Mémoires*, 3.
[30] *Confidences*, 54.

simply because their present stupidity is no longer capable of comprehending their former genius.

Vous n'attendez pas de moi, j'imagine, la phrase par où toutes les confessions débutent: 'Je ne me rappelle rien de mon enfance.' Moi, je m'en souviens au contraire; mais je crois que c'est une exception. . . . Vous savez que les métamorphoses de l'individu enfermé dans le sein maternel imitent celles de la race au cours de l'évolution. Ce principe s'applique à la vie morale. . . . Au fait, si les hommes arrivés à la maturité ont tant de peine à retrouver le moindre souvenir de leur enfance, c'est peut-être tout bonnement que leur bêtise actuelle n'est plus capable de comprendre leur génie passé.[31]

Justifications for publishing autobiographies constitute, indeed, one of the principal opening gambits. Some writers present themselves as typical, offering their own life-stories as a kind of template for their fellows, and simultaneously demanding from their reader a comprehending complicity: 'What I am, all my contemporaries must also be, apart from certain slight differences.' (*Ce que je suis, tous mes contemporains doivent l'être, sauf les nuances.*)[32] Others, either explicitly or covertly, give as their reason for writing a sense of their own uniqueness. Marie d'Agoult, writing under the pseudonym Daniel Stern with which she signed so many articles of art criticism, together with her confessional novel *Nélida*, indulges in considerable breast-beating to vindicate the publication of her memoirs, although a well-established tradition of eighteenth-century women memorialists might well have dispensed her from any such need:

I was a woman and, as such, not obliged to conform to virile sincerity. Since neither my birth nor my sex had called me to play an active role in politics, I had no account to render to my fellow citizens and I could keep to myself the painful secret of my inner struggles . . . At other moments the voice that spoke to my conscience changed its tune. It found in the very fact that I was a woman a decisive reason for speaking out. When a woman has made a life for herself, I would think at such times, and when that life is not controlled by the common rule, she becomes responsible for it, more responsible than a man in all eyes. When that woman, through mere chance or through some talent or other, has come into the spotlight, she has contracted at the same time virile duties.

J'étais femme, et comme telle, non obligée aux sincérités viriles. Ma naissance et mon sexe ne m'ayant point appelée à jouer un rôle actif dans la

---

[31] *Confessions*, 9.
[32] Ibid., 8.

politique, je n'avais aucun compte à rendre à mes concitoyens, et je pouvais garder pour moi seule le douloureux secret de mes luttes intérieures. . . . En d'autres moments la voix qui parlait à ma conscience changeait d'accent. Elle trouvait dans mon sexe même une raison décisive de parler. Lorsqu'une femme s'est fait à elle-même sa vie, pensais-je alors, et que cette vie n'est pas gouvernée suivant la règle commune, elle en devient responsable, plus responsable qu'un homme aux yeux de tous. Quand cette femme, par l'effet du hasard ou de quelque talent, est sortie de l'obscurité, elle a contracté, du même instant, des devoirs virils.[33]

The industrialist Richard-Lenoir bases his decision to write partly on the need to record a general change in living conditions and partly on the conviction that, at least to some degree, he has been responsible for those changes through the power of his own personality. Looking back to a childhood in the Calvados of the late eighteenth century, he remarks that 'when today you see the almost universal well-being and the kind of luxury that has extended even into our rural areas, you have no inkling of what a farm could be like in those days, or of the poverty-stricken state of the peasant' (*en voyant aujourd'hui le bien-être presque général et l'espèce de luxe qui s'est glissé jusque dans nos campagnes, on ne se doute pas de ce que pouvaient être alors une ferme et l'état misérable du paysan*),[34] and he adds of himself as a young boy:

Already the liveliness of my imagination could be detected in a thousand different ways . . . I already felt a kind of repugnance at the thought of shuffling along the well-worn routes: had a clever observer followed me in all my actions, he would have foreseen the active life I was destined to lead, and he would have recognized even in my tricks and my premature calculations the germ of the speculative genius which, I can say this without vainglory, was one day to give a new impetus to French industry.

Déjà l'activité de mon imagination se faisait remarquer de mille manières . . . Je sentais déjà une espèce de répugnance à me traîner dans les routes battues: l'observateur habile, qui m'eût suivi dans toutes mes actions, eût pressenti la vie active à laquelle j'étais destiné, et il aurait reconnu jusque dans mes espiègleries et mes calculs prématurés le germe de ce génie spéculatif, qui, je puis le dire sans orgueil, devait un jour donner un nouvel essor à l'industrie française.[35]

---

[33] *Mes souvenirs*, p. viii.
[34] *Mémoires*, 2.
[35] Ibid., 9.

Richard-Lenoir, who rose from his obscure peasant background to become the first to set up a cotton mill[36] in France, and whose name is immortalized in a Paris street, certainly convinces his readers that they are dealing with a child whose exceptional native wit and entrepreneurial skills point forward to the success of the adult. His conviction of the continuity between child and adult provides him with a further reason for writing his autobiography, together with the sheer pleasure of remembering, since, as he says, 'while these events may not offer any powerful interest to outsiders, I cannot refuse myself the pleasure of retracing them; for these old memories appear in my childhood as portents of the future' (*ces événements, quoiqu'ils n'offrent pas peut-être un intérêt puissant aux étrangers, je ne puis me refuser au plaisir de les rétracer; car ces vieux souvenirs apparaissent dans mon enfance comme des présages de l'avenir*).[37]

Wordsworth's belief that the child is indeed father to the man is, perhaps predictably enough, offered by several writers as grounds for exploring their own childhoods, despite the fear of being mocked for introducing puerilities. There are numerous variations on the basic theme that 'if I tell this so many years later, the reason is that neither the child, nor the head, nor the old person has changed in thought or heart' (*si je le dis, après tant d'années, c'est que ni l'enfant, ni la tête, ni la vieillesse, n'ont changé de pensée ni d'amour*),[38] or, as Stendhal idiosyncratically puts it: '*il y a plus, il y a bien pis*, I am *encore* in 1835 the man of 1794' (there is more, there is far worse, in 1835 I am still the man of 1794).[39] The artist Elisabeth Vigée-Lebrun, who also adopts the common trope of writing for a specific reader—friend, child, descendent—which mitigates the immodesty of the enterprise, spells out her conviction that her early years have presaged her entire life,[40] and the feminist Suzanne Voilquin, writing in 1866, adopts the same two devices: 'To let you understand my life, dear child, I shall need to spend a few pages describing my first years for you; the past gives birth to the future; logic demands that this be the case.' (*Pour comprendre ma vie, je dois, chère enfant, t'en développer en quelques pages les*

---

[36] See also Stearns, *Paths to Authority*.

[37] *Mémoires*, 10–11.

[38] Bosco, *Un oubli moins profond*, 53.

[39] *Vie de Henry Brulard*, 188.

[40] *Souvenirs*, 2.

*premières années; le passé enfante l'avenir; la logique le veut
ainsi.*)[41] Voilquin has an even more pressing need than Vigée-
Lebrun to justify her life, in both senses of the word, for while
painting could be seen as an extension of the drawing-room skills
suitable for a woman, Suzanne Voilquin's decision to acquire
medical knowledge went well beyond the pale of acceptability for a
woman in her social class. Other authors of autobiographies felt
themselves in equally acute need of some form of defence: thus the
murderer Lacenaire, whose hand Gautier describes with such eager
revulsion in *Émaux et Camées*, is intent on using his highly
intelligent autobiography to show, through the tenacious memories
of childhood, the path of cause and effect between his father's
refusal to love him and his subsequent criminal activities.[42]

   If in many memoirs some sort of justification acts as a starting-
point, it is also true that the search for a valid beginning frequently
mirrors the writer's own search for the stage at which they become
the individual they now feel themselves to be as adults. In this
regard the multiple beginnings of Proust's *A la recherche du temps
perdu* may be exemplary, but they are not unique. It is at least a
tenable suppostion that for many the first step in that slow progress
towards self-definition, or at least the first step revealed to the
reader, is encapsulated by the title itself. While one suspects that the
various titles that incorporate some form of generalizing definition
—'Childhood and Education of a Peasant in the Eighteenth
Century' (Jamerey-Duval) or 'The Cry of a Child from the
Auvergne' (Sylvère)—are the suggestion or even the creation of an
editor or publisher, others seem more revealing. Few titles reflect
the self-assurance of Joyce in *Portrait of the Artist as a Young Man*
or Henry Handel Richardson in *Myself when Young*. While some
attempt to defuse, through self-mockery, their fears of a mocking
reception, as Stendhal does in choosing the title *Souvenirs
d'égotisme*, others select a title that appears to shift the central
focus from the personality to the intellect, an example being
Quinet's *Histoire de mes idées*. Others seize on the possibility of
suggesting the universal nature of their own experience and thus of
classifying a collection of personal memories under the rubric *sub
specie aeternitatis*. Hence, no doubt, the proliferation of memoirs
described as being 'of a little girl' (Mme Michelet), 'of a

---

[41] *Souvenirs d'une fille du peuple*, 4.
[42] See e.g. Lacenaire, *Mémoires*, 36–9.

journeyman' (Perdiguier), or, in slightly different versions of the same device, 'of Léonard' (Nadaud) or 'of half a century' (Houssaye). The uncertainty concerning the very nature of auto-biography is reflected in titles incorporating the word novel (roman): *The Novel of My Childhood*, *The Novel of My Friend*, *The Novel of a Little Girl*, the last two suggesting, as does *Memoirs of Another Life*, the desire to avoid the charge of egotism that Stendhal so deliberately and provocatively courts.

In this search for an opening, the act of recapturing the first memory, or isolating the moment when the child first becomes aware of its identity, informs innumerable autobiographies and adds to the image of nineteenth-century childhood yielded by the written records. Yet if adults in search of their earliest memories are certainly looking through the wrong end of the telescope, to use P. Laslett's suggestive phrase, most of them are also filtering those memories through the lens of literature. In reading them, one begins to wonder to what extent such elements of an autobiography have become a literary trope, included mainly because there has arisen during the course of the century a mythology of childhood so tenacious as to create, through a kind of spontaneous generation, the need, rather than the reality, of a clearly isolatable and locatable first memory.[43] While this may raise salutary doubts about the historical experience of being a child in the nineteenth century, it does not necessarily distort our study of a literary topos.

One example of the point where the lens through which we are looking may be more literary than historical concerns those first memories associated with pain, since Cellini's autobiography offers us a singularly memorable instance of such a combination. (There is an earlier memory in Cellini's *Life*, but it is specifically described as being related to him at a subsequent date.) This episode is worth quoting in full:

One day when I was about five years old, my father was sitting in a ground-floor room of ours in which washing had been going on, and where a large fire of oak logs had been left. Giovanni [Cellini's father], his viola on his arm, was playing and singing by himself near the fire—for it was very cold. Looking into the fire he chanced to see in the middle of the most ardent flames a little creature like a lizard disporting itself in the midst of the

[43] On the question of the first memory see Vercier, 'Le Mythe du premier souvenir', and for a truly stunning example see Schweitzer's affirmation in *Aus meiner Kindheit* that his first memory is of the devil.

intensest heat. Suddenly aware of what it was, he called my sister and me and pointed it out to us children. Then he gave me a sound box on the ears, which made me cry bitterly, on which he soothed me with kind words, saying, 'My dear little fellow, I did not hurt you for any harm you had done, but only that you might remember that the lizard in the fire is certainly a salamander, which has never been seen for a certainty by any one before.' Then he kissed me and gave me some farthings.[44]

My argument here is not, of course, that this is the sole or specific source of anecdotes concerning first memories associated with pain, but rather that it provides an exemplary illustration of the trope, tying together the clarity with which small details are recalled—the fire, the washing, the music—, the shock associated with the beating, and a clearly formulated statement about the union of pain and memory. Nor am I arguing for the fictional basis of all such instances, but instead seeking to suggest that the inclusion of similar experiences in earlier autobiographies may well have encouraged even those reluctant to reveal much of their childhood to insert a similar episode in their own work.

Whatever the case, numerous autobiographies contain variations on the novelist Julien Green's affirmation: 'My first memory is one of physical pain.' (*Mon premier souvenir est un souvenir de douleur physique*.)[45] George Sand recalls being dropped by her maid when she was 2, in a passage which binds together the physical and the emotional:

This is the first memory of my life and it dates from very early childhood. I was 2 years old, a maid dropped me from her arms on to the corner of the chimneypiece. I was frightened and hurt my forehead. This shock, this disturbance of my nervous system, made me aware that I was alive and I saw clearly, I still see, the reddish marble of the chimneypiece, my blood as it flowed, the distraught face of my nursemaid.

Voici le premier souvenir de ma vie, et il date de loin. J'avais deux ans, une bonne me laissa tomber de ses bras sur l'angle d'une cheminée, j'eus peur et je fus blessée au front. Cette commotion, cet ébranlement du système nerveux ouvrirent mon esprit au sentiment de la vie, et je vis nettement, je vois encore, le marbre rougeâtre de la cheminée, mon sang qui coulait, la figure égarée de ma bonne.[46]

Henri Boucher also links a very early memory with pain, showing the clarity with which he recalls small details which would otherwise be irrecoverable:

[44] *Autobiography*, 7–8.
[45] *Partir avant le jour*, 9.   [46] *Histoire de ma vie*, i. 530.

As for the top of the stair well, the door to our apartment on the left, and the dining-room one saw on entering, they have . . . been rescued from oblivion as the result of the time I fell on to the landing in escaping from being pursued around the big table. I split my cheek open on a pot of flowers.

Quant au haut de l'escalier, la porte de notre logement à gauche et la salle à manger en entrant, ont . . . été sauvées de l'oubli par suite d'une chute que je fis sur la palier en échappant à une poursuite que m'avait été faite autour de la grande table. Je me fendis la joue sur un pot de fleurs.[47]

For her part, Judith Gautier recalls, as an early, although not first, memory, twisting her ankle and being carried home under a night sky of such splendour that for her the beauty of the stars became inextricably linked with memories of pain: 'I have never remembered that physical pain, experienced for the first time on that day, without its immediately being veiled by the splendour of my first view of the stars.' (*Jamais je ne me suis souvenue de cette première souffrance physique, endurée ce jour-là, sans quelle ne fût aussitôt voilée par cette splendeur; la première vision des étoiles.*)[48] (Whether a post-Freudian writer would dare link so clearly beauty and pain is at least open to question.) A similar linking of pain and pleasure can be found in Champfleury, who, after visiting the theatre, is left with an indelible memory of two lines—'Trestaillon commands/ That we should spare no one' (*Trestaillon l'ordonne/ N'épargnons personne*)—not, he hastens to add, because of their lyricism, but because he fell down the stairs on leaving the theatre and was consoled by an amiable actress: 'the emotion my fall had caused her still swelled her breast and this delightful sight made me forget the horrible rogues of Trestaillon's band.' (*l'émoi que lui avait causé ma chute soulevait sa poitrine et cette agréable vue me faisait oublier les affreux scélérats de la bande de Trestaillon.*)[49] Champfleury, moreover, specifically refers to Cellini in relating this anecdote: 'this had the same result as the salamander Benvenuto Cellini saw when he was very young and which brought him such a fierce cuff from his father, together with the admonishment: "You'll remember the salamander."' (*il en arriva comme pour la salamandre qu'aperçut tout jeune Benvenuto Cellini, et qui lui valut un si rude soufflet de son père avec cette admonestation: 'Tu te*

---

[47] *Souvenirs d'un parisien*, 13.
[48] *Le Collier des jours*, 95.
[49] *Souvenirs*, 7.

souviendras de la salamandre.')[50] The mythical salamander, therefore, serves as an icon of the ways in which intertextual reference, explicit or implicit, facilitates for many nineteenth-century autobiographers the incorporation of the personal into the literary.

FINDING THE SELF

Although these early memories capture a moment in the child's development, they do not necessarily constitute the point when the author feels for the first time fully in touch with his or her own self. Many of the autobiographers are concerned, overtly or covertly, with the questions of when the child becomes fully aware of itself as independent individual and how its future career is determined. The belief in the existence of a determining moment, and the pain associated with it, a belief shared by many writers, is evoked with particular intensity and melancholy by Julien Green:

All of us have experienced that singular moment when we feel ourselves abruptly separated from the rest of the world through the fact that we are ourselves and not that which surrounds us. . . . At that moment I left paradise. It was the melancholy hour when the first person singular makes its entry into human life to claim the front of the stage until we breathe our final breath.

Tous les hommes ont connu cet instant singulier où l'on se sent brusquement séparé du reste du monde par le fait qu'on est soi-même et non ce qui nous entoure. . . . Je sortis à ce moment-là d'un paradis. C'était l'heure mélancolique où la première personne du singulier fait son entrée dans la vie humaine pour tenir le devant de la scène jusqu'au dernier soupir.[51]

Ironically, it is the writers most alert to the complexities of childhood for whom questions concerning the discovery of self pose the greatest problems, as they reveal themselves aware, to use Kipling's sardonic assessment, that 'no-one, the owner least of all, can explain what is in a growing boy's mind',[52] or, to quote C. S. Lewis's more sober reminder, 'we all remember that our childhood, as lived, was immeasurably different from what our elders saw'.[53]

---

[50] *Souvenirs*, 6.
[51] *Partir avant le jour*, 23.
[52] *Stalky & Co.*, p. x.
[53] 'On Three Ways of Writing for Children', 209.

Finding a means of translating into metaphor the child's awareness of self often seems, therefore, at least as important as noting the time or cause of its precipitation. George Sand recalls her childhood puzzlement at hearing an echo of her own voice, and her explanation that she must be double, surrounded by an unseen but ever-watching *me* who replies whenever spoken to.[54] Judith Gautier also focuses on the notion of doubling when she attempts to find an image for the awareness of self:

The little person, unknown and solitary, who lived deep within me had no intention of being discovered. . . . This was the first time I had attempted to explain myself to myself as regards this special state in which I felt that I was two people.

La petite personne, inconnue et solitaire, qui était au fond de moi n'entendait pas être découverte. . . . C'était la première fois que j'essayais de m'expliquer avec moi-même, sur cet état particulier, où il me semblait être dédoublée.[55]

And a similar image occurs to Hermant, in recalling how he looked forward to going to school: 'I felt sure that once I went to school my only problem would be in deciding who to love, and I observed myself somewhat maliciously, already split in two.' (*je comptais bien qu'une fois au collège, je n'aurais que l'embarras du choix pour aimer, et je m'observais avec un peu de malice, déjà dédoublé.*)[56] In many of these cases, so it would seem, we have a development of what Lacan has termed the mirror stage, a stage, in other words, where the child endeavours to explore its own individuality by fleshing out the image its mirror has provided, and realizes its position as separate from a world it had previously considered an extension of itself.

Many writers trying to indicate the nature of their own childhoods, and in particular attempting to find the point where they recognize themselves, if only in embryo, as the individuals under observation, record the extent to which their sense of personality arises from an awareness of their difference in comparison to others, as opposed, say, to the world of nature or of books. This may, of course, be closely allied to their initial reason for writing their memoirs. Philarète Chasles, for example, asserts: 'my first awakening was neither literary nor *bookish*, as Montaigne

[54] *Histoire de ma vie*, i. 573.
[55] *Le Collier des jours*, 70.
[56] *Confessions*, 14.

puts it, but caused by *the sight of my fellows.*' (*mes premiers éveils ne furent pas littéraires ou* livresques, *comme dit Montaigne, mais causés par* le spectacle de mes semblables.)[57] But this assertion needs to be understood in conjunction with the justification in his opening remarks that 'a man is of interest and his life of worth only through his relations with the age in which he was born' (*un homme n'intéresse et sa vie n'a de prix que par ses rapports avec l'époque où il est né*) and that 'The moral wounds the world inflicted on me are deep; and that pain, that others would not feel, has to be explained, has to be salvaged from irony and insult' (*les blessures morales que le monde m'a laissées sont profondes; et cette douleur que d'autres ne ressentiraient pas, il faut l'expliquer, il faut l'arracher à l'ironie et à l'injure*).[58] Here, in other words, is a man who, like Rousseau, is profoundly susceptible to the judgements of others, painfully in need of their approval, and almost masochistically courting the danger of further rejection.

For many, of course, the other who first impinges on the child's desires and who plays the greatest role, positive or negative, in shaping it, is a parent. Not all autobiographers have succeeded in finding a means of conveying the complexity of parent–child relationships, particularly if the adolescent's need to impose him or herself has created a bitterness through which the child's earlier feelings can no longer be easily discerned. There is no lack of evidence to justify R. Coe's assertion that 'until one starts to explore the literature of the Childhood, it is difficult to conceive in how many different ways it is possible for a father to forfeit his teenage child's esteem, love or reverence, and in how many ways he can realize his vocation for failure'.[59] But here again placing the autobiographical works in the wider literary context raises the question of whether the Romantic image of the misunderstood individual, whose value grows in direct proportion to the lack of comprehension shown by his or her nearest and dearest, has not invaded the memoirs as well as the confessional novels.

Moreover, in considering how these relationships can be evoked in autobiographies, the reader needs also to bear in mind Hal Porter's pertinent question: 'at what age does one actually see,

---

[57] *Mémoires*, i. 14.
[58] Ibid., 1 and 3.
[59] *When the Grass was Taller*, 144.

rememberably, one's mother, the full-length portrait?'[60] While there is little point in producing from the records a vast bouquet of examples and counter-examples of such relationships, the parallels between the growth of the analytical novel, from *Adolphe* and *René* to *A la recherche du temps perdu* and beyond, and the increased emphasis on early impressions in autobiographies, do not seem merely fortuitous and can more clearly be grasped by examing the ways in which some of these writers sought to reveal their own relationships with parents. Paul Adam sketches for us with considerable economy a portrait of his father seen from the child's-eye view, as 'a man of rigid features, normally dresed in soft black material. His lips rarely parted to smile or speak.' (*un homme aux traits rigides, habillé à l'ordinaire de souples draps noirs. Ses lèvres s'écartaient peu pour le rire ou la parole.*)[61] This physical portrait associated with the child's very early memories is later expanded by an evocation of the kind of upbringing he attempted to impose on his son:

My father intended to guide my upbringing according to evangelistical rigidity. His mania for thwarting my pleasures and tastes and contradicting what I said was a real sport and, in his eyes, an excellent exercise for breaking my will. Little by little I came to feel for him sincere hatred.

Mon père entendait conduire mon éducation selon le mode de rigidité évangeliste. Sa manie de contrarier mes plaisirs ou mes goûts, de contredire mes propos, était un sport véritable, et, à son sens, une excellente gymnastique pour me rompre la volonté. Je lui vouai peu à peu une haine sincère.[62]

Not all those who wrote autobiographies were willing to give direct expression to the unhappy emotions their fathers aroused in them. J. Isaac, for instance, seems to be operating a curious transference of emotions from himself to his sister, when he records that his father's severity was such that

children did not have the right to speak at table unless they were addressed directly. My younger sister . . . later admitted to me that her fear of my father had terrorized all her childhood and her early youth.

---

[60] *The Watcher on the Cast-Iron Balcony*, 48.
[61] *Les Images sentimentales*, 7.
[62] Ibid., 74.

les enfants n'avaient pas le droit de parler à table, à moins qu'on ne leur adressât la parole. Ma soeur cadette . . . m'a avoué plus tard que la crainte du père avait terrorisé toute son enfance et sa prime jeunesse.[63]

Even fathers whose reputation among adults was that of an easy-going bon viveur could not always respond to the emotional needs of their children. Judith Gautier, who was left with a wet-nurse for years because of her mother, Ernesta Grisi's, acting commitments, describes her first remembered meeting with her father as involving a presumably jocular threat by him to stick her to the ceiling with a ceiling wafer: 'My father had hardly any inkling that this scene left me with an indelible memory and a pretty long-lasting sense of rancour.' (*Mon père ne se doutait guère que j'emportais de cette scène un souvenir ineffaçable et une assez longue rancune.*)[64] (A story which casts a curiously ironic light on Gautier's own more than slightly fatuous statement in a review of Gavarni's *Les Enfants terribles*: 'Of course children are no angels, but nor are they devils. You only need to wash them frequently and whip them occasionally to make of them very pleasant little creatures, very sweet and chubby, quite capable of being found charming even by people who are not their mothers.' (*Certes les enfants ne sont pas des anges, mais ce ne sont pas non plus des diables. Il n'y a qu'à les débarbouiller souvent et à les fouetter quelquefois pour en faire de petits êtres fort gentils, fort mignons et fort poupins, très dignes d'être trouvés charmants par d'autres même que par leurs mères.*)[65] The most moving of such testimonials comes from an English source, Edmund Gosse's truly remarkable book, *Father and Son*:

while it was with my Father that the long struggle which I have to narrate took place, behind my Father stood the ethereal memory of my Mother's will, guiding him, pressing him, holding him to the unswerving purpose which she had formed and defined. And when the inevitable disruption came, what was unspeakably painful was to realize that it was not from one but from both parents that the purpose of the child was separated.[66]

Indeed, mothers do not come off much better than fathers, whatever the sex of the writer: one need only think of the mothers in Vallès's *L'Enfant*, or Renard's *Poil de carotte* or indeed in

[63] *Expériences de ma vie*, 21.
[64] *Le Collier des jours*, 18.
[65] *Souvenirs de théâtre*, 179–83.
[66] *Father and Son*, 14.

Juliette Adam's *Le Roman de mon enfance*. But of course there are exceptions: Stendhal's passionate love for his mother, the cult of the father in Mme Michelet's autobiography (which explains of course the relationship with her husband), Marie d'Agoult's reverence for her father, or the tender and very productive relationship between George Sand and her mother, described in the following terms: 'my mother instinctively and quite naïvely opened up for me the world of beauty by sharing all her impressions with me from my tenderest years.' (*ma mère m'ouvrait instinctivement et tout naïvement le monde du beau en m'associant dès l'âge le plus tendre à toutes ses impressions.*)[67] And of course it needs to be emphasized that for many the root cause of difficulty in the relations with parents can be traced back to the habit of sending children away to wet-nurses and leaving them there often for some considerable time, Rousseau's pleas on maternal breast-feeding notwithstanding.

The awareness of self is inevitably bound up with a sense of gender which, at least for many male writers, proves less difficult to explore than the question of parental influence. Renan, confessing that 'from a very early stage I had a keen appreciation of little girls' (*très tôt, le goût des jeunes filles fut vif en moi*), adds the double-edged rider:

Of course I saw my own intellectual superiority; but from then on I felt that a very beautiful or very good woman completely solves for herself the problem that we, for all our mental strength, only worsen.

Je voyais bien ma supériorité intellectuelle; mais, dès lors, je sentais que la femme très belle ou très bonne résout complètement, pour son compte, le problème qu'avec toute notre force de tête nous ne faisons que gâcher.[68]

Hermant, an only child, affirms straightforwardly that 'I placed a very high value on everything that seemed to me specifically male and a very low value on everything that seemed to me to be female' (*j'estimais très haut tout ce qui me semblait plus particulièrement mâle, et très bas ce qui me semblait femelle.*[69] And Julien Benda, seeking the roots of his clerical soul[70] in a childhood spent in the 1870s, notes: 'I also extracted from the feelings my father aroused in me the idea that, in a household, it is the man who by rights has

[67] *Histoire de ma vie*, 556.
[69] *Confessions*, 10.
[68] *Souvenirs*, 113–14.
[70] *La Jeunesse d'un clerc*, 69.

the first role, and that the woman must only be a "follower" ' (*je tirais aussi des sentiments que m'inspirait mon père l'idée que, dans le ménage, c'est à l'homme qu'appartient de droit le premier rang, la femme n'y devant être qu'une personne 'à la suite'*), adding, heavy-handly, 'moreover I have always been favourable to female emancipation but through justice not gallantry' (*j'ai d'ailleurs été toujours acquis à l'émancipation de la femme, mais par justice, non galanterie*).[71] Mme Michelet expresses her awareness of gender in terms of limitation, restriction, and being forced in a direction alien to her interests: 'Daughters belong to their mothers. I could not pursue my own tastes nor the tendency of my heart, which would have led me far more to work with my father.' (*Les filles appartiennent à leur mère. Je ne pouvais suivre mes goûts, ni la tendance de mon cœur, qui m'auraient portée beaucoup plus à travailler avec mon père.*)[72] For some children the awareness of different standards for the two sexes was from an early stage not merely a means of self-definition but a convention enabling the child to manipulate the adult. The young George Sand, for example, notes that while Deschartres, her brother's preceptor, beats the boy cruelly, he punishes little girls merely with verbal abuse; she, therefore, deliberately sets out to draw Deschartres's fire and thus protect her brother.

The need to define oneself in relation to a sibling is frequently recorded, though rarely with the frank aggression and precocious sexual awareness of Alexandre Weill:

I recall an outburst of pride, dating from my fifth year. I had five sisters, three older and two younger (I have seven now). The second, who was called Ruth, constantly teased me. I did not like her. I was the only son until I was 8 years old. She was jealous. One day she insisted in front of my mother that, for all that she was a girl, she would never yield to me and that she could do everything I could. . . . Noisily opening the window, I retreated to the middle of the room and launched a rainbow through the casement. 'Well do that!' I said to her.

Je me rappelle un accès de fierté, dès l'âge de cinq ans. J'avais déjà cinq sœurs, trois plus âgées et deux plus jeunes (j'en ai sept). La seconde qui s'appelait Ruth me taquinait toujours. Je ne l'aimais pas. J'étais fils unique jusqu'à l'âge du huit ans. Elle était jalouse. Un jour elle prétendait devant

[71] *La Jeunesse d'un clerc*, 15.
[72] A. Michelet, *Mémoires d'une enfant*, 147.

ma mère que, toute fille qu'elle était, elle ne me céderait jamais le pas et qu'elle saurait faire tout ce que je ferais. . . . Ouvrant la fenêtre avec fracas, puis, reculant au milieu de la chambre je lâchai un arc-en-ciel à travers la croisée: 'Fais cela', lui dis-je![73]

How much is packed into that brief passage! The designation of Ruth as second sister, forced to give precedence both to an older sister and, still more humiliating and unjust, to a younger brother; the brief surfacing of Alexandre's own jealousy at the birth of the brother who stripped him once and for all of that title of only son, a jealousy not specifically acknowledged but revealed by the introduction of information unnecessary to our understanding of the anecdote in question; the heightening of tension due to the mother's presence; the violence ('noisily') and crudeness of the boy's response; and finally the unnecessarily aggressive nature of the challenge, for the mother's subsequent burst of laughter indicates that the struggle for possession of her affection had already been won by the little boy.

The conviction that siblings have taken all the parents' affections hangs over many autobiographical childhoods. Hal Porter, in his acerbic account of an Australian childhood, theorizes somewhat eccentrically that 'perhaps an eldest son exhausts a mother's fire, burns out the last of her virginal flames with the more outrageous flames of the newer, untried masculinity that supplements and at the same time destroys the father's older, tried-out and chewed-over masculinity'.[74] For Chateaubriand things were more straightforward. If there was little hope that he, as second son, could gain the affection of a father whose sole passion was his name,[75] it was clear that maternal love was a strictly limited commodity: 'all [my mother's] affection was concentrated on her first-born son; not that she did not cherish her other childen, but she revealed a blind preference for the young comte de Combourg.' (*toutes les affections [de ma mère] s'étaient concentrées dans son fils aîné; non qu'elle ne chérît ses autres enfants, mais elle témoignait une préférence aveugle au jeune comte de Combourg.*)[76] And he adds, with the heartless selfishness of childhood and a fair degree of snobbery: 'It is true that I did indeed have, as a boy, and as the last-born . . . some

[73] *Ma jeunesse*, 8–9.
[74] *The Watcher on the Cast-Iron Balcony*, 120.
[75] *Mémoires d'outre-tombe*, i. 26.
[76] Ibid., i. 33–4.

privileges over my sisters; but by and large I was abandoned to the care of the servants.' (*J'avais bien, il est vrai, comme garçon, comme le dernier venu . . . quelques privilèges sur mes sœurs; mais en définitive, j'étais abandonné aux mains des gens.*)[77] Mme Michelet, whose passionate love for her father seems undiminished by his judgement, expressed in her presence, that 'my princess will always be ugly but she will be intelligent' (*ma princesse sera toujours laide, mais elle sera intelligente*),[78] found her American mother's affections already full invested in two older and, so it would seem, prettier children:

Two older children had preceded me, both born in America and all the more dear as a result. . . . These pretty and admired children, who adorned my mother so well, would perhaps have been all she needed for happiness.

Deux aînés m'avaient précédée, tous deux nés en Amérique et d'autant plus chers. . . . Ces jolis enfants admirés, qui paraient si bien ma mère, auraient peut-être suffi à son bonheur.[79]

The need for self-definition in response to such apparent rejection is even more sharply present in the child abandoned, however briefly, by a mother enabled by his birth to sell her milk elsewhere. Although, of course, he does not claim to have a personal memory of the event, Toinou's bitterness is evident even in the apparent humour and the carefully polished syntax of his statement: 'The maternal breasts set off for the city to bring joy to a so-called little sister whose name I can no longer remember.' (*Les seins maternels partirent vers la grande ville faire la joie d'une prétendue petite sœur dont je ne puis me rappeler le nom.*)[80] Although he cannot deny her existence, he takes what revenge he can in refusing her an identity.

Some writers, however, present as unproblematic the whole question of self-definition in relation to other children, even in circumstances that might strike us as extraordinary. Angélina Bardin, an *enfant trouvée* who began earning her living at 13, offers a comic, unpretentious autobiography in which her abandonment by her natural parents is in no way tragic:

I was the thirteenth in Mother Gomard's home, a numbered number, to tell the truth. The others weren't numbered as I was. They were called by their

[77] *Mémoires d'outre-tombe*, i. 34.
[78] A. Michelet, *Mémoires d'une enfant*, 62.
[79] Ibid., 4.   [80] Sylvère, *Toinou*, 1.

given names and their family name. And that was that. But I had my
number as well, inscribed on a little medallion in the middle of a bone
necklace.

J'étais la treizième chez maman Gomard, un numéro numéroté, à vrai dire.
Les autres ne l'étaient pas comme moi numérotés. Ils s'appelaient de leurs
prénoms et de leur nom de famille. Un point, c'est tout. Mais moi, j'avais
en plus mon numéro, inscrit sur une petite médaille, au milieu d'un collier
d'os.[81]

Predictably, there are also autobiographies in which affection for
a sibling is a source of self-assurance that is presented as playing a
more important role in the formation of the individual than
parental or filial love. Loti says of his sister, for instance, that 'she
adored me and I admired her unreservedly, which gave her supreme
power over my childish imagination' (*elle m'adorait et je l'admirais
sans réserves, ce qui lui donnait sur mon imagination d'enfant un
ascendant suprême*),[82] while the decision taken by Suzanne
Voilquin's mother to put her 9-year-old daughter in charge of a
new-born sister is, not surprisingly, offered as a decisive moment in
the girl's development:

This precocious maternity, which caused me, like all exclusive emotions,
both joy and pain, became a salutary stimulant for my youth and nourished
my heart. Through this purest of emotions I came to understand my duty.

Cette précoce maternité, qui me causa, comme tous les sentiments
exclusifs, joie et douleur, devint un stimulent salutaire pour ma jeunesse et
un aliment pour mon cœur. Ce sentiment si pur me fit comprendre mon
devoir.[83]

For some, it is a threat to, or separation from, a beloved parent
or nurse that precipitates the child into self-awareness. Judith
Gautier's desire to protect a much-loved nurse underpins her
earliest memories, from her remembered feelings of anxiety when
the nurse has to draw water from a well, to her recollections of
walking past a cake-shop, determinedly looking the other way, so

---

[81] *Angélina*, 11.

[82] *Prime jeunesse*, 33.

[83] *Souvenirs d'une fille du peuple*, 15. One should note that such a move was far
from being eccentric or unique: foundlings were not infrequently given to girls of the
aristocracy to bring up, as happened, for instance, when Mme de Genlis was
preceptress to the royal children. George Sand draws on the custom in her novel *Les
Maîtres-Sonneurs*, and Mme Michelet affirms that, when very young, she was put in
charge of her baby brother (*Memoires d'une enfant*, 33).

that the nurse will not buy her a cake that she cannot afford. Separation from the nurse produces in the child what is clearly a desire to punish herself for the unknown sin that has caused this rejection:

> Since I had fallen from grace and was deprived of my dear nurse, who was still the only person I loved, I had become very hard on myself, stoically enduring the consequences of my behaviour; I suffered privations and even physical pain without complaint.

> Depuis que j'étais déchue de ma royauté et privée de la chère nourrice, toujours seule aimée, je devenais très dure pour moi-même, subissant stoïquement les conséquences de mes actes; j'endurais les privations et jusqu'à la souffrance physique sans me plaindre.[84]

For many, and particularly for boys, separation was the result of being sent away to school. Lamartine, for whom the garden at Milly, where he spent his infancy, was part of the very fabric of his being, describes being sent to college at 12 in terms of a new and far more painful birth:

> I entered it as a man condemned to death enters his last cell. The false smiles, the hypocritical caresses of the schoolmasters who wanted to imitate a father's heart in exchange for money cut no ice with me. I understood all that was venal in that stimulated tenderness. My heart broke for the first time in my life, and when the iron gate closed between my mother and me, I felt I was entering another world and that the honeymoon of my early years had gone, never to return.

> J'y entrai comme le condamné à mort entre dans son dernier cachot. Les faux sourires, les hypocrites caresses des maîtres de cette pension, qui voulaient imiter le cœur d'un père pour de l'argent, ne m'en imposèrent pas. Je compris tout ce que cette tendresse de commande avait de vénal. Mon cœur se brisa pour la première fois de ma vie, et quand la grille de fer se referma entre ma mère et moi, je sentis que j'entrais dans un autre monde, et que la lune de miel de mes premières années était écoulée sans retour.[85]

The critic D. Nisard, born, as he puts it, in May 1806 between the battle of Austerlitz and the battle of Iéna,[86] describes being taken to college by his father, who had promised to come back and make his

---

[84] *Le Collier des jours*, 84. Despite the pleas of Rousseau and others in this regard, the use of wet-nurses was still extremely widespread in 19th-century France: see Badinter, *L'Amour en plus*.

[85] *Confidences*, 110–111.

[86] *Souvenirs*, 23.

final farewells before leaving the town. Fearing that he will not be able to control his emotions, his father leaves without performing this final ceremony and Nisard comments: 'I thought I could feel my heart melting, or rather I felt as if I were being born. . . . That day was the true day of my birth.' (*Je crus sentir mon cœur se fondre, ou plutôt je le sentis naître. . . . Ce jour-là fut mon véritable jour de naissance.*)[87] And, rather later, the poet Francis Jammes notes, also with regard to a separation caused by the need to go away to school:

I left my mother with such grief that I still feel, forty years later, that sense of being torn away that gave me nightmares and fevers for the months I spent apart from her. I can now confess this martyrdom to her, at a time when she is almost 80, and my past bitterness mingles with the smell exuded by a stick cut from a holly tree by my father on one of our autumnal rambles.

Je quittai ma mère avec une telle douleur que je ressens encore, après quarante ans, cet arrachement qui me donna des cauchemars et la fièvre durant les mois que je passai loin d'elle. Ce martyre, je le lui confirme, aujourd'hui qu'elle va être octogénaire, et je mêle mon amertume passée au parfum qui s'exhalait d'un bâton de houx, coupé par mon père, dans l'une de nos promenades d'automne.[88]

In much autobiographical writing, therefore, the school becomes a figure for the inevitable separation of the growing child from a beloved parent, and one that enables the displacement of responsibility for that separation from the self to the parent. What is perhaps most remarkable about these anecdotes is the intensity of the child's feeling as it bursts dialogically through the adult writer's controlled language.

Several writers record that sense of a discovery of self that is like a rebirth occurring much earlier, often as the result of a rebellion against authority. This, too, could be conceived of as part of the Romantic cliché of the misunderstood genius, encapsulated in a formula of Baudelaire's that undoubtedly gains much in virulence for drawing on personal experience:

It is a good thing for each of us, once in our lives, to experience the oppression of an odious tyranny; such an experience teaches us to hate it! How many philosophers have been engendered by the seminary! How

[87] Ibid., 178.
[88] *De l'âge divin*, 137.

many rebellious natures have been born through contact with a cruel and punctilious Empire soldier!

Il est bon que chacun de nous, une fois dans sa vie, ait éprouvé la pression d'une odieuse tyrannie; il apprend à la haïr! Combien de philosophes a engendrés le séminaire! Combien de natures révoltées ont pris vie auprès d'un cruel et ponctuel militaire de l'Empire![89]

Lacenaire dates the self-creating movement of revolt from the time he realized his father would never love him:

It was at this time in my life that there took place within me a miraculous alteration, without anyone realizing it or even guessing that it had happened. Great and intense ideas came to me. I became a man, but for myself alone, at the age of 8.

C'est à cette époque que se fit en moi un changement miraculeux, et sans que personne pût s'en apercevoir, ni même s'en douter. Des idées grandes et fortes se présentèrent à moi. Je devins un homme, mais pour moi seul, à l'âge de 8 ans.[90]

Edmund Gosse, who no doubt had less urgent reasons than Lacenaire to shift the blame for his personality to other shoulders than his own, notes his own revolt more calmly as he affirms: 'through thick and thin I clung to a hard nut of individuality, deep down in my childish nature. To the pressure from without I resigned everything else, my thoughts, my words . . . but there was something which I never resigned, my innate and persistent self.'[91]

Among the experiences that mark the individual, even if they are not necessarily distinguished as uniquely important, are the moments when the child becomes aware of death, or at least attempts to penetrate the meaning of the word and its euphemisms. Few are content to remain at the loftily adult, if poetic, level that Chateaubriand adopts when he asserts from the age of 7 he watched death 'enter that house of peace and benediction, making it gradually more and more solitary, closing one bedroom and then another, bedrooms that would never open again, (*entrer sous ce toit de paix et de bénédiction, le rendre peu à peu solitaire, fermer une chambre et puis une autre qui ne se rouvrait plus*).[92] George Sand makes a more sustained attempt to trace the child's slow realization of human mortality. Referring to the accidental death of her father

---

[89] *Œuvres complètes*, ii. 29.
[90] *Mémoires*, 39.
[91] *Father and Son*, 141.
[92] *Mémoires d'outre-tombe*, i. 39.

when she was 4, she states: 'I had . . . understood death but it seems that I did not believe that it was eternal. I could not imagine an absolute separation.' (*J'avais . . . compris la mort, mais apparamment je ne la croyais pas éternelle. Je ne pouvais me faire l'idée d'une séparation absolue.*)[93] It is only through observing the reactions of others that the little girl gradually begins to comprehend the notion of a permanent separation:

the life of the emotions had awakened in me on the birth of my little blind brother, when I saw my mother's grief. Her despair at the death of my father had further developed me in that direction and I began to feel myself subjugated by that affection when the idea of a separation burst upon me in the midst of my age of gold.

la vie du sentiment s'était éveillée en moi à la naissance de mon petit frère aveugle, en voyant souffrir ma mère. Son désespoir à la mort de mon père m'avait développée davantage dans ce sens et je commençai à me sentir subjuguée par cette affection quand l'idée d'une séparation vint me surprendre au milieu de mon âge d'or.[94]

For the young Marouzeau too, the meaning of death is revealed by the reactions of adults:

I had seen the death, at the age of 19, of a brother loved more than anything else. I was 8 years old. Since that time I have never known my father or mother in any other state than that of devouring grief. . . . And I lived to the age of manhood without my dead brother's name ever having been spoken in our house.

J'ai vu mourir à dix-neuf ans un frère aimé par-dessus tout. J'avais huit ans. Depuis je n'ai plus connu mon père et ma mère que dévorés de souffrance. . . . Et j'ai vécu jusqu'à l'âge d'homme sans que le nom du frère mort ait été prononcé dans la maison.[95]

Stendhal conveys with elliptical poignancy the child's gradual awareness of the meaning of death and the insensitivity of adults in their responses to the little boy's questions:

I was much more surprised than distressed. I did not understand death, I barely believed in it.
　　'What!' I said to Marion, 'Won't I ever see her again?'
　　'How can you see her again, if she's taken to the cemetary?' . . .
　　That night's entire dialogue is still with me and I could transcribe it here

---

[93] *Histoire de ma vie*, i. 598.　　　　　　　　[94] Ibid., i. 604–5.
[95] *Une enfance*, 33.

if I wanted to. That was the real beginning of my moral existence. I must have been about six and a half.

J'étais beaucoup plus étonné que désespéré, je ne comprenais pas la mort, j'y croyais peu.

'Quoi, disais-je à Marion, je ne la reverrai jamais?'

—Comment veux-tu la revoir, si on l'emportera [sic] au cimetière? . . .

Tout le dialogue de cette nuit m'est encore présent, et il ne tiendrait qu'à moi de le transcrire ici. Là véritablement a commencé ma vie morale, je devais avoir six ans et demi.[96]

Childish curiosity about the nature of death is encapsulated by Hermant in a recollection whose simplicity no doubt renders it all the more intense:

I remember that at the age of 5 or 6, I thought that life might perhaps be a dream and I can still see myself, little as I was, leaning dangerously out of a window, tempted to die out of curiosity, but restrained by that healthy and positive taste for life that was already part of my nature.

Je me rappelle qu'à cinq ou six ans, je pensais que la vie est peut-être un rêve et je me vois encore, tout petit, dangereusement penché hors d'une fenêtre, tenté de mourir par curiosité, mais retenu par ce goût sain et positif de vivre que j'avais déjà.[97]

It is, perhaps, Pierre Loti who evokes with the greatest subtlety the child's sense of the mystery of death, preserving to some degree the simplicity of the little boy's phraseology while still retaining the underlying complexity of the question that perplexes him:

At that point there passed through me one of those sad little illuminations that sometimes go through children's minds, as if to allow them to question with a furtive glance the dimly perceived abysses, and I made this observation: How can grandmother be in heaven, how can such a doubling be understood, since what remains to be buried is still so much herself and retains, alas!, *her very expression*?

Alors passa en moi une de ces tristes petites lueurs d'éclair, qui traversent quelquefois la tête des enfants, comme pour leur permettre d'interroger d'un furtif coup d'œil des abîmes entrevus, et je me fis cette réflexion: Comment grand'mère pourrait-elle être au ciel, comment comprendre ce dédoublement-là, puisque ce qui reste pour être enterré est tellement elle-même, et conserve, hélas! jusqu'à *son expression*?[98]

---

[96] *Vie de Henry Brulard*, 48.
[97] *Confessions*, 11.
[98] *Le Roman d'un enfant*, 90.

For some, an inability to comprehend the meaning of death is transferred to another element of language. Jean-Jacques Coulmann, for instance, whose childhood was marked by the very early deaths of his mother and a slightly older brother, focuses not on them, but on the death from tuberculosis of a girl next door, recounting that he overheard that she expired 'at the moment of *twilight*' (*au moment du* crépuscule), and he adds: 'at that time I didn't understand what the word meant, and in a strange way it became combined in my mind with the sad circumstances under which I learnt it.' (*je ne comprenais pas alors ce que voulait dire ce mot, qui s'attacha en quelque sorte pour moi à la triste circonstance où j'avais appris à le connaître.*)[99]

The awareness of difference between the self and others, and the understanding of the limitations placed on the child's ambitions by social position, sexual status, or historical and physical realities, are shown by most autobiographies, predictably enough, as gradual and universal processes: several writers, however, are also eager to discover the point at which their individual destiny first began to take shape, or to isolate the experience that most indelibly marked their personality. Chateaubriand has little hesitation in locating that experience in his education:

I do not know whether the harsh education I received was good in theory, but it was adopted by my family without any purpose and as the natural result of their natures. What is certain is that it made my way of thinking less like that of other men; what is even more sure is that it imprinted on my emotions a melancholy bent, which was born in me as a result of habitual suffering from my earliest years, the years that should be carefree and joyous.

J'ignore si la dure éducation que je reçus fut bonne en principe, mais elle fut adoptée de mes proches sans dessein et par une suite naturelle de leur humeur. Ce qu'il y a de sûr, c'est qu'elle a rendu mes idées moins semblables à celles des autres hommes; ce qu'il y a de plus sûr encore, c'est qu'elle a imprimé à mes sentiments un caractère de mélancolie née chez moi de l'habitude de souffrir à l'âge de la faiblesse, de l'imprévoyance et de la joie.[100]

What is perhaps most remarkable about this passage is the determination with which Chateaubriand builds up his personal fable of a destiny shaped by forces beyond the individual's control,

[99] *Réminiscences*, i. 5.
[100] *Mémoires d'outre-tombe*, i. 58.

a destiny that has led to a life of melancholy and despair but that could so easily—and this is what makes for the sense of tragedy—have been one of radiant happiness. For all the force of character claimed in the early passages of the *Mémoires d'outre-tombe*, Chateaubriand is here explicitly denying himself any choice in the formation of his own temperament and in doing so is establishing himself firmly in the Romantic mould of the hero swept along by mighty forces against which he is powerless to struggle. Canler, who was to become chief of police, is far more phlegmatic about the shaping power of early experience. Recalling the effect exerted on him by the prison at Namur, to which his father was appointed governor when Canler was 4 years old, he adopts a down-to-earth and moralistic tone in which the need to convince his adult reader no doubt has much to do with the refusal to suggest in any way what the child's own immediate impressions were:

So I found myself at the age of 4 in a prison where the most complete isolation and the harshest discipline were the punishment inflicted on soldiers who had failed in their duty or in the laws of honour. The memory of that age makes me recognize how deeply the impressions of childhood influence the ideas that later develop in the adult.

Je me trouvai donc, à l'âge de quatre ans, dans une prison où la séquestration la plus complète et la discipline la plus rigoureuse sont la punition infligée aux soldats qui ont manqué à leurs devoirs ou failli aux lois de l'honneur. Le souvenir de cette époque m'a fait reconnaître combien les impressions de jeune âge influent sur les idées qui se développent plus tard chez l'homme.[101]

Philarète Chasles, whose father, so he tells us, educated him as if he were founding a republic,[102] started working on his memoirs at the same time as creative writers such as Balzac and Stendhal were shifting the emphasis away from the tragic forces controlling man's destiny, and towards the role of the individual's will-power. It is at least arguable that this literary shift combines with expectations which, in the republican Chasles, were very much at variance with those of the monarchist Chateaubriand, to produce a quite different image of how the individual's nature is formed. Chasles insists that he was, from birth, 'a *free* soul, a *liberated* man, a spirit aware of its *will*' (*une âme* libérée, *un homme* délivré, *un esprit qui a eu*

[101] *Mémoires*, 4.
[102] *Mémoires*, i. 6: on Chasles see Pichois's study, *Philarète Chasles*.

conscience de sa volonté),[103] yet there is something reminiscent of
the Baudelairean *tedium vitae* in his choice of decisive moment and
its effect on him: recounting that at 14 he was incarcerated in the
Conciergerie as a result of a political crime of which he was not in
fact guilty, he describes the experience as an 'excellent life lesson for
a nineteenth-century man, a lesson that teaches him to believe
neither in the hallucinatory dreams of modern philanthropists nor
in the sublimity of the new institutions' (*une leçon excellente pour
la vie d'un homme du dix-neuvième siècle, leçon qui lui apprend à
ne croire ni aux rêves hallucinés des philanthropes modernes, ni à la
sublimité des institutions nouvelles*),[104] and he adds the rider:
'when I left France for England, three days after leaving prison, I
already had the veiled and deep awareness of French decadence.'
(*quand je quittai la France pour l'Angleterre, trois jours après ma
sortie de prison, j'avais déjà l'instinct sourd et profond de la
décadence française.*)[105] That Chasles's autobiography manip-
ulated biographical truth matters little here: what is at issue is the
determination with which he creates his own mythology of the
self.

Not all experiences that are seen as seminal in the child's
development are, of course, as grandiose as these last two. The
future historian Michelet affirms that a visit to the museum of
monuments left him with an intense intuition of history,[106] while
that poet of the ocean and the exotic, Pierre Loti, combines the
simplicity of the child's imagery with the poetic complexity of the
adult's understanding in conveying to his reader the disturbing
magic of the expression 'the colonies' in the ears of a 6-year-old
boy:

how disturbingly, how magically it sounded in my childish ears, that simple
phrase: 'the colonies', which, in those days, summoned up in my mind all
those hot, distant places, with their palm trees, their great flowers, their
negroes, their animals, their adventures. From the combination of these
things there arose an overall impression that was completely accurate, an
intuition of their dreary splendours and their debilitating melancholy.

ce qu'il avait de troublant et de magique, dans mon enfance, ce simple mot:
'les colonies', qui, en ce temps-là, désignait pour moi l'ensemble des
lointains les plus chauds, avec leurs palmiers, leurs grandes fleurs, leurs

---

[103] *Mémoires*, i. 21.   [104] Ibid., i. 106.
[105] Ibid., i. 110.   [106] J. Michelet, *Ma jeunesse*, 44–5.

nègres, leurs bêtes, leurs aventures. De la confusion que je faisais de ces choses, se dégageait un sentiment d'ensemble absolument juste, une intuition de leur morne splendeur et de leur amollissante mélancolie.[107]

The exuberant Berlioz traces his own passion for travel and adventure to long hours spent poring over maps in childhood, with a sharpness of focus in his description that carries particular conviction:

I spent long hours before globes of the earth, intensely studying the complex tracery formed by the islands, capes, and straits of the Southern Sea and the Indian archipelago; reflecting on the creation of those distant lands, on their vegetation, their inhabitants, their climate, and seized with a burning desire to visit them.

je passais de longues heures devant des mappemondes, étudiant avec acharnement le tissu complexe que forment les îles, caps, et détroits de la mer du Sud et de l'archipel indien; réfléchissant sur la création de ces terres lointaines, sur leur végétation, leurs habitants, leur climat, et pris d'un ardent désir de les visiter.[108]

Reading, too, as I shall be exploring in a later chapter,[109] can precipitate the child's sense of awakening to individuality, an awakening which, in retrospect, the adult perceives as determining his or her future career. Alexandre Weill, to quote only one example, twice in the course of his autobiography spotlights his translation of *Genesis* at the age of 5 as the moment when he discovered his own identity:

from my earliest childhood, from the age of 5, when I had read and translated the first chapter of Genesis, I was aware that I had a loftier mission. Although I was still a child, I said to myself: 'No, all that is not as it should be.'

dès mon bas âge, dès cinq ans, après avoir lu et traduit le premier chapitre de la Genèse, j'ai pressenti une mission plus haute. Enfant encore, je me suis dit: Non, tout cela n'est pas comme cela devrait être.[110]

Later he confirms: 'reading and translating the story of the world's creation tore me from the most attractive games of my childhood and opened my soul to reflections, to doubts which soon became a real danger for me.' (*la lecture et la traduction de la création du monde m'arrachèrent aux jeux les plus attrayants de mon jeune âge*

---

[107] *Le Roman d'un enfant*, 83.
[109] See Chapter 4.

[108] *Mémoires*, 4–5.
[110] *Ma jeunesse*, i. 9.

et livrèrent mon âme à des reflexions, à des doutes qui devinrent bientôt pour moi un vrai danger.)[111]

In an age preoccupied with the individual, with the nature of the personality and the mind, the autobiographies serve to focus our attention on the central topoi that recur with remarkable predictability in almost all first-person narrations, particularly in the less-charted and frequently stormy waters of childhood. Moreover, they indicate the ease with which recurrent images and archetypes not only facilitate, but also, more negatively, shape the individual's search for self. The ways in which certain recurrent images and archetypes dominate fiction in the course of the century form the basis of my next chapter.

[111] Ibid., i. 34.

2
Observing Childhood

Rousseau discovered and explored the world of childhood, insisted that adequate attention be given to children's abilities and needs, but for nearly a century real human children continued to be virtually excluded from both adult and children's literature.

(I. Jan, *On Children's Literature*)

For the whole of the nineteenth century, children, whether angels or victims, were to be given only a secondary role in the novel, a role strictly limited by the adult gaze . . . Everywhere the child remains a prisoner of stereotypes.

Durant tout le dix-neuvième siècle les enfants, anges ou victimes, garderont dans le roman un rôle secondaire, étroitement limité par le regard adulte . . . L'enfant demeure partout prisonnier de stéréotypes.

(A. Richter, 'L'Enfant dans la littérature fantastique moderne')

Around 1850 the figure of the child makes a massive entrance into literature.

Autour de 1850, la figure de l'enfant entre massivement dans la littérature.

(M. J. Chambart de Lauwe, *Un monde autre*)

THE problems encountered by the writers of autobiographies in evoking their childhood suggest certain reasons for what is felt by Jan and Richter to be the rarity of children in nineteenth-century literature. Indeed, the linguistic hazards of the challenge are acknowledged by no less a manipulator of the French language than Victor Hugo, who speaks of 'that sweet and adorable language of children, whose charm, like the splendour of a butterfly's wing, disappears when one attempts to make it permanent' (*ce doux et adorable language des enfants dont la grâce, pareille à splendeur de l'aile des papillons, s'en va quand on veut la fixer*).[1] Above all, however, the first decades of the century

---

[1] *Les Misérables*, i. 521.

are marked both by a degree of condescending mawkishness sufficiently alien to the post-modernist mentality to make it difficult for us to penetrate the surface emotionalism, and by the archetypes that Romanticism created around the notion of childhood. Part of the difficulty of deciding at what point children cease to appear merely as symbols of innocence or of evil, as angels or devils, lies in defining what I. Jan refers to as 'real human children', but a more important part, I would argue, concerns the problematics of a fictional re-creation of an experience in which we have all participated but which remains at once too intimate and too alien to permit of an easy transformation into literary terms—as Jung asks: 'Have you ever heard of a hammer beating itself?'[2] Nevertheless, it will be my contention in what follows that both Jan and Richter are too trenchant in their judgements and that the balance began to shift far earlier than they suggest. In this chapter I want to explore above all the question of the relationship between the narrative voice and the child, in those works where children and childhood play a minor or secondary role, in order to see whether that relegation really carries with it a restrictive stereotyping, or whether the use of familiar images and myths is merely part of a process facilitating a more original and profound penetration of childhood. Such an approach, of course, also implies an exploration of the nature of the intended reader and of the kind of complicity that the narrative voice attempts to establish with the reader thus addressed.

LOOKING DOWN ON ROMANTICISM'S CHILDREN

For many writers active in the first decade of the nineteenth century, the vision of childhood is bound up both with the search for purity and freshness of vision that marks much of German Romanticism, and with the legacy of Wordsworth's conviction that the child's intensity of experience cannot be recaptured by the adult, since experience dulls our sensitivity:

> There was a time when meadow, grove and stream,
> The earth, and every common sight,
> To me did seem
> Apparelled in celestial light,

[2] *Analytical Psychology*, 141–2.

The glory and the freshness of a dream.
It is not now as it hath been of yore; -
Turn whereso'er I may,
By night or day,
The things which I have seen I now can see no more.[3]

Intensity of experience does not, however, preclude the possibility of childhood melancholy, for if the child truly is father to the man, the brooding sense of isolation, the inexplicable mental suffering that became known as the *mal du siècle*, must already be present in the child, if only in the form of 'a little sorrow deep in the heart' (*un peu de tristesse au fond du cœur*).[4] The pattern of sensitivity and melancholy, which was to be followed by innumerable *enfants du siècle*, is set in France by Chateaubriand, who, in *René*, encapsulates with highly poetic and suggestive brevity the sense of an original and irreparable fault, the failure to win parental love, and the awareness of an initial exile that stamps its indelible mark on the rest of the hero's life:

I cost my mother her life when I was born; I was torn from her womb with iron. I had a brother, whom my father blessed, because he saw in him his elder son. As for me, abandoned from an early age to outsiders, I was brought up far from the family home.

J'ai coûté la vie à ma mère en venant au monde; j'ai été tiré de son sein avec le fer. J'avais un frère, que mon père bénit, parce qu'il voyait en lui son fils aîné. Pour moi, livré de bonne heure à des mains étrangères, je fus élevé loin du toit paternel.[5]

We have already seen the extent to which the two themes of sibling rivalry and the effect of being sent away to a wet-nurse are commonly expressed causes of youthful misery in the autobiographical childhoods. Such a passage suggests, therefore, the degree of cross-fertilization that takes place between fictional writing and memoirs, each bolstering the other's conception of what is admissible. Moreover, the high death rate of women in childbirth is easily absorbed into a myth of original sin, not merely in Chateaubriand, but in numerous later writers, and finds a particular twist in Maupassant, for whom it allows the analysis of a bereaved husband adoring in his child both his own characteristics

---

[3] Wordsworth, 'Ode: Intimations of Immortality from Recollections of Early Childhood'.
[4] Chateaubriand, *René*, 135.
[5] Ibid., 133.

and those of a beloved wife lost in giving birth, only to discover that
the child is not his own.

Chateaubriand also adds weight to the association of childhood
and purity, as well as to the sweetness of childhood memories, an
association which in *René* is saved from the saccharine silliness its
presentation attains in some writers, both by the acknowledgement
that the pleasure of memory by no means implies the unadulterated
pleasure of the experience as lived, and by the beauty of the
language in which the experience is related. The games of
childhood, for instance, are here presented with a dignity and
seriousness that suggest an attempt to relive the past, rather than
look back on it from the condescending heights of adulthood, even
if one might suspect that sympathy is dependent on choosing
childhood pursuits that continue little changed in adulthood:

Sometimes we would walk in silence, listening to the muted moaning of
autumn or the sound of the dry leaves we crushed under our melancholy
steps; sometimes, in our innocent games, we would pursue the swallow in
the field, the rainbow arching over the rain-swept hills; sometimes, too, the
spectacle of nature would inspire us to murmur lines of poetry.

Tantôt nous marchions en silence, prêtant l'oreille au sourd mugissement
de l'automne ou au bruit des feuilles séchées que nous traînions tristement
sous nos pas; tantôt, dans nos jeux innocents, nous poursuivions
l'hirondelle dans la prairie, l'arc-en-ciel sur les collines pluvieuses;
quelquefois aussi nous murmurions des vers que nous inspirait le spectacle
de la nature.[6]

Although this attempt to enter into childhood might now strike us
as somewhat portentous, Chateaubriand's achievement in this
regard instantly becomes more evident if we compare the passage
just quoted with one from a far less gifted imitator, Du Camp, who,
in *Mémoires d'un suicidé*, explicitly presents as a natural son of
René, educated by Antony and Chatterton,[7] a protagonist whose
childhood is typified in the following evocation:

when I look back to my remotest memories, the first image [of my mother]
that I see is of her dressed in black, mourning for my father, in a great park
in the country, walking under old tree-covered walks and dragging me
along by the hand, while I called to a little dog that I would martyrize with
my solicitude.

   [6] Ibid., 134.
   [7] *Mémoires d'un suicidé*, 18. Antony is Dumas's hero, Chatterton the protagonist
of Vigny's play inspired by the English poet.

je la [ma mère] revois d'abord, en mes souvenirs les plus éloignés, vêtue de noir, en deuil de mon père, dans un grand parc à la campagne, marchant sous de vieilles charmilles et me traînant par la main, pendant que j'appelais un petit chien que je martyrisais de ma sollicitude.[8]

Here the narrative voice is unquestionably external to the scene, an observer looking on at the relationship between mother and child, suggesting in the word 'dragging' (*traînant*) an impatience indicative more of the adult hero's response to children than of the child's own awareness, and conveying in the expression 'martyrize with my solicitude' (*martyrisais de ma sollicitude*) a judgement that is equally beyond the child's abilities. Moreover, the sharpness of focus Chateaubriand brings to bear on his evocations of the natural world suggests a love of natural beauty for its own sake, where Du Camp's 'old tree-covered walks' smacks more of a desire to pay fleeting lip-service to nature while the central preoccupation is unmistakably and overwhelmingly with the self.

Among the poetic works of the great French Romantics, Lamartine's *Harmonies poétiques et religieuses*, first published in 1830, has little success in entering the mind of childhood. It contains a 'Hymne de l'enfant', which is nothing short of ponderously and condescendingly adult in its creaking attempts to find images within the child's purview—'They say that this gleaming sun/ Is merely a plaything for you' (*On dit que ce brillant soleil/ N'est qu'un jouet de ta puissance*)[9]—and a 'Souvenir d'enfance' which is entirely focused through grown-up eyes, even when dealing with the theme that most frequently allows a return to infancy, that of food:

> A table rich with the gifts that autumn paraded,
> Where the fruits of the garden, where milk and honey,
> Seasoned with the care taken by an attentive mother,
> Charmed the guests through their rural luxury.

> Table riche des dons que l'automne étalait,
> Où les fruits du jardin, où le miel et le lait,

---

[8] *Mémoires d'un suicidé*, 27.

[9] *Harmonies poétiques et religieuses*, VII. One suspects that it is Lamartine's embarrassment with the subject that has led to the clumsiness of expression in the first two lines: 'O Father whom my father adores/ Thou whom one names only on one's knees' (*O père qu'adore mon père,/ Toi qu'on ne nomme qu'à genoux*). It has to be said, however, that Lamartine's contemporaries may well have read this poem quite differently. Durand, for instance, sings its praises in *Le Règne de l'enfant*.

Assaisonnés des soins d'une mère attentive,
De leur luxe champêtre enchantaient le convive.[10]

Nevertheless, in a passage from *Jocelyn*, which dates from 1836, Lamartine appears to share with Chateaubriand a desire to capture the essence of his hero's past in terms that preserve both the playful and the serious side, the insouciance as well as the dignity of childhood. Admittedly, there is something rather laboured in the careful symmetries, a hint of embarrassment in the way in which the description threatens to slide away from the child's view towards the easier theme of the adult's view of nature, and occasionally an inappropriate word or image indicative of the difficulty the poet experiences in returning to the mind of childhood. Yet the sincerity of the experiment is certainly evident, all the more so as this is a passage not indispensable to the understanding of the work as a whole. If Lamartine has found the challenge problematic, in other words, it seems indisputable that he has, nevertheless, attempted to respond to it, especially in the following lines:

> As a child, I sometimes spent whole days
> In the garden, in the meadows,
> In a few green pathways
> Worn into the hillsides by the village cattle,
> All veiled in hawthorn and wild brambles,
> My dog at my side, my book in my hand,
> Resting with no need to rest, wayfaring where there was no way,
> Sometimes reading, sometimes stripping a twig,
> Following with inattentive gaze the fluttering insect,
> The water flowing in the sunlight like little diamonds,
> Or my ear glued to sounds of buzzing;
> Then, choosing a resting place in the shelter of a hedge,
> Like a crouching hare frightened by barking,
> Or lying in the meadow, where flowering grasses
> Drowned me in a bed of mystery and odours,
> And curved over me curtains of dim shadow,
> I gave my eyes and my heart back to my reading.

> Enfant, j'ai quelquefois passé des jours entiers
> Au jardin, dans les prés, dans quelques verts sentiers
> Creusés sur les coteaux par les boeufs du village,
> Tout voilés d'aubépine et de mûre sauvage,

[10] *Harmonies poétiques et religieuses*, XXIII.

> Mon chien auprés de moi, mon livre dans la main,
> M'arrêtant sans fatigue et marchant sans chemin,
> Tantôt lisant, tantôt écorçant quelque tige,
> Suivant d'un œil distrait l'insect qui voltige,
> L'eau qui coule au soleil en petits diamants,
> Ou l'oreille clouée à des bourdonnements;
> Puis, choisissant un gîte à l'abri d'une haie,
> Comme un lièvre tapi qu'un aboiement effraie,
> Ou couché dans le pré, dont les gramens en fleurs
> Me noyaient dans un lit de mystère et d'odeurs,
> Et recourbaient sur moi des rideaux d'ombre obscure,
> Je reprenais de l'œil et du cœur ma lecture.[11]

One might well ask why, when John Clare had so economically conjured up the past in 'Childhood', and Wordsworth had already shown the way in his presentation of bird-nesting, ice-skating, and hallooing children, Lamartine should find it so patently difficult to seize on an imagery and vocabulary evocative of childhood pursuits, for if the peeling of the stick touches a chord, the image of the water flowing in little diamonds is not far short of pedestrian, and the phrase 'a bed of mystery and odours' (*un lit de mystère et d'odeurs*) lacks conviction. Clearly the problem for Lamartine lies only partly with the desire to move an adult reader rather than concentrate on entering into the mind of the child: the overriding difficulty is much more concerned with the crippling restrictions on poetic vocabulary that still plagued French writers in the first decades of the nineteenth century, and with Lamartine's own preference for a sentence structure tied to the alexandrine line or the distich.[12] Nevertheless, it could be argued that what matters here is less an awareness of difficulties unresolved than an acknowledgement that the easy option, that of adopting the condescendingly adult viewpoint, has not been chosen. Moreover, a stanza from 'La Vigne et la maison', first published some twenty years later, is rather more successful, even if the doubtful taste of the last line is reminiscent of Greuze:

> Their fair hair blowing free in the mountain wind,
> The girls, putting both hands over their eyes,
> Would throw cries of joy to the mountain echo,
> Or cross their pious fingers on their growing breasts.

[11] Lamartine, *Jocelyn*, quatrième époque.
[12] On this see Houston, *The Demonic Imagination*, 17–20.

Leurs blonds cheveux épars au vent de la montagne,
Les filles, se passant leurs deux mains sur les yeux,
Jetaient des cris de joie à l'écho des montagnes,
Ou sur leurs seins naissants croisaient leurs doigts pieux.[13]

Given the stylistic difficulties of presenting the child's vision, given also perhaps the dichotomy between the expressed conviction of childhood innocence and a lived experience of something rather different, many minor Romantics chose the safer course of treating the theme of the death of a child. It was, moreover, in an age of high infant mortality and a somewhat mawkish sensibility, a subject of considerable popularity.[14] Typical examples are Émile Deschamps's sonnet 'A une mère qui pleure':

Like a thief in the night, greedy death
Slipped into your home . . . And now he sleeps under the grass,
The lovely little child, he who took so little place
In the house and who leaves so great a gap!

Comme un voleur de nuit, chez vous, la mort avide
S'est glissée . . . Et voilà qu'il dort sous le gazon
Le beau petit enfant, lui qui dans la maison
Tenait si peu de place, et laisse un si grande vide![15]

and 'L'Ange et l'enfant', by Jean Reboul, whom no less a poet than Lamartine invoked as a minstrel friend in his poem 'Le Génie dans l'obscurité'. Reboul's poem depicts an angel with a radiant face inviting a child to fly away with him, lest earthly existence sully his innocence, and concludes with the dubious taste of the following lines:

And, with these words, the angel,
Beating his white wings, took flight
Towards the eternal dwellings . . .
Poor mother! . . . Your son is dead.

Et, secouant ses blanches ailes,
L'ange à ces mots a pris l'essor
Vers les demeures éternelles . . .
Pauvre mère! . . . ton fils est mort.[16]

Where the theme of the death of a child is concerned, such lapses of taste are indeed not unique to minor writers. No less a poet than

---

[13] *Méditations poétiques*, 419.
[15] In Lacomble, *Perles*, 4.
[14] See Ariès, *L'Homme devant la mort*.
[16] Ibid., 47. Original ellipses.

Hugo himself, in *Les Contemplations*, announces accusingly to a grieving mother that she must have painted so beautiful a picture of heaven to her child that he left earthly life to reach it more quickly.[17]

Yet whatever obstacles the poets encountered, a far more sardonic prose voice could be heard as early as 1829 treating the theme with an entirely provocative lack of effusiveness. Mérimée's 'Mateo Falcone', which, when it first appeared in *La Revue de Paris*, carried the subtitle 'Mœurs de la Corse', is a briskly told tale of treachery, honour, and rough justice, in which the 10-year-old Fortunato, bribed first into hiding a bandit and then into betraying him for a larger prize, brings such dishonour to the family house and name that his father shoots him, for all he is the only son. What is remarkable about Mérimée's approach to his topic is his refusal to accept any of the contemporary clichés concerning children. Fortunato is presented neither as innocent nor, for that matter, as evil; no attempt is made to gloss over his turpitude on the grounds that he is too young to know what he is doing; Mérimée does not even seek to make the child likeable. It is, of course, this apparently unemotional tone that makes the final explosion so shocking.

The tale begins with an evocation of the wild and inhospitable countryside before presenting the domestic scene of Fortunato guarding the family home during his parents' brief absence. The calm of this tableau is suddenly shattered by gunshots and the arrival of the wounded bandit. When the bandit, Gianetto, finds the boy unmoved by his pleas for help, he attempts to appeal to family honour: 'You are not Mateo Falcone's son! Are you going to let me be arrested in front of your house?' (*Tu n'es pas le fils de Mateo Falcone! Me laisseras-tu donc arrêter devant ta maison?*) The narrative voice informs us that the child appears moved, but narration is challenged by representation when Fortunato's response suggests a different interpretation: 'What will you give me if I hide you?' (*Que me donneras-tu si je te cache?*)[18] The child's cunning in hiding Gianetto in a pile of straw, the stroke of imagination that leads him to put a cat and her kittens on top of the straw, and the care with which he removes traces of blood, all point to a very different image of childhood from that conveyed by many

---

[17] *Les Contemplations*, 'A la mère de l'enfant mort', Bk. iii. poem 14.
[18] Mérimée, *Romans et nouvelles*, 228.

of Mérimée's contemporaries. So, too, does the consummate skill with which Fortunato feigns stupidity when the soldiers arrive in search of the bandit. But the grain of cupidity already revealed leads to Fortunato's downfall when the adjutant offers him a silver watch in exchange for revealing Gianetto's hiding place. Where a lesser contemporary might have chosen an animal image to depict the child's greed as innocence, and the theme of food to evoke a healthily innocuous appetite, Mérimée's tale is far more concerned to spotlight the element of cunning:

Fortunato, ogling the watch out of the corner of his eye, looked like a cat being offered a whole chicken. As it feels it's being teased, it doesn't dare put out its paw, and from time to time turns its eyes away so as not to succumb to the temptation.

Fortunato, lorgnant la montre d'un coin de l'œil, ressemblait à un chat à qui l'on présente un poulet tout entier. Comme il sent qu'on se moque de lui, il n'ose y porter la griffe, et de temps en temps il détourne les yeux pour ne pas s'exposer à succomber à la tentation.[19]

And Mérimée, briefly and with apparent ease, enters the child's mind to convey the intensity of the temptation in terms of a sensual seduction:

the tip of his fingers touched it; and its full weight was in his hand even though the adjutant didn't let go of the end of the chain . . . The face was coloured sky blue . . . the case was newly polished . . . in the sun it seemed made of fire . . .

le bout de ses doigts la toucha; et elle pesait tout entière dans sa main sans que l'adjudant lâchât pourtant le bout de la chaîne . . . Le cadran était azuré . . . la boîte nouvellement fourbie . . . au soleil, elle paraissait toute de feu . . . [20]

If 'Mateo Falcone' is, for all its brevity, so powerful a work, the reasons lie partly in the contrast between the coldness of the narrative voice and the violence of what is narrated, partly in the balance between an external, largely unsympathetic presentation of Fortunato, and this moment of identity between narrative view and the child's experience, and partly in the briefly posed, but none the less telling, relationship set up with the reader. Indeed, the opening paragraphs seem to be doing little more than creating a landscape

[19] Ibid., 231.
[20] Ibid., 232. Original ellipses.

that will provide a physical symbol of the emotions revealed in the course of the narration, and the invitation they offer to the bourgeois reader of *La Revue de Paris* to imagine himself in more romantic guise appears nothing more than a playful wink from writer to audience: 'if you have killed a man, take to the maquis of the Porto-Vecchio.' (*si vous avez tué un homme, allez dans le mâquis de Porto-Vecchio.*)[21] Yet the invitation is, in effect, a time-bomb, suddenly acquiring explosive power when the murder takes place, a murder that has nothing romantic about it, that is perpetrated against a child, and that, for all Mérimée may wrap it round in terms of Corsican codes of honour, is clearly intended to tear the wraps off the relationship between fathers and sons. The sense of oppression and fear that many autobiographies record hanging over children because of their father's nature seems to find explosive release here, even if that release is permissible only by transferring the role of victim from father to son, whereas children dream of killing their father.

Between these two poles of the sugary effusion with which many minor Romantics treated childhood, and Mérimée's sardonic matter-of-factness, Nerval finds, in *Sylvie*, a note of bitter-sweet clarity, moving with apparent ease between the adult's and the child's viewpoint, and bringing a deceptive appearance of spontaneity to his evocations of the past. Of course Neval is using his depiction of childhood songs and dances to suggest the continuing existence of what he considers most profoundly French, indicating with the lightest of touches the kind of syncretism he explores at greater length elsewhere, notably in 'Les Chimères'. But that symbolic purpose is not allowed to detract from the clarity of the passage's surface purpose, which is the analysis of why a moment experienced in childhood should persist so strongly in the adult's memory. While permitting himself a moment of gentle mockery directed at the mobility of children's (and, implicitly, adults') affections (his narrator says of the little girl Sylvie that he loved and saw only her, until he heard Adrienne sing)[22] Nerval allows neither mockery nor condescension to distort the depiction of Adrienne's song and the beauty of the natural surroundings:

As she sang, darkness fell from the great trees and the growing moonlight fell on her alone, isolated from our attentive circle.—She fell silent, and no-

---

[21] Mérimée, *Romans et nouvelles*, 225.
[22] Nerval, *Œuvres complètes*, i. 245.

one dared break the silence. The lawn was covered with moist, impercept-
ible mist, which deposited white drops on the tips of the grasses. We
thought we were in paradise.

A mesure qu'elle chantait, l'ombre descendait des grands arbres, et le clair
de lune naissant tombait sur elle seule, isolée de notre cercle attentif.—Elle
se tut, et personne n'osa rompre le silence. La pelouse était couverte de
faibles vapeurs condensées, qui déroulaient leurs blancs flocons sur les
pointes des herbes. Nous pensions être en paradis.[23]

Sylvie, moreover, also conveys the humour of childhood memories
in a passage of dialogue between Sylvie and the narrator that
captures with uncloying sureness of touch the rhythms and the
vocabulary of the spoken language:

'Do you remember that you taught me to fish for crayfish under the bridges
of the Thève and the Nonette?' 'And do you remember your milk-brother,
who pulled you out the *waarter* one day?' 'Big curlylocks! He was the one
who told me you could walk across it . . . that *waarter*!'

Te rappelles-tu que tu m'apprenais à pêcher des écrevisses sous les ponts de
la Thève et de la Nonette?—Et toi, te souviens-tu de ton frère de lait qui t'a
un jour retiré de *l'ieau*.—Le grand frisé! c'est lui qui m'avait dit qu'on
pouvait la passer . . . *l'ieau*![24]

And at the one point where the evocation of children's misappre-
hensions threatens to slip into the condescending and gushing tone
adopted in such compendiums as Deschanel's *Le Bien et le mal
qu'on a dits des enfants*, Nerval adroitly adds an acerbic judgement
that destroys any hint of the saccharine: the narrator's *frère de lait*
recalls:

'You were a lot more worried about your watch than about yourself,
because it didn't work any more: you said, "The animal has *drownded*, it
doesn't say tick tock any more; what is my uncle going to say? . . . " "An
animal in a watch!" said old Dodu, "That's what they make children
believe in Paris!" '

'Tu étais bien plus inquiet de ta montre que de toi-même, parce qu'elle ne
marchait plus; tu disais: "La bête est *nayée*, ça ne fait plus tic tac; qu'est-ce
que mon oncle va dire? . . . "—Une bête dans une montre! dit le père Dodu,
voilà ce qu'on leur fait croire à Paris, aux enfants!'[25]

---

[23] Ibid., i. 245.
[24] Ibid., i. 264. Original ellipses.
[25] Ibid., i. 268. Original ellipses.

ALTERING THE FOCUS

If children and childhood play only a minor role in the works of the writers considered so far, two Romantics, Victor Hugo and Marceline Desbordes-Valmore, allow them a far more central place in their writings.

Throughout his career, Hugo, who conceived it as the poet's priestly duty to speak for those whose voice was not heard—the poor, the downtrodden, the suffering—had fulminated against the abuse of children; long before Ferry made free, secular education obligatory, Hugo had begun arguing for the realization of this great ambition of the revolutionaries of 1789. The depth of his love for his oldest daughter, Léopoldine, is beyond doubt, as witness *Les Contemplations*, where he attempts to make meaning of a world and a God that could destroy his daughter on her honeymoon, although the delight he took in his grandchildren may strike some as smacking of opportunism, providing the rather unconvincing inspiration for him to write *L'Art d'être grand-père*, with its affectionate, indeed doting, depiction of the deeds and sayings of his very young grandchildren. Moreover, the sincerity and depth of an emotion is no guarantee that it can be adequately translated into language: as Lear painfully learns, Cordelia's inability to heave her heart into her mouth does not mean that her love is as wanting as her tongue. What one discovers in exploring those of Hugo's poems that deal with children is how seldom he is able to set aside his awareness of himself as watching and commenting adult. As a result it is only rarely that he succeeds in conveying the world of childhood rather than the adult's myth of childhood, however complex that myth might be when filtered through a mind of the intricacy of Hugo's.[26] This is hardly surprising, for what makes Hugo's best poetry so powerful, and his worst poetry so pretentious, is of course the quality of the mind through which his poems are presented and the relationship he establishes with his reader. Moreover, the ability to adapt that mind thematically, lexically, and syntactically to the depiction of childhood is not something that either developed or deteriorated in the course of his career.

[26] J. P. C. de Boer, *Victor Hugo et l'enfant*, provides a far more favourable, not to say hagiographic, reading of Hugo's response, although he, too, emphasizes that Hugo uses the theme to explore his own adult personality rather than evoking childhood itself.

Although one might well argue that *L'Art d'être grand-père* is one of the weakest of his books of poetry, the reasons for that, I would suggest, have little to do with the period in his life at which it was written, and more to do with the failure to discriminate between the moving and the mawkish, with an inability in this case to transpose the purely personal into the more generally human.

Nevertheless, although the pitfalls of writing poetry about children were, for a poet of Hugo's frame of mind, enormous and multifarious, he did produce several works in which what I. Jan might well recognize as real, human children do indeed feature. *Les Orientales*, for instance, which first appeared in January 1829, could well be seen to contain an unintentional *mise en abyme* of much of Romanticism's poetry about children: while the adult onlooker surveys the destruction left after the Turks have passed through a Greek village, and with equal pity and condescension offers the sole surviving child baubles, lilies, and fruit, the child has entirely different needs in mind:

> 'Friend', said the Greek child, the child with the blue eyes,
> 'I want powder and bullets.'

> —Ami, dit l'enfant grec, dit l'enfant aux yeux bleus,
> Je veux de la poudre et des balles.[27]

The deliberate choice of those hackneyed indicators of innocence, the blue eyes, the contrast between what the adult imagines the child to be feeling—'your vague unhappiness' (*tes chagrins nébuleux*)—and the sharply focused, murderous impulses of the child itself, between the silliness of the adult's attempts to reach the child's intellectual level—'that tree which is so big/ That a horse, galloping without stopping, takes/ A hundred years to come out of its shadow' (*cet arbre si grand,/ Qu'un cheval au galop met, toujours en courant,/ Cent ans à sortir de son ombre*)—and the dignified simplicity of the child's expression, all combine to throw Romanticism's image of childhood powerfully into doubt. But the kinds of questions it raises may well have been too disturbing to be allowed to remain as resolutely centre-stage as they are here. Hugo's next book of poetry, *Les Feuilles d'automne*, does more to establish the archetype of childhood innocence than to explore the intuition touched on here, an intuition that may perhaps have been

[27] *Les Orientales*, XVIII.

allowed to surface only because the child in *Les Orientales* was not, after all, French.

   The poem numbered xv in *Les Feuilles d'automne*, for example, is above all an affirmation of the power of poetic inspiration to draw on the sights and sounds of everyday, domestic life, and a rejection of the image of the poet retiring to the soundproofed isolation of an ivory tower. While the person who has attempted to drive the boisterous, laughing children away from the poet's study argues that 'Their noisy games will obliterate/ The sacred words whispered by the Muse,/ Those pure songs in which the soul swoons' (*ils s'effaceront à leurs bruyants ébats/ Ces mots sacrés que dit la muse tout bas,/ Ces chants purs où l'âme se noie*), the poet himself claims to prefer their presence to all that fame can offer:

> Oh! I much prefer my joy and pleasure,
> And all my family with all my leisure,
>   Even if ungrateful and mobile fame,
> Together with my poetry, disturbed by this familiar laughter,
> Were to flee like a flock of birds flying away
>   Before a swarm of scholars!

> Oh! que j'aime bien mieux ma joie et mon plaisir,
> Et toute ma famille avec tout mon loisir,
>   Dût la gloire ingrate et frivole,
> Dussent mes vers, troublés de ces ris familiers,
> S'enfuir, comme devant un essaim d'écoliers
>   Une troupe d'oiseaux s'envole![28]

There is, particularly in the last two lines of this stanza, a sense of light-heartedness, conveyed in the sweeping rhythm, the unstraining image, the playful choice of the interchangeable nouns '*troupe*' and '*essaim*' and also, I suspect, in the etymological pun that links '*essaim*' to its Latin root '*examen*'. Moreover, the poet can all the more easily put his future glory at risk in that the presence of the children, far from driving poetry away, serves rather to intensify it: 'Childhood with its cheerful colours/ Gives our lines their poetry as dawn/ Gives the dew to the flowers' (*L'enfance aux riantes couleurs/ Donne la poésie à nos vers, comme aux fleurs/L'aurore donne la rosée*). What is happening here, of course, is an intensification of the mythical image of the child, an incorporation of its voice into the great concert of nature whose secret music it is the poet's task to capture in poetry.

---

[28] *Les Feuilles d'automne*, xv.

Les Feuilles d'automne explores further aspects of the Romantic myth of childhood in the poem numbered xx, which begins: 'Dans l'alcôve sombre'. In this poem it is the innocence and happiness of childhood that Hugo seeks to exemplify, partly through a series of images offered as studding the child's dreams, and partly through the thoughts of the adult onlooker contemplating the child as it sleeps. The two angles of vision are linked by an extended metaphor based on water and by a rhythm that succeeds in suggesting both the child's delight and the onlooker's sense of the inexorable passing of time:

> Lakes of delight
> Where the fish glides
> And the wave forms furrows
> Around the golden reeds.
> Child, dream on! Sleep, my loved ones!
> Your young soul does not know
> Where all your days go.
> Like a frond of dead sea-weed
> You slip away, uncaring!
> The current carries you on,
> But you sleep for ever.

> Des lacs de délice
> Où le poisson glisse,
> Où l'onde se plisse
> A des roseaux d'or.
> Enfant, rêve encor!
> Dors, ô mes amours!
> Ta jeune âme ignore
> Où s'en vont tes jours.
> Comme une algue morte
> Tu vas, que t'importe!
> Le courant t'emporte,
> Mais tu dors toujours![29]

Moreover, the dichotomy between the two perceptions is, if only briefly, broken down when the child's dream turns to nightmare with the vision of angels, weeping because they have foreknowledge of human destiny. After all, both memories of our own childhoods, and the experience of children around us, combine with the autobiographical record to suggest the frequency with which

---

[29] Ibid., xx.

children, even when very young, are tormented by nightmares.
C. S. Lewis states: 'I remember nothing earlier than the terror of
certain dreams. It is a very common trouble at that age, yet it still
seems to me odd that petted and guarded childhood should so often
have in it a window opening on what is hardly less than Hell.'[30]
And Julien Green, acknowledging a similar experience, asks:
'Where do these childhood nightmares come from? Out of what
abysses?' (*D'où montent ces cauchemars de l'enfance? De quels
gouffres?*)[31] Hugo's subversion of the myth of innocent happiness
may be fleeting and its purpose may be primarily that of
introducing the image of the mother reassuring the child with her
kisses, but it nevertheless admits the child, however tentatively, into
the human experience of poems such as 'La Pente de la rêverie' and
'Ce que dit la bouche d'ombre'.

'Lorsque l'enfant paraît', however, adopts a resolutely adult,
and, one might well argue, male, view of children. For all the
warmth of expression, there is something curiously remote (not to
say comic) about the image of grave discussions concerning God,
poetry, and the fatherland being abandoned when the child is
brought out of the nursery and put briefly on show. The child in
this poem is stripped of all individuality to become a mere cipher of
innocence and joy, an embodiment of future hope, a source of
physical pleasure for the adults rather than a person in its own
right:

> How beautiful the child is, with his sweet smile,
> His gentle good faith, his voice which wants to say everything,
>> His quickly calmed tears,
> As he gazes in astonishment and delight,
> Offering in all he has his young soul to life
>> And his mouth to kisses.

> Il est si beau, l'enfant, avec son doux sourire,
> Sa douce bonne foi, sa voix qui veut tout dire,
>> Ses pleurs vite apaisés.
> Laissant errer sa vue étonnée et ravie,
> Offrant de toutes parts sa jeune âme à la vie
>> Et sa bouche aux baisers![32]

---

[30] *Surprised by Joy*, 15.   [31] *Partir avant le jour*, 28.
[32] *Les Feuilles d'automne*, XIX.

This is not to deny the poem's power to move its readers, the beauty and simplicity of its imagery, or the ease with which Hugo varies the rhythms and capitalizes on the restrictions and possibilities of the metrical form. What is at issue here is the extent to which poems that appear to focus on children are instead dominated by the adult's desire—conscious or not—to create a mythology of childhood, of the relationships between children and adults, and of the nature of the child's experience.

After all, much of what is *sui generis* in Hugo's work, and probably all of its power, derives from his vacuum-like ability to suck into his own personality everything external to himself. This can be clearly seen operating in another poem ostensibly about children in *Les Voix intérieures*, 'Regardez: les enfants se sont assis en rond'. Here, two Romantic icons combine, that of the child as cherub and that of the mother as angel, but the real core of the poem appears only after these gentle images have been dilated on in such a way as to give particular impact to the final verse, with its less than felicitous metaphor:

> And I who see them all before my eyes, mother and children,
> While the little ones are as joyous beside me
>   As birds on the shore,
> My heart growls and boils, and I feel slowly opening,
> Like a lid lifted by a foaming flood,
>   My brow full of dreams.

> Et moi qui, mère, enfants, les vois tous sous mes yeux,
> Tandis qu'auprès de moi les petits sont joyeux
>   Comme des oiseaux sur les grèves,
> Mon coeur gronde et bouillonne, et je sens lentement,
> Couvercle soulevé par un flot écumant,
>   S'entr'ouvrir mon front plein de rêves.[33]

While poems of this sort can be found in almost all Hugo's collections, there is also evidence of a desire to add to the optimistic myth a far more pessimistic awareness of what for many children was the grim reality of existence in nineteenth-century France. 'Melancholia', in Hugo's collection *Les Contemplations*, points forward to the eloquent indictment of *Les Misérables* with its evocation of working children:

---

[33] *Les Voix intérieures*, xx.

Where are they going these children, of whom not one laughs?
These gentle, thoughtful beings wasted by fever?
These 8-year-old girls we see walking on their own?
They are going to work under grindstones for fifteen hours a day;
They are going to repeat eternally from dawn to evening
The same movement in the same prison.

Où vont tous ces enfants dont pas un seul ne rit?
Ces doux êtres pensifs que la fièvre maigrit?
Ces filles de huit ans qu'on voit cheminer seules?
Ils s'en vont travailler quinze heures sous des meules;
Ils vont, de l'aube au soir, faire éternellement
Dans la même prison le même mouvement.[34]

This use of literature to plead the cause of exploited children
reaches its apogee, where Hugo is concerned, in the portrayal of
Cosette in *Les Misérables*, where it combines with a robust sense of
the child's resilience in the presentation of Gavroche.

Hugo's novel, first published in 1862, includes in its vast,
labyrinthine structure various portraits and sketches of children:
the pampered Eponine and Azelma, the lonely, love-starved
Marius, the perky, rain-soaked, hairy little lad who defines himself
as Navet, Gavroche's friend.[35] Moreover, it seizes on these and
other children to feed some of the novel's numerous digressions,
those that deal with the nature of the gamin, for instance, or those
concerned with depicting the germ of maternal love in the way a
little girl plays with her doll. What is remarkable, given both the
slight attention paid to the child in contemporary fiction, and
the way in which children are represented in Hugo's poetry, is the
extent to which even those figures of children that are clearly
symbolic or metonymic—Cosette, for instance, standing as a
symbol of down-trodden humanity, while Gavroche exemplifies the
gamin—are fleshed out in ways that lend them individuality. Even
so minor a figure as Petit-Gervais, whose sole function in the novel
is to precipitate the crime that will for ever condemn Jean Valjean,
is rounded out from the lay-figure of the '*petit savoyard*', with the
traditional symbols of the hurdy-gurdy and the box of samples on
his back, through the description of him playing knuckle-bones as
he walks across the vast, deserted plain.[36] Equally, the two little

---

[34] *Les Contemplations*, bk. 3, poem II.   [35] *Les Misérables*, iii. 137.
[36] *Les Misérables*, i. 172–4. But see l'abbé Bugniot's *Les Petits Savoyards* for a
considerably less sanguine view of the fate of these wandering children.

Thénardier boys Gavroche takes under his wing surface again
somewhat later in the novel to allow a discourse on the beauty of
the Luxembourg gardens, normally out of bounds to waifs and
strays. But in the elder of the two Hugo indicates, with the briefest
of touches, a Gavroche in the making.[37] And the very young
Eponine, who is later to play such an important role as the
delinquent adolescent transformed by unrequited love, allows
Hugo to experiment with the possibilities of capturing both the
child's power of imagination and the structures, rhythms, and
vocabulary of a little girl's imaginary world. Dressing the cat up as
a baby, Eponine dazzles her sister with the following story:

We'll imagine this is my little girl. I'll be a lady. We'll pretend I come to see
you and you'll look at her. Little by little you'll see her moustaches, and
that'll surprise you. And then you'll see her ears, and then her tail, and
that'll surprise you. And you'll say to me, 'Heavens above!' And I'll say to
you: 'Yes, Madam, that's the sort of little girl I've got. Little girls are like
that these days.'

Ce serait ma petite fille. Je serais une dame. Je viendrais te voir et tu la
regarderais. Peu à peu tu verrais ses moustaches, et cela t'étonnerait. Et
puis tu verrais ses oreilles, et puis tu verrais sa queue, et cela t'étonnerait. Et
tu me dirais: Ah! mon Dieu! et je te dirais: Oui, madame, c'est une petite
fille que j'ai comme ça. Les petites filles sont comme ça à présent.[38]

The child's delight in lists—'and then you'll see . . . and then you'll
see'—evident is so many nursery songs and children's books, the
pleasure in copying adult discourse, and the enjoyment of the
absurd are all concisely and sharply evoked here in a description
that has nothing condescending about it. Nevertheless one might
note here a passage in Baudelaire's *Morale du joujou* on 1853 that
seems a prophetic rejection of Hugo's image of childhood games.
Evoking the powerful imagination of the child at play, Baudelaire
adds the rider:

What I am talking about here are not those little girls who play at being
ladies and calling on each other, introducing their imaginary children and
talking about their clothes. Those poor little girls are imitating their
mamas: they are already preparing for their immortal future puerility, and
you can be certain that none of them will become my wife.

Je ne veux pas parler de ces petites filles qui jouent à la madame, se rendent

---

[37] *Les Misérables*, iii. 275–82.
[38] Ibid., i. 521.

des visites, se présentent leurs enfants imaginaires et parlent de leurs toilettes. Les pauvres petites imitent leurs mamans: elles préludent déjà à leur immortelle puérilité future, et aucune d'elles, à coup sûr, ne deviendra ma femme.[39]

Hugo's handling of the scene, together with Baudelaire's subsequent delight in little boys playing at war, surely only a different version of future puerility, suggests, however, that here the younger poet's view of childhood is clouded by adult misogyny.

   Equally, for all Hugo's tendency to reduce Cosette to symbol, she is also allowed to appear as individual subject, even if that subjectivity is overshadowed in later passages when she becomes the object of Jean Valjean's paternal love and of Marius's physical and emotional love. In the scene where she fetches water, staggering through the dark wood to reach the well, a series of physical gestures and sensations combines with a powerful imagination to convey the child's response to fear: the scratching of her scalp that indicates her perplexity as she hesitates between fear of the dark and fear of the Thénardier couple, the certainty that she can hear animals and see ghosts in the black woods, the sensation of cold water on her hands and legs, the device of counting aloud to allay her terror,[40] all succeed in creating Cosette as individual. Yet, at the same time, Hugo seizes on the chance to transform this episode into an archetypal vision of mankind faced with the terror of darkness, given a further turn of the screw by the very fact that Cosette is a mere child: 'this penetration of the darkness is inexpressibly sinister in a child. Forests are apocalypses and when a little soul beats its wings under their monstrous vault you hear the sound of death.' (*cette pénétration des ténèbres est inexprimablement sinistre dans un enfant. Les forêts sont des apocalypses et le battement d'ailes d'une petite âme fait un bruit d'agonie sous leur voûte monstrueuse.*)[41] However great the tendency to slip from the depiction of Cosette as individual to the depersonalizing transformation of little girl into icon, this passage is indisputably among the first to succeed in entering at any length into the mind of a child, and to do so without being patronizing. None the less it is characteristic both of Hugo and of the age in which he was writing that when he comes to evoke Cosette's happiness once Jean Valjean

---

[39] *Œuvres complètes*, i. 583.
[40] Whether Cosette would actually know how to count is highly dubious.
[41] *Les Misérables*, i. 502–3.

has rescued her, he is content merely to offer an external judgement, and one that, moreover, the passage in the woods serves powerfully to undermine: 'Children accept joy and happiness immediately and on familiar terms, for they themselves are by nature happiness and joy.' (*Les enfants acceptent tout de suite et familièrement la joie et le bonheur, étant eux-mêmes naturellement bonheur et joie.*)[42] Hugo's attraction to the sombre, the terrifying, the monstrous is enabled, in other words, by his equally strong belief in man's natural penchant for the joyous, the reassuring, the beautiful, as, indeed, Esmeralda and Quasimodo together exemplify.

Gavroche is also a complex amalgam of the symbolic and the individual. Entering the novel first as the crying baby ignored by selfish parents, his first major task in *Les Misérables* is to present the archetype of the gamin, that Parisian phenomenon that many other nineteenth-century writers would also attempt to portray.[43] Out of the complex network of allegories and symbols associated with the gamin, Gavroche surges forth in his own right in the scene where he discovers the two little boys wandering unprotected through Paris. Here Hugo captures with consumate skill the combination of condescension and sympathy, the desire to teach and the desire to show off, that mark the slightly older child's response to those who are slightly younger, together with the characteristic irritation when adults assume patronizing airs:

'White bread, waiter! Well-washed grub! It's my treat!'

The baker could not help smiling, and as he cut the white bread, he looked at them with a pity that offended Gavroche.

'Hey you, baker's boy!' he said, 'What are you weighing us up for like that?'

If all three of them had been put together they would hardly have made full weight.

When the bread had been cut, the baker put the coin in the till and Gavroche said to the children: 'Nosh!'

The little boys looked at him in astonishment. Gavroche burst out laughing. 'Gosh, it's true, they're so little they don't know what that means yet!'

And he said again: 'Eat.'

'Du pain blanc, garçon! du larton savonné! Je régale.'

---

[42] Ibid., i. 557.
[43] See e.g. Lamothe-Langon's sentimental novel *Le Gamin* and the boys Garofoli trains in H. Malot's *Sans famille*. See also Chapter 5, 230–3.

Le boulanger ne put s'empêcher de sourire, et tout en coupant le pain blanc, il les considérait d'une façon compatissante qui choqua Gavroche.

'Ah, ça, mitron! dit-il, qu'est-ce que vous avez donc à nous toiser comme ça?'

Mis tous trois bout à bout, ils auraient fait à peine une toise.

Quand le pain fut coupé, le boulanger encaissa le sou, et Gavroche dit aux deux enfants: 'Morfilez.'

Les petits garçons le regardèrent interdits. Gavroche se mit à rire: 'Ah! tiens, c'est vrai, ça ne sait pas encore, c'est si petit!'

Et il reprit: 'Mangez.'[44]

Even more powerful is the imaginative and baroque description of the children sheltering in the dilapidated statue of the elephant that Gavroche has transformed into his personal palace:

The smaller of the two clung to his brother and murmured:

'It's dark.'

This word made Gavroche cry out in indignation. The petrified air of the two kids made a sharp shock essential.

'What are you playing at!' he cried. 'Is this a joke? We're turning up our noses, are we? You need the Palace, I suppose? Are you a pair of asses? Go on, answer. I warn you I'm not one of your oafs. Look, are you Lord and Lady Muck?'

A little roughness is a good thing when you're frightened. It's reassuring. The two children came closer to Gavroche. Gavroche, paternally moved by such trust, switched from fierce to gentle and turned to the smaller of the two.

'Silly', he said, giving the insult a caressing tone, 'It's outside that it's dark.'

Le plus petit se recogna contre son frère et dit à demi-voix:

—C'est noir.

Ce mot fit exclamer Gavroche. L'air pétrifié des deux mômes rendait une secousse nécessaire.

—Qu'est-ce que vous me fichez? s'écria-t-il. Blaguons-nous? faisons-nous des dégoûtés? vous faut-il pas les Tuileries? Seriez-vous des brutes? Dites-le. Je vous préviens que je ne suis pas du régiment des godiches. Ah çà, est-ce que vous êtes les moutards du moutardier du pape?

Un peu de rudoiement est bon dans l'épouvante. Cela rassure. Les deux enfants se rapprochèrent de Gavroche. Gavroche, paternellement attendri de cette confiance, passa du 'grave au doux', et s'adressant au plus petit:

—Bêta, lui dit-il en accentuant l'injure d'une nuance carressante, c'est dehors que c'est noir.[45]

[44] *Les Misérables*, ii. 562.   [45] Ibid., ii. 562.

Although it is clear that part of the pleasure underlying the creation of this scene derives from the possibilities of exploring the gamin's slang, it is also indisputable that it seeks to reveal, through a mimetic rather than analytical presentation, both the psychology of childhood fears and the nature of the friendships that spring up so easily among the very young. Nevertheless, in the case of Hugo, it would seem that the desire to depict and explore childhood, although it plays a greater and more complex role than in the majority of his predecessors, is always secondary in importance to the imperative need to create, extend, and deepen a personal, labyrinthine myth dependent on the transformation of individual into icon.

Baudelaire, in exploring the difference between the presentation of the child in Hugo and in the poet Marceline Desbordes-Valmore, offers the following evaluation:

Victor Hugo has expressed magnificently, as with all he expresses, the beauties and joys of family life but it is only in the poetry of the ardent Marceline that you will find a mother's warmth for her brood, a warmth that some of the sons of women, less ungrateful than the others, still recall with delight. Were I not afraid that too animal a comparison might be seen as lacking in respect towards this adorable woman, I would say that I find in her the grace, the restlessness, the suppleness, and the violence of the female, the she-cat or the lioness who loves her little ones.

Victor Hugo a exprimé magnifiquement, comme tout ce qu'il exprime, les beautés et les enchantements de la vie de famille mais seulement dans les poésies de l'ardente Marceline vous trouverez cette chaleur de couvée maternelle, dont quelques-uns, parmi les fils de la femme, moins ingrats que les autres, ont gardé le délicieux souvenir. Si je ne craignais pas qu'une comparaison trop animale fût prise pour un manque de respect envers cette adorable femme, je dirais que je trouve en elle la grâce, l'inquiétude, la souplesse et la violence de la femelle, chatte ou lionne, amoureuse de ses petits.[46]

Admired by Sainte-Beuve, Verlaine, Aragon, and Bonnefoy, Marceline Desbordes-Valmore's poetry is marked above all by the spontaneity and intensity with which it evokes the delights and despair of love and loss: the love of woman for man, mother for child, friend for friend, the sense of loss when the lover ceases to love, when the friend departs or dies, when the child grows up and

---

[46] *Œuvres complètes*, ii. 147.

leads its own life. Despite the relative narrowness of her thematic range and the somewhat repetitive nature of her imagery, her poetry conveys a sense of immediacy, of entering directly into the experience of another mind, and, in a domain which, in the nineteenth century, was dominated by men, offers a rare example of the very different response of a woman to sexual and maternal love.[47]

For all the intensity of her expression of maternal love, it is nevertheless the case that very often the evocation of childhood and children in her poems is above all a springboard into meditations on adult sufferings or on the passing of time. Thus, in contemplating the studious nature of her daughter Ondine and wondering whether the laurels the school has awarded her will lead to real happiness, Marceline Desbordes-Valmore finds a remarkable formulation for the mother's painful realization of her daughter's alterity:

> Oh! how I missed you, young soul of my soul!
> What fear I felt at the departure of a flame
> I had placed on earth, and which stemmed from me,
> And which went away all alone. Oh! Ondine, what fear!

> Oh! que vous me manquiez, jeune âme de mon âme!
> Quel effroi de sentir s'éloigner une flamme
> Que j'avais mise au monde, et qui venait de moi,
> Et qui s'en allait seule! Ondine! quel effroi![48]

Not only do the wreaths cover the child's hair, denaturing the natural beauty created by her mother—'They hid your hair that I had made so beautiful', (*Ils cachaient vos cheveux que j'avais faits si beaux*)—but the child's passion for knowledge affirms a character quite different from that encapsulated in the name bestowed on her by the poet: throughout this poem the element of water conveyed by the nickname Ondine conflicts with the imagery of fire and flames evoking her character to suggest an awareness—conscious or not—that the adult's view of the child can never coincide entirely with that of the child. If Léopoldine forces Hugo to reach a similar awareness, through her marriage, he chooses to express it in

---

[47] For studies of her poetry see the monographs of Jasénas and Moulin, and Bonnefoy's preface to his edition of selections from her works. The best edition of her poetry is that of M. Bertrand.
[48] *Poésies*, 212.

quite different terms, by shifting the focus away from the child's otherness and on to the depiction of the small child still dependent, both physically and intellectually, on the adult.

As is the case with most Romantics, Marceline Desbordes-Valmore's meditation on the child also prompts memories of her own past. In a poem whose imagery and rhythms attempt to capture the mobility of the little girl, Ondine, the 'joyous child who leaps on to the earth' (*l'enfant joyeux qui bondis sur la terre*), recapitulates her mother's past to become a symbol of eternal childhood:

> When I see you slipping past, dancing so gracefully,
> I feel my wandering soul float beside you:
> I watch myself live, a silent shade;
> My days of purity, under your features, pass before me yet again!
>
> Quand je t'y vois glisser dansante et gracieuse,
> Je sens flotter mon âme errante autour de toi:
> Je me regarde vivre, ombre silencieuse;
> Mes jours purs, sous tes traits, repassant devant moi![49]

Here, the water imagery inevitably connected with Ondine serves both to contrast the joyous mobility of the child with the static nature of the adult, and also to trigger those hysterical tears that Baudelaire saw as central to Marceline Desbordes-Valmore's poetic universe:[50]

> Everything weeps! The innocent victim swept away by the torrent
> And those who, when they pray, can pray only of their repentance.
>
> Tout pleure! et l'innocent que le torrent entraîne,
> Et ceux qui, pour prier, n'ont que leurs repentirs.[51]

If the sight of Ondine is sufficient to precipitate the poet back into her own childhood, so also is the power of affective memory, that source of fascination for so many of her contemporaries, notably Nerval and Baudelaire. The return to memories of childhood is accompanied here by a rather rosy series of images, and a total conformity to the Romantic notion of the child's beauty and purity:

> The breath of a wild flower,
> As it passed close by my heart,
> Carried me away to the river bank

---

[49] Ibid., 94.   [50] *Œuvres complètes*, ii. 149.   [51] *Poésies*, 95.

Where a short time ago I too was a flower:
As in the depths of a prism where everything changes,
Where everything appears before my eyes,
I see a child with angel's eyes:
He was my little beloved!

L'haleine d'une fleur sauvage,
En passant tout près de mon cœur,
Vient de m'emporter au rivage,
Où naguère aussi j'étais fleur:
Comme au fond d'un prisme où tout change,
Où tout se révèle à mes yeux,
Je vois un enfant aux yeux d'ange:
C'était mon petit amoureux![52]

The little beloved comes complete, predictably, with a halo of golden hair, blue eyes, and brief words of tenderness,[53] a carefully and too consciously created counterpart to those later *'amoureux'* who have played so fast and loose with the adult poet's heart.

Although the image of the child is sometimes used primarily as a particularly potent device for entering more profoundly into the adult's experience, other poems reflect a more energetic attempt to recreate the child's own imagination and to find corresponding metaphors and rhythms. If, in doing so, Desbordes-Valmore is able to avoid the pitfalls of sentimentality, it is above all because she attempts to shift her horizon to the child's gaze, rather than remaining at the Olympian heights of adulthood. Recalling her voyage to Guadeloupe, when she was 11, for example, she finds a series of images for an imagined submarine world, which, for all the adult nature of some of the vocabulary—*'épurant'*, *'bénir'*, *'front calme'*, etc.—nevertheless captures the excitement and joy of the child's vision of a different existence:

I thought that a fairy, purifying the surge,
In order to trace a glowing path to the ship,
Burnt golden lamps under the deep waves
And I, to bless her for it, stretched out my hand to her.
My fascinated eyes saw the lovely mermaid
Wander, untouched by water, in her damp palace.
I saw her calm brow bedecked with diamonds
And I saw her charming feet slip through the cool crystal.

---

[52] *Poésies*, 121.   [53] Ibid.

Je croyais qu'une fée, en épurant les ondes,
Pour tracer au navire un lumineux chemin,
Brûlait des lampes d'or sous les vagues profondes
Et moi, pour l'en bénir, je lui tendais la main.
A mes yeux fascinés la belle Néréide
Errait, sans se mouiller, dans son palais humide.
Je voyais son front calme orné de diamants,
Et dans le frais cristal glisser ses pieds charmants.[54]

And while 'Un ruisseau de la Scarpe' is again primarily an exploration of the transience of human existence, it also offers a series of sharply etched vignettes of children, particularly in the depiction of them playing in the stream:

School children of those days, you lively, noisy flock,
Where are they now, the presents you threw into the flowing water?
The open book, sometimes your shoes as ships,
And your little gardens of moss and shrubs?

Ecoliers de ce temps, troupe alerte et bruyante,
Où sont-ils vos présents jetés à l'eau fuyante?
Le livre ouvert, parfois vos souliers pour vaisseaux,
Et vos petits jardins de mousse et d'abrisseaux?[55]

Moreover, in 'L'Enfant au miroir' Desbordes-Valmore responds to the challenge of allowing the child to speak directly in a rhythm reflecting the mobility of a little girl's imagination. While she avoids the embarrassing stiffness of Lamartine's 'Hymne de l'enfant au révcil', and succeeds in conveying the girl's impatience, despite the limitations imposed by the metrical structures adopted, one might well feel that she nevertheless oversimplifies the child's thought in her desire to remain within the vocabulary of childhood:

It's cool in the dark wood,
And it's beautiful, too,
To dance like a shadow
Beside the water!
Children of my age,
Always running,
Should spend all their days
In the country!

C'est frais dans le bois sombre,
Et puis c'est beau

De danser comme une ombre
Au bord de l'eau!
Les enfants de mon âge,
Courant toujours,
Devraient tous au village
Passer leurs jours![56]

Whatever problems she, like her contemporaries, might encounter in entering the child's mind, she is nevertheless particularly gifted in her ability to convey the adult's amusement and delight in watching children play, and, unlike Hugo, prefers to suggest that pleasure without linking it to some more wide-ranging metaphysical meditation. The image of children proudly shouting out to clouds and startled birds the songs they have learnt,[57] and above all, perhaps, the depiction of the little boy too full of energy to want to go to bed, lose none of their spontaneity and lightness of touch by being forced to carry any weighty meaning. Indeed, the child in 'Le Coucher d'un petit garçon' makes short work of the silliness of the adult's rational or mendacious arguments for sending him off to bed:

'Go to bed, little Paul. It's raining. Night has fallen, the
   time has come for sleep.
Wolves are on the rampart. The dog has just barked.
The bell says "Sleep" and the guardian angel weeps
When children are noisy so late around the hearth.'
'I don't want to go to sleep all the time. And I like
Making my sabre sparkle in the light of the evening fire.
And I'll kill the wolves! I'll kill them myself!'
And the naughty little boy, completely naked, flings
   himself on to a chair.

Couchez-vous, petit Paul! Il pleut. C'est nuit: c'est l'heure.
Les loups sont au rempart. Le chien vient d'aboyer.
La cloche a dit: 'Dormez!' et l'ange gardien pleure,
Quand les enfants si tard font du bruit au foyer.

'Je ne veux pas toujours aller dormir et j'aime
A faire étinceler mon sabre au feu du soir
Et je tuerai les loups! Je les tuerai moi-même!'
Et le petit méchant, tout nu! vint se rasseoir.[59]

[56] *Poésies*, 236.   [57] Ibid., 194.
[58] Ibid., 197   [59] Ibid., 99.

Above all, however, she succeeds in conveying the visceral intensity of the relationship between mother and daughter, and the amount of emotional support it offers the adult. Indeed, the language she uses to depict this love is all but identical with that used to evoke sexual love, particularly, for example, in the poem entitled 'Ma fille' in the collection called *Les Pleurs*: 'How soft your hair is! Spread it over my tears/ Like a golden veil over a black memory.'[60] (*Que tes cheveux sont doux! étends-les sur mes larmes,/ Comme un voile doré sur un noir souvenir.*)

For Marceline Desbordes-Valmore, therefore, the child is both a means of projection into the future and a recapitulation of the adult's past, a source of emotional support in despair, and a flesh-and-blood creature, having its own desires and its own separate personality. Her poetry offers us a rare image of a woman's view of children and childhood, one that is too intense and idiosyncratic to suffer the limiting judgement that it stands for a universal female response, but a presentation whose spontaneity and warmth provide a unique insight into the relationships between a woman and her past, and a mother and her daughter.

SHIFTING THE VIEWPOINT TOWARDS REALISM

In his vast canvas depicting the artist's studio, the Realist painter Gustave Courbet presents, on the left, a series of allegorical models and, on the right, groups of his friends. None of these, however, looks at either the painter, posing in splendid Assyrian profile, or his painting. The figures who do appear absorbed by pictorial art are the half-draped model, a child who stands gazing intently at the work on the easel, and a second child, lying flat on his stomach sketching.[61] The future of art, Courbet implies, lies neither in its subject-matter nor in its intended audience, but in children. In this, Courbet's vision partly coincides with, partly extends, the Romantic image of the intensity of childhood experience. Indeed, the boys in Courbet's painting could stand as icons not merely of the Realists' focus on the appetites, both physical and intellectual, of children,

---

[60] Ibid., 96.
[61] Baudelaire is depicted in the painting as lost in a book, which could conceivably be a collection of prints, but Baudelaire is in any case convinced of the close relationship between artists and children.

but also of the way in which the Realists absorbed much of the mythology of Romanticism, however different might have been their purposes and techniques.

In the Preface to *La Comédie humaine*, Balzac signals the growing interest in childhood as a literary topos, and in education as a political and social problem, when he designates the works included in the *Scènes de la vie privée* as concerned above all with childhood, adolescence, and their errors and misdemeanours.[62] Although the very fact that he should choose to highlight, not the joys or pleasures or innocence of childhood, but its transgressions, suggests a marked shift in his perception of the child, it is no guarantee that the pre-adolescent child will figure largely in Balzac's writing. Indeed, one could argue that the claims he makes concerning the theme of childhood in the Preface stem less from the realities of the *Scènes de la vie privée* than from the will to impose a logical structure on a somewhat recalcitrant group of novels. Moreover, the novelist's overriding interest in the passions aroused by sexual desire and money would seem a priori to relegate childhood to a minor role, even if, in 'L'Enfant maudit', he evokes a remarkably intense relationship between mother and son:

To see his mother approaching, to hear from afar the rustle of her dress, to wait for her, kiss her, speak to her, listen to her, caused him sensations that were so intense that often a delay or the slightest fear gave him a consuming fever.

Voir venir sa mère, entendre de loin le frôlement de sa robe, l'attendre, la baiser, lui parler, l'écouter, lui causaient des sensations si vives, que souvent un retard ou la plus légère crainte lui causaient une fièvre dévorante.[63]

Furthermore, where the figure of the child is explored at any length in Balzac's writing, it is almost invariably strongly marked by the Romantic image of the misunderstood individual, doomed to suffer even at the hands of those who should most offer love and comprehension. Even if we leave aside the melodramatic 'L'Enfant maudit', with its image of the child utterly rejected by his father,

---

[62] *Œuvres complètes*, i. 14.
[63] *Œuvres complètes*, ix. 694–5. The compensatory autobiographical nature of this description is self-evident, and its physical intensity is swiftly thrust under by the affirmation that 'with the form of a child and the mind of a man, he was equally angelic from both points of view' (*enfant par la forme, homme par l'esprit, il était également angélique sous les deux aspects.*) (695).

what prevails in the picture of childhood conveyed by *La Comédie humaine* is unhappiness, isolation, and mental and physical suffering. Rogron, in *Pierrette*, seems to sum up the metality of many Balzacian parents, with his comment: 'It'd be a funny state of affairs if parents put themselves out for their children!' (*Ce serait drôle de se gêner pour ses enfants!*)[64] Nevertheless, what distinguishes Balzac's image from the Romantic myth is the relentless way in which he infuses into this vision of the misunderstood child the social and physical realities of the situation. Seizing on the contemporary practice of sending children off to wet-nurses, so often portrayed in the nineteenth-century autobiographies, he elaborates on the bare facts to create a potent symbol of alienation:

sent to a wet-nurse in the country who does not charge too much, these wretched children return with the horrible education provided by a village, having cried lengthily and often for their wet-nurse's breast while she was in the fields. During this time she would have locked them in one of those dark, damp, and low rooms which the French peasants use as dwellings.

mis en nourrice à la campagne et à bas prix, ces malheureux enfants revinrent avec l'horrible éducation du village, ayant crié longtemps et souvent après le sein de leur nourrice qui allait aux champs, et qui, pendant ce temps, les enfermait dans une de ces chambres noires, humides et basses qui servent d'habitation au paysan français.[65]

The attempt to find a physical correlative for the child's sense of abandonment and loneliness is also present in the opening pages of *Le Lys dans la vallée*. Prefacing this picture with a more than slightly melodramatic call for a poet to tell of 'the grief of the child whose lips have suckled a bitter breast and whose first smiles have been repressed by the consuming fire of a severe gaze' (*les douleurs de l'enfant dont les lèvres suçent un sein amer, et dont les sourires sont réprimés par le feu dévorant d'un œil sévère*),[66] Balzac's first-person narrator, Félix de Vandenesse, depicts himself abandoned under a tree, with only a star for company, and, somewhat later,

---

[64] Ibid., iii. 662. Some thirty years later Zola was to depict a young father saying of his children: 'With these little creatures one starts worrying immediately they suffer the slightest pain' (*Avec ces petits êtres, on s'inquiète tout de suite, pour le moindre bobo*) (*Les Rougon-Macquart*, v. 86), although there we are dealing not only with a different period but with a different class, the wealthy middle class.

[65] *Œuvres complètes*, iii. 661.

[66] Ibid., viii. 771.

forced to measure the paucity of his mother's love for him in the scantiness of the lunch she provides for him to take to school.[67]

Perhaps because he perceives a direct parallel between the child and the *poète maudit*, Balzac also differs from many Romantics in that he does not look down on children, but rather seeks to indicate, both with Félix de Vandenesse and with Louis Lambert, whose experiences we shall explore in a subsequent chapter, the degree to which the child, for all its apparent fragility, is capable of the passions and convictions of the adult. Félix, for example, argues that 'the certainty that these acts were unjust inspired in him prematurely a sense of pride, that fruit of reason, which no doubt stemmed the evil tendencies that such training encouraged' (*la certitude de ces injustices excita prématurément dans [son] âme la fierté, ce fruit de la raison, qui sans doute arrêta les mauvais penchants qu'une semblable éducation encourageait*).[68] Equally, the mystery and beauty of the night sky awaken in him feelings no less acute than they might be in an adult:

One evening, tranquilly curled up against a fig-tree, I was watching a star with that curious passion that seizes hold of children, and to which my precocious melancholy added a kind of sentimental intelligence.

Un soir, tranquillement blotti sous un figuier, je regardais une étoile avec cette passion curieuse qui saisit les enfants, et à laquelle ma précoce mélancolie ajoutait une sorte d'intelligence sentimentale.[69]

And although one might argue that *Le Lys dans la vallée* encourages an autobiographical mode of reading to such an extent as to make Félix a special case, Balzac is, characteristically, careful to indicate in the above passage that this 'curious passion' is a general tendency in children and not unique to his narrator. One final analytical comment rounds out Balzac's depiction of children:

A tyrannical refusal whets a child's appetite all the more intensely than an adult's; children have over their elders the advantage of thinking of nothing but what has been forbidden and that makes it irresistibly attractive to them.

Les défenses tyranniques aiguisent encore plus une passion chez les enfants que chez les hommes; les enfants ont sur eux l'avantage de ne penser qu'à la chose défendue, qui leur offre alors des attraits irrésistibles.[70]

---

[67] See also Chapter 4, 202–3.
[68] *Œuvres complètes*, viii. 772.   [69] Ibid., viii. 772–3.
[70] Ibid., viii. 773. Compare some of the monomaniac longings of Sophie in Mme de Ségur's famous children's novel, *Les Malheurs de Sophie*.

Monomania, that typically Balzacian theme, is, then, nowhere so likely to be present as in childhood. While Balzac shows little interest, therefore, in recapturing the language children use, and is most concerned to reveal the unhappiness of childhood, the down-to-earth nature of his imagery and the refusal to patronize them gives his depictions a freshness and, despite their melodramatic nature, a degree of conviction that few of his contemporaries achieved.

Flaubert, too, had interests, ambitions, and a vision of the novel's potential that led him to include children only occasionally in his work, even then granting them only a minor role. Given the magnitude of the task he set himself in terms of creating for the novel a style allowing the narrative voice to remain external and invisible but constantly present, a technique that would enable him to convey the emotions of characters incapable of expressing themselves with the analytical fluency of traditional novelistic heroes and heroines, given also his creation of a diegetic space and time creating an emotional rather than a strictly realistic climate, it is hardly surprising that Flaubert—at a time when, as we have seen, children were in any case a relative rarity in French literature—should not have sought out that particular challenge as well. It could certainly be the case, however, that his technical achievements were a critical enabling factor for works written later in the century in which the minds and the world of children are explored more deeply. Moreover, when he does introduce images of childhood, he does so with a characteristic refusal to veer into the maudlin, and an equally typical questioning of the current *idées reçues*. Not surprisingly, in his dictionary of clichés, Flaubert includes under the heading 'children' the concisely cynical recommendation that one should show great tenderness to them, when anyone else is present.

Taking a malicious delight in the plethora of theories concerning the upbringing of children,[71] Flaubert evokes with robust concision the conflict in views between Charles Bovary's mother and father, using the passage not merely to lay the foundation of Charles's character, but also to indicate both the lack of harmony between the married couple, and the way in which adults inflict on their children the penalties of their own failed ambitions. As with so much of *Madame Bovary*, these early passages point forward to

---

[71] On these see e.g. Donzelot, *La Police des familles*, 22.

Emma's own response to her child, her hopes for a male infant in whom she can live out dreams of a kind of life inaccessible to women, and the contrasting moods of excessive tenderness and straightforward neglect that mark her treatment of her daughter. While Charles's mother spoils the child and dreams of him occupying high positions in law or civil engineering, his father, we are told, has a more virile idea of childhood, consisting, so it would appear, of making him go to bed without a fire in his room, teaching him to swig rum, and encouraging him to hurl insults at religious processions. Little Charles, of course, remains unscathed both by maternal tenderness and paternal free-thought, indulging instead in the normal activities of childhood, evoked by Flaubert in a brief but dense passage that indicates perfectly clearly that, where childhood is concerned, he could an he would:

He used to follow the ploughmen, and throw clods of earth at the crows to make them fly away. He ate blackberries along the ditches, herded the turkeys with a stick, made hay at harvest time, ran about in the woods, played hopscotch in the church porch on rainy days and, on great feast-days, begged the beadle to let him ring the bells, so that he could hang full weight on the long rope and feel himself carried away with the bell in its flight.

Il suivait les laboureurs, et chassait, à coups de mottes de terre, les corbeaux qui s'envolaient. Il mangeait des mûres le long des fossés, gardait les dindons avec une gaule, fanait à la moisson, courait dans les bois, jouait à la marelle sous le porche de l'église, les jours de pluie, et, aux grandes fêtes, suppliait le bedeau de lui laisser sonner les cloches, pour se pendre de tout son corps à la grande corde et se sentir emporter par elle dans sa volée.[72]

There is in this passage both a doffing of the cap to Flaubert's great master, Rabelais, who in *Pantagruel* sums up with such memorable gusto the pursuits of childhood, and a response to one of the many challenges the novelist sets himself in the course of *Madame Bovary*, that of seizing on a handful of sensory images and using them to make his readers feel to the very core of their beings the experience he is describing.[73]

The child has a further role to play in *Madame Bovary* in acting as yet another area where Emma's expectations, culled mainly from reading, are brought so abruptly and unglamorously down to earth

---

[72] *Madame Bovary*, 8.   [73] *Correspondance*, ii. 449.

by the realities she encounters. Basing her image of passionate motherhood on Victor Hugo's character, Sachette, in *Notre-Dame de Paris*, Emma forgets that here the violence of maternal feeling is dependent on the absence of the child, who has been stolen by gypsies. Emma, however, has to deal with the physical presence of her child, with its cries, its vomit, its needs, and it independence. And Flaubert is not above using Berthe to give a further turn to the screw in the tale of havoc Emma's death and debts leave behind her: Berthe is put in the care of an aunt whose poverty forces her to send the child to earn her living in a cotton mill. In other words, with the theme of childhood, as with many contemporary interests, Flaubert is able to exploit both the reader's anticipation, based on clichées and *idées reçues*, and his own awareness of other, and often darker, aspects of those themes.

That awareness is very much in evidence in the character of Louise Roque in *L'Éducation sentimentale*. Here, Flaubert throws into question the Romantic dichotomy in which woman is either angel or demon, Madonna or prostitute. With remarkable brevity he establishes the characteristics of Louise's parents, to explain, in part, her own nature: the hard-nosed, ambitious petit-bourgeois father rising in social status through the wealth he accumulates, and the lethargic, queenly mother in whom Flaubert suggests a smouldering passion. The spontaneity and intensity of Louise's nature are also, however, shown as a product of her early experiences, when she is neglected by her mother, spoilt by her nurse, and spurned by the town's children, whose parents find revenge for the humiliation M. Roque's rise to power has inflicted on them in forbidding their offspring to play with the little girl. We first encounter her when Frédéric is gazing vacantly over the hedge that runs between the two gardens, in a passage that depicts her in terms redolent of early Impressionism:

A little red-headed girl of about 12 years old was there all alone. She had made herself ear-rings from rowan berries, her grey stuff bodice revealed shoulders that were slightly bronzed by the sun, jam stains soiled her white skirt, and there was about her the kind of grace one finds in a young animal, making her both wiry and slight. The presence of a stranger no doubt astonished her, for she had stopped abruptly, her watering can in her hand, and she gazed at him with her clear greeny-blue eyes.

Une petite fille d'environ douze ans, et qui avait les cheveux rouges, se trouvait là, toute seule. Elle s'était fait des boucles d'oreilles avec des baies

de sorbier, son corset de toile grise laissait à découverte ses épaules, un peu
dorées par le soleil, des taches de confitures maculaient son jupon blanc, et
il y avait comme une grâce de jeune bête sauvage dans toute sa personne, à
la fois nerveuse et fluette. La présence d'un inconnu l'étonnait, sans doute,
car elle s'était brusquement arrêtée, avec son arrosoir à la main, en dardant
sur lui ses prunelles, d'un vert-bleu limpide.[74]

In this succinct description, Flaubert conveys the child's natural
coquetry, in the rowan berries hanging from her ears, her isolation
and the degree to which the adults neglect her, in the fact that she is
all alone and that her skirt is stained with jam. All this is seen
through the focus of Frédéric's mind, as the 'no doubt' informs us:
subsequent developments suggest to the reader a different interpretation for the intensity with which she gazes on the young man who
has suddenly appeared before her. As with his renderings of
Charles's early boyhood, Flaubert also depicts with pithy and
painterly clarity the games of this lonely little girl: 'she lived alone,
in her garden, where she would play on the swing, run after
butterflies, then suddenly stop to look at the rose beetles that were
attacking the rose bushes.' (*elle vivait seule, dans son jardin,
se balançait à l'escarpolette, courait après les papillons, puis
tout à coup s'arrêtait à contempler les cétoines s'abattant sur les
rosiers.*)[75] There is in this description an inescapable echo of
Watteau's paintings or of the many lesser-known dreams of
happiness, those of Baron or Papety, for instance, that were so
common in the 1840s, where the swing and the butterflies signal
both pleasure and the ephemeral, while Flaubert's addition of the
rose beetles with their sturdy carapaces suggests something rather
more earthy and less ethereal. Above all, Louise serves as a means
to explore the love a child can experience, a love which, Flaubert
insists, combines 'the purity of a religion and the violence of a need'
(*la pureté d'une religion et la violence d'un besoin*).[76] The challenge
she sets the novelist is partly that of rejecting the simplistic myth of
childhood purity by showing how innocence can coexist with the
intensity of passion, and partly that of indicating her mind and her
nature uniquely through what is accessible to Frédéric, suggesting
her thoughts only through what she says or her facial expression.

The same sardonic delight in debunking current theories of
education and showing how such theories are formed for the

---

[74] *L'Éducation sentimentale*, 105.
[75] Ibid., 111.   [76] Ibid., 292.

benefit of adults rather than children surfaces in the chapter Flaubert devotes to education in *Bouvard et Pécuchet*. There the blind but benevolent desire to give two children a chance in life regardless of their abilities or personalities crumbles against the passive but immovable resistance of the children themselves, whose bored incomprehension raises between adult and child an unsurmountable wall.

Conventional conceptions of childhood and children also come under attack in the middle of the nineteenth century from the sardonic, complex mind of Baudelaire. As with Flaubert, much of the virulence of Baudelaire's attack on Romantic clichés lies in the fact that he is himself so steeped in Romanticism, and so sharply aware of the extent to which Romanticism's vigour has been sapped by the ease with which the bourgeoisie have harnessed it for their own purposes. The characteristic bipolarity of his thought, moreover, produces a series of images of childhood in which the legacy of Romanticism, particularly its dark, satanic side, confronts a more pragmatic vision, Byron illustrated by Daumier, perhaps. There can be no doubting the importance Baudelaire attaches to the role of childhood in forging the individual, and to the intensity of the child's experience as the source of subsequent artistic vision. His first full-length study of Poe adds the following suggestion to the article by John Daniel from which Baudelaire extracted so much of his information:[77]

the character, the genius, the style of a man are formed by the apparently unexceptional circumstances of his youth. If all those who have occupied the world's stage had noted their childhood impressions, what an excellent dictionary of psychology we would have!

le caractère, le génie, le style d'un homme est formé par les circonstances en apparence vulgaires de sa première jeunesse. Si tous les hommes qui ont occupé la scène du monde avaient noté leurs impressions d'enfance, quel excellent dictionnaire psychologique nous posséderions![78]

Even when he refuses to adopt the familiar biographical criticism of the day in his study of the poet Pierre Dupont, and implicitly mocks the innumerable 'childhoods of famous men' written for children,[79]

[77] On this see the number of the *Cahiers de l'Herne* devoted to Poe in 1974, Richard, *Edgar Allan Poe journaliste et critique*, and my *Baudelaire's Literary Criticism*.

[78] *Œuvres complètes*, ii. 253.

[79] Louise Colet, for example, published a work with this title in 1858.

he nevertheless insists on the importance of childhood in the subsequent development of the artist or writer: 'The childhood and youth of Pierre Dupont were like the childhood and youth of all those destined to become famous. They are very simple and they explain the subsequent years.' (*L'enfance et la jeunesse de Pierre Dupont ressemblent à l'enfance et à la jeunesse de tous les hommes destinés à devenir célèbres. Elle est très simple, et elle explique l'âge suivant.*)[80] And in the study of Constantin Guys entitled 'Le Peintre de la vie moderne', he seizes on the opportunity to explore the relationship between the child and the genius, in terms that reveal how much the Wordsworthian conviction concerning the intensity of childhood experience has in common with Baudelaire's own vision:

the child sees everything as *new*; it is always *intoxicated*. Nothing is so reminiscent of what is termed inspiration as the joy with which children absorb shape and colour . . . The man of genius has solid nerves; the child's nerves are weak. In the former, reason has assumed a considerable place; in the latter, sensitivity occupies almost the entire individual. But genius is merely *childhood regained* through an act of will, childhood which now, in order to express itself, possesses virile organs and an analytical mind that enables it to impose order on the sum of the material unconsciously amassed.

L'enfant voit tout en *nouveauté*; il est toujours *ivre*. Rien ne ressemble plus à ce qu'on appelle l'inspiration, que la joie avec laquelle l'enfant absorbe la forme et la couleur . . . L'homme de génie a les nerfs solides; l'enfant les a faibles. Chez l'un, la raison a pris une place considérable; chez l'autre, la sensibilité occupe presque tout l'être. Mais le génie n'est que *l'enfance retrouvée* a volonté, l'enfance douée maintenant, pour s'exprimer, d'organes virils et de l'esprit analytique qui lui permet d'ordonner la somme de matériaux involontairement amassée.[81]

That this notion is central to Baudelaire's æsthetic, and not merely suggested by the characters of Poe or Guys, is further confirmed by his addition of the following lines to his translation of De Quincey's *Confessions of an English Opium-Eater*:

All biographers . . . have realized the importance of anecdotes concerning the childhood of an artist or writer. But in my view this importance has never been sufficiently stressed. Often, when we look at works of art, not in

---

[80] *Œuvres complètes*, ii. 27–8.   [81] Ibid., ii. 690.

their easily comprehensible *materiality* . . . but in the soul that has been invested in them, in the atmospheric impression they convey, in the spiritual light or darkness they shed over our souls, I have felt myself penetrated by what one might term a vision of their creator's childhood. Certain minor sorrows, certain little delights that the child has felt and that have been magnified out of all proportion by an exquisite sensitivity, later become for the adult, whether he knows it or not, the germ of a work of art.

Tous les biographes ont compris . . . l'importance des anecdotes se rattachant à l'enfance d'un écrivain ou d'un artiste. Mais je trouve que cette importance n'a jamais été suffisamment affirmée. Souvent, en contemplant des ouvrages d'art, non pas dans leur *matérialité* facilement saisissable . . . mais dans l'âme dont ils sont doués, dans l'impression atmosphérique qu'ils comportent, dans la lumière ou dans les ténèbres spirituelles qu'ils déversent sur nos âmes, j'ai senti entrer en moi comme une vision de l'enfance de leurs auteurs. Tel petit chagrin, telle petite jouissance de l'enfant, démesurément grossis par une exquise sensibilité, deviennent plus tard dans l'homme adulte, même à son insu, le principe d'une œuvre d'art.[82]

While the seeds of this æsthetic are certainly to be found in the Romantic image of childhood, and while Baudelaire subscribes to that image so far as to claim that 'the fertile mind of childhood makes everything delightful' (*le cerveau fécond de l'enfance rend tout agréable*),[83] he nevertheless conveys the extent to which the lived experience differs from the imaginative reconstruction through the sudden vehemence of a passage in which he comments on Poe's tale 'William Wilson':

The hours spent in the school prison, the uneasiness felt by the weak and abandoned child, the terror inspired by the teacher, our enemy, the hatred of bullying schoolmates, the loneliness of the heart, all the tortures experienced by children, all these were unknown to Edgar Poe.

Les heures du cachot, le malaise de l'enfance chétive et abandonée, la terreur du maître, notre ennemi, la haine des camarades tyranniques, la solitude du cœur, toutes ces tortures du jeune âge, Edgar Poe ne les a pas éprouvées.[84]

As the sentence structure suggests, and the poet's early letters,

---

[82] Ibid., i. 497–8. Compare also M. Stäuble's edition, 220–3, in which Baudelaire's additions and alterations are clearly signalled.
[83] *Œuvres complètes*, ii. 258.   [84] Ibid., ii. 257.

together with comments in *Mon cœur mis à nu*, confirm, if Poe did
not experience these horrors, Baudelaire himself did.[85]

It is not surprising, therefore, that in Baudelaire's poetry we find
echoes of this belief in the vigour of childhood experience and its
vital effect on the range and nature of the adult's creative
production. The early poems of 'Spleen et Idéal' offer a Byronic
image of the poet rejected and condemned, even in infancy, by his
horrified mother, yet still capable of transforming into delight all
that he experiences:

> The disinherited child, enraptured by the sun,
> Finds again in all he drinks and all he eats
> Ambrosia and rosy nectar.

> L'Enfant déshérité s'enivre de soleil,
> Et dans tout ce qu'il boit et dans tout ce qu'il mange
> Retrouve l'ambroisie et le nectar vermeil.[86]

Yet the Gothic virulence of Baudelaire's image of childhood is only
one aspect of his complex vision. In 'Tableaux parisiens', as a letter
to Mme Aupick clarifies,[87] the violent hatred of those surrounding
the poet, and the elevated nature of the child's pleasures, are
replaced by the calm and silent beauty of evenings spent in the
house on the outskirts of the city:

> And in the evenings, the sun, behind the window pane
> Where its superb stream of rays was halted,
> Seemed like a great open eye in the curious heavens,
> Contemplating our long and silent dinners
> As it generously shed its beautiful, candle-like reflections
> On the frugal cloth and the serge curtains.

> Et le soleil, le soir, ruisselant et superbe,
> Qui, derrière la vitre où se brisait sa gerbe,
> Semblait, grand œil ouvert dans le ciel curieux,
> Contempler nos dîners longs et silencieux,
> Répandant largement ses beaux reflets de cierge
> Sur la nappe frugale et les rideaux de serge.[88]

Despite the calm of this image, there is nevertheless an echo of the
isolation Baudelaire claims to have felt even in childhood—'a
feeling of solitude from childhood on. Despite my family—and

---

[85] See Pichois's note, Ibid., ii. 1208.   [86] Ibid., i. 7.
[87] *Correspondance*, i. 445.   [88] *Œuvres complètes*, i. 99.

especially when surrounded by schoolmates—a feeling that I was destined to eternal loneliness' (*sentiment de solitude, dès mon enfance. Malgré la famille,—et au milieu des camarades, surtout,— sentiment de destinée éternellement solitaire*)[89]—and a sense, too, of the unbridgeable gap between mother and child that underlies the poignant question asked in the prose poem 'Les Veuves': 'Which is the sadder and the more saddening widow, the one who drags by the hand a toddler with whom she cannot share her dreams or the one who is completely alone? I do not know . . . ' (*Quelle est la veuve la plus triste et la plus attristante, celle qui traîne à sa main un bambin avec qui elle ne peut pas partager sa rêverie, ou celle qui est tout à fait seule? Je ne sais . . .*)[90]

   If Baudelaire's vision of the relationship between adult and child is predicated on an intellectual gulf, it certainly does not preclude a sense of the powerful physical attraction the son feels for his mother. This is expressed not only in a letter the adult Baudelaire wrote to his mother, in which he recounts that he experienced a period of passionate love for her in the days of her widowhood (when Baudelaire was 7 years old),[91] but also in the poem 'La Géante', where the infant's vision of his mother's comparative vastness combines with a more adult erotic awareness in such a way as to create a myth of a young giantess over whom the poet can roam at leisure and 'Sleep nonchalantly in the shadow of her breasts/ Like a peaceful hamlet at the foot of a mountain' (*Dormir nonchalamment à l'ombre de ses seins,/ Comme un hameau paisible au pied d'une montagne*).[92] This conviction of the child's ability to experience erotic drives and impulses—a conviction that subverts the hackneyed view of childhood innocence so conscientiously bolstered up even by someone as imaginative as Hugo—finds its clearest expression, in Baudelaire's writing, in the prose poem 'Les Vocations', where four children, idly chatting together, reveal both their characters and what Baudelaire would term their destiny. Here the element of challenge that marks so much of the poet's work, both creative and critical, is very much in evidence as Baudelaire not only combines a relatively simple syntax with a range of images within a boy's experience, in order to enter directly into the child's mind, but also shows through external description the physical effect that the memory is exerting. Eyes wide open in

[89] Ibid., i. 680.
[91] *Correspondance*, i. 445.
[90] Ibid., i. 293. Original ellipses.
[92] *Œuvres complètes*, i. 23.

astonishment, hair back-lit by the setting sun in such a way as to give him a form of sulphurous halo of passion, the child recounts a night when he had to share a bed with his maid and, sleepless, ran his hand over her arms and neck, finding her skin 'so soft, so soft that you'd think it was made of writing paper or silk paper' (*si douce, si douce, qu'on dirait du papier à lettre ou du papier de soie*).[93] Stopping through fear not only of waking her but also of '*je ne sais quoi*', the boy then plunges his head into the mane of her hair, finding it smells just as good as flowers at evening time. There is in this passage a blend of innocence and passion, a refusal to condescend in referring to childhood experience, and an ability to find a language that remains within the grasp of a child while still achieving considerable poetic resonance, that makes it an extraordinary achievement in the literature of the nineteenth century.

   While other prose poems may not quite reach such heights, they none the less serve to round out the image of the child and to undermine even further the standard myth. At a time when several journalists were devoting articles to nostalgically sentimental descriptions of children's toys,[94] Baudelaire, in 'Le Joujou du pauvre', paints a totally unsentimental picture of rich child and poor child ignoring the artificial and splendid toy in favour of the caged rat. Equally clear-sighted is his version of a typical comparison between child and animal when he describes the effect of giving poor children a simple toy:

You will see their eyes open enormously wide. At first they will not dare take it, they will doubt the reality of their good fortune. Then their hands will swiftly seize the present, and they will take flight, like cats that go and eat far from you the morsel of food you have given them, for they have learnt to be wary of mankind.

Vous verrez leurs yeux s'agrandir démesurément. D'abord ils n'oseront pas prendre; ils douteront de leur bonheur. Puis leurs mains agripperont vivement le cadeau, et ils s'enfuieront comme font les chats qui vont manger loin de vous le morceau que vous leur avez donné, ayant appris à se défier de l'homme.[95]

---

[93] *Œuvres complètes*, ii. 333.

[94] Hippolyte Rigault, for instance, contributed a study on 'Les Jouets d'enfants' to the *Journal des débats* in 1856. Jacques Stella's famous *Les Jeux et les plaisirs de l'enfance* goes back to 1667. See Clarétie, *Les Jouets de France, leur histoire, leur avenir*.

[95] *Œuvres completes*, i. 304.

Of course Baudelaire's purpose here is quite other than in those poems in which he conveys the world of childhood from the child's view. In this poem, a resolutely external view allows for the operation of irony, directed not at the child, but at adults who see as natural the social divisions exemplified by the ironwork gate that physically separates the boys who have found a common sympathy in playing with the rat. Nevertheless, the political point does not detract from the acerbically down-to-earth nature of the presentation of the children and their needs. The meditation on toys included in this prose poem encapsulates a longer discussion published in 1853 under the title 'Morale du joujou' in which Baudelaire insists even more forcefully on the relationship between the child's imagination, revealed in games, and that of the artist:

all children talk to their toys; toys become actors in the great drama of life, reduced by the dark-room of their little minds. Children bear witness through their games to their great gift of abstraction and their high powers of imagination. They play without toys. . . . The ease with which their imagination can find satisfaction shows just how spiritual children are in their artistic conceptions. The toy is the child's first initiation into art or rather it is the first realization of art for the child, and, when maturity comes and they can achieve their desires, they will not feel the same warmth, nor the same enthusiasm, nor the same belief.

tous les enfants parlent à leurs joujoux; les joujoux deviennent acteurs dans le grand drame de la vie, réduit par la chambre noire de leur petit cerveau. Les enfants témoignent par leurs jeux de leur grande faculté d'abstraction et de leur haute puissance imaginative. Ils jouent sans joujoux. . . . Cette facilité à contenter son imagination témoigne de la spiritualité de l'enfance dans ses conceptions artistiques. Le joujou est la première initiation de l'enfant à l'art, ou plutôt c'en est pour lui la première réalisation, et, l'âge mûr venu, les réalisations perfectionnées ne donneront pas à son esprit les mêmes chaleurs, ni les mêmes enthousiasmes, ni la même croyance.[96]

In this passage Baudelaire captures with bitter poignancy that sense of a lost paradise of intensity and beauty that Wordsworth conveys in his famous ode but that tends in the hands of most French Romantics to melt into a sickly sweetness because in them it lacks the transforming power of a fully convinced imagination.

Equally free of sugary sentiment is the portrayal of childish passions in 'Le Gâteau', where the fraternal smiles of the children in

---

[96] Ibid., i. 582–3.

'Le Joujou du pauvre' are replaced by a destructive battle for a morsel of bread, seen as so white by a child used to black bread as to justify his description of it as 'cake'. Here, too, the focus is on the adult and his reactions, the pompously judgemental attitude he adopts when a simple act on his part could separate the children by providing for both of them. A social statement about bourgeois hypocrisy when faced with the crime of the lower classes, this prose poem is also a wry assessment of clichéd responses to fraternal feelings and to childhood passions more generally.

It is in this context, too, that 'La Corde' achieves its full resonance. A cynical questioning of the *idée reçue* of maternal love,[97] this prose poem, with its central image of the child suicide, also gives an unexpected and powerful twist to the topos of childhood melancholy, for whereas the hackneyed view attaches a degree of pleasure to that sorrow, the prose poem evokes strange crises of unhappiness from which the only possible escape is through the few physical pleasures available to the boy, pilfered sugar and liqueurs. There is nothing to suggest that these recurrent bursts of despair are any less painful than they would be in the manic-depressive adult, and the way in which the narrative voice focuses, not on the distress of seeing the child dead, but on the practicalities of dealing with the corpse, merely strengthens the sense of shock the reader feels, particularly if that pragmatic response is set in the context of the emotional poems about dead children that were so much the current coin of the time. Nor should we accuse Baudelaire of morbidity, as T. S. Eliot does, but rather see him as responding to the climate of an age when, as Chevalier points out in his study of crime, suicide in the working class had reached such proportions as to be regarded as an illness, and had inspired such studies as Brière de Boismont's *De l'influence de la civilisation sur le suicide* and Saint-Marc Girardin's *Du suicide et de la haine de la vie*.[98]

The writers of the middle of the century, then, are beginning to bring to the presentation of childhood a refreshing acerbity and wry humour, as well as a range of linguistic possiblities, that prepare the way for the far greater richness of the theme as it develops under the Third Republic.

---

[97] Like Flaubert in *Madame Bovary* and George Sand in *Les Maîtres Sonneurs*, Baudelaire here raises issues that have more recently exercised the minds of such feminists as E. Badinter and S. Firestone.

[98] See Chevalier, *Classes laborieuses et classes dangereuses*, 341–2.

CHANGING THE HORIZON

The fall of Napoleon III as a result of the 1870–1 Franco-Prussian War enabled the rise to power of a group of people, primarily Protestant, whose interests were more sharply focused on certain aspects of childhood, particularly education and child labour, than had been the case with the Second Empire. Changes in medical and especially psychological knowledge also altered the general perception of childhood, and coloured, if they did not destroy, the Romantic topoi of purity, innocence, intensity of vision, and pleasurable melancholy. More importantly from our point of view, the shift in the perceptions of the role played by childhood in the adult's subsequent development also meant that attempts to explore the mind and world of the child were no longer seen as primarily the domain of the woman, lacking in seriousness, mere digressions from the more solemn artistic purpose of charting the human condition. Moreover, the novelists working towards the end of the century could draw on a wide range of techniques culled from the accumulated experience of autobiography and the analytical novel, and could combine these with their desire to rival the growing prestige of science, to produce an apparently more realistic image of the child's experience. Now intensity of experience is often replaced by boredom, purity by evil, carefree innocence by a sharply perceptive awareness of the physical and social facts of existence. Among the many portraits of children produced in these final decades, those in the works of Edmond de Goncourt, Maupassant, and Zola are representative of the devices typically employed, at least where the child plays only a minor role. Goncourt's novel, *Chérie*, is concerned less with exploring the nature of childhood than with reinforcing a myth of female sexual and personal dependence on men. Nevertheless, in doing so, it suggests drives and needs very different from those that tended to be attributed to little girls in the earlier part of the century. Openly drawing on the autobiographical record, it shows the effect on the child of the lack of maternal love,[99] revealing in Chérie, not a cipher of sweetness and light, but a being subject to uncontrollable bursts of anger that indicate a depth of passion which, unfulfilled, will lead to her very early death.[100] All of this is presented from the

---

[99] *Chérie*, 35. The reference here is to Mme Michelet's autobiography.
[100] Bizarre though it may seem, there is a clear parallel here with Mme de Ségur's

viewpoint of a narrator capable of observation but not explanation, remaining resolutely alien from the central character, adult where she is a child, male where she is female. Indeed, there is almost an unintentional parody here of the scientific method of observation, for the observer is so preoccupied with emphasizing her alterity that he leaves his reader with the distinct impression that he himself has never been a child: childhood, he pontificates, 'in the memory of the man or woman who thinks back to it, resembles a vast empty space, in which four or five small events appear, surging up with a kind of photographic clarity' (*en la mémoire de celui ou de celle qui se souvient, ressemble à un grand espace vide, dans lequel quatre ou cinq petits événements se lèvent, se surgissent dans une espèce de netteté photographique*).[101] While no doubt facilitating the novelist's task, this statement seems to accept at surface value the protestations of many autobiographers rather than offer any quantifiable truth. What appears to be happening in *Chérie*, in other words, is that the driving need to create a fiction of female subjugation to physical forces has led to the creation of a new image of childhood, one in which innocence, pleasure, and gentle melancholy have no place, but where they are supplanted by an equally restricting depiction, and above all a depiction predicated on the otherness of both childhood and the child.

In the case of Maupassant a vigorous personal myth also underlies the delineation of childhood, but the writer's fascination with the possibilities of a psychological portrait of his characters, together with his skill in signalling that psychology through physical gestures and patterns of behaviour, enable him to create images of children that are both individual and arresting. Maupassant's ambivalent attitude towards women, the contradictions between his disgust at the generative act and his sensual response to the pleasure of love-making, and the deeply ingrained uncertainties concerning his own identity, which spill over in his tales of cuckoldry and contested paternity, all feed into his presentation of the child. That presentation is, predictably, further coloured by his conviction that most people are driven by greed, cruelty, and fear.

Although he most frequently uses an external focus to depict children, he also experiments with the possibilities and problems

Sophie in her famous children's book, first published in 1859. Sophie is also shown as subject to wild anger.   [101] *Chérie*, 69.

of presenting the tale from the child's viewpoint. 'Monsieur Parent', for instance, is concerned above all with the responses of the man who adores his son as an extension of himself, until he discovers that his paternity is thrown in doubt by his wife's adultery. The child is, therefore, little more than an object in this tale, and his responses matter only in so far as they affect the protagonist. Nevertheless, Maupassant does not reduce him to a mere cardboard cut-out, but uses him to arouse our sympathies for the observing father. Thus, the tale opens with a description of the child playing: 'Little Georges, on all fours in the path, was creating mountains of sand. He gathered the sand up in both hands, made it into a pyramid, then planted on the top a chestnut leaf.' (*Le petit Georges, à quatre pattes dans l'allée, faisait des montagnes de sable. Il le ramassait de ses deux mains, l'élevait en pyramide, puis plantait au sommet une feuille de marronnier.*)[102] Whereas when Hugo describes children playing he tends to infuse the description with the emotions felt by the adult onlooker, while Flaubert, in recording the games of Charles or Louise, transmits the delight felt by the child, Maupassant here succeeds in remaining totally neutral, describing the little boy with the same analytical coolness that he would use for an animal or an object, in order to intensify the depth of the father's emotions: 'M. Parent was watching his son squatting in the dust: he followed the child's slightest gestures with love, and seemed to be blowing kisses to him whenever Georges moved.' (*M. Parent regardait son fils accroupi dans la poussière: il suivait ses moindres gestes avec amour, semblait envoyer des baisers du bout des lèvres à tous les mouvements de Georges.*)[103] This does not mean, however, that the child is a mere cipher. Indeed, Maupassant's observant eye and linguistic virtuosity enable him to portray the little boy with concise and unemotional force, particularly, perhaps, in describing his response when the maid storms from the room and slams the door behind her: 'Georges, at first surprised, began to clap his hands in delight and puffing out his cheeks he made a great "boom" with all the strength of his lungs in imitation of the noise made by the door.' (*Georges, surpris d'abord, se mit à battre des mains avec bonheur, et, gonflant ses joues, fit un gros 'boum' de toute la force de*

[102] *Contes et nouvelles*, in *Œuvres complètes*, ii. 580.
[103] Ibid., 581.

ses poumons pour imiter le bruit de la porte.)[104] Like the self-possessed, independent children of many Impressionist paintings, Georges suddenly leaps into sharp focus here, free of the restrictions of stereotype and archetype.

'Le Papa de Simon', however, while rising to the challenge of depicting the world of childhood, does not succeed in keeping Maupassant's personal 'family story' entirely at bay. Included in one of Maupassant's most ironic and observant collections, *La Maison Tellier*, this tale is as drily unemotional in its presentation of children as the title story is unhypocritical about prostitutes and 'Histoire d'une fille de ferme' is unromantic in its portrait of country life. The cruelty children can inflict on another child who is somehow different from them is conveyed in animal imagery, the banality of which merely intensifies its power, as does the cluster of alliterative 'p', 'b', and 'k' sounds: *'ces fils des champs, plus proches des bêtes, éprouvaient ce besoin cruel qui pousse les poules d'une basse-cour à achever l'une d'entre elles aussitôt qu'elle est blessée.'* (these boys of the land, who were closer to animals, felt the same cruel need that drives the hens in a fowl yard to kill off one of their number as soon as it is wounded.)[105] Such images, although they fall within the child's experience, are nevertheless obviously the product of an external commentary, which occasionally also includes a judgement beyond the child's awareness, as happens in the following description:

these rascals, whose fathers were for the most part bad-tempered drunkards and thieves who mistreated their wives, jostled each other as they crowded closer and closer to him, as if they, who were legitimate, wanted to squeeze to death the child who was an outlaw.

ces polissons, dont les pères étaient, pour la plupart, méchants, ivrognes, voleurs et durs à leurs femmes, se bousculaient en le serrant de plus en plus, comme si eux, les légitimes, eussent voulu étouffer dans une pression celui qui était hors la loi.[106]

Elsewhere in the tale, however, free indirect discourse allows for the presentation of an internal narrative focus in the passage where the child contemplates drowning himself. The brief sentences, the

---

[104] *Contes et nouvelles*, in *Œuvres complètes*, ii. 584.
[105] *Contes et nouvelles*, in *Œuvres complètes*, ii. 75.
[106] Ibid., 75–6.

repetitions of words and rhythms, the emphasis on the physical effects of emotion are all clearly intended to convey the thought-processes of a child:

It was very warm, very pleasant. The gentle sun warmed the grass. The water glinted like a mirror. And Simon experienced moments of bliss, of that languor that follows tears, moments when all he wanted to do was to fall asleep there, in the warmth.

Il faisait très chaud, très bon. Le doux soleil chauffait l'herbe. L'eau brillait comme un miroir. Et Simon avait des minutes de béatitude, de cet alanguissement qui suit les larmes, où il lui venait de grandes envies de s'endormir là, dans la chaleur.[107]

With the arrival of the workman, Philippe, who takes the child home, however, the tale switches focus away from Simon to the relationships developing between Simon, his mother, and the man. Here one suspects that Maupassant's childhood wish for a father of his own invades the austerity of tone adopted hitherto, transforming the final paragraphs into something dangerously close to a tear-jerker:

'My father', said [Simon] in a clear voice, 'is Philippe Rémy, the smith, and he's promised to pull the ears of anyone who hurts me.'

This time, no-one laughed, because Philippe Rémy the blacksmith was well known, and he was the sort of father everyone would have been proud of.

'Mon papa, dit-il [Simon] d'une voix claire, c'est Philippe Rémy, le forgeron, et il a promis qu'il tirerait les oreilles à tous ceux qui me feraient du mal.'

Cette fois, personne ne rit plus, car on le connaissait bien, ce Philippe Rémy, le forgeron, et c'était un papa, celui-là, dont tout le monde eût été fier.[108]

Somehow, one feels, like Dr Rieux faced with Grand's image of publishers applauding a new writer in Camus's *La Peste*, that things do not happen quite like that.

It is perhaps in Zola's novels that we encounter the greatest range of characteristics attributed to children. This is hardly surprising, given his fascination with humanity's most basic urges and his desire to reveal the workings of inherited characteristics through the generations. There is in his writing, moreover, an evident

---

[107] Ibid., 77.

[108] Ibid., 82.

delight in rising to the challenge of depicting children, both mentally and physically, and a painterly attention to colour and form that again recalls the numerous children portrayed by such contemporaries as Renoir, Berthe Morisot, and Mary Cassatt. Pauline, in *Le Ventre de Paris*, is sketched in ways that show her both as heir to the Rougon-Macquart characteristics and as individual child:

She was a superb 5-year-old, with a plump, round face, who took very much after her beautiful mother. In her arms she carried an enormous ginger cat, which sprawled luxuriously, paws hanging down, and the little girl hugged it in her small hands, bending under its weight, as if she feared that this ill-clad gentleman was going to steal it from her.

C'était une superbe enfant de cinq ans, ayant une grosse figure ronde, d'une grande ressemblance avec la belle charcutière. Elle tenait, entre ses bras, un énorme chat jaune, qui s'abandonnait d'aise, les pattes pendantes et elle le serrait de ses petites mains, pliant sous la charge, comme si elle eût craint que ce monsieur si mal habillé ne le lui volât.[109]

Children's games also provide the opportunity for exploring the nature of childhood, and especially, in Zola's case, for revealing the gravity with which these games can be invested. Marjolin and Cadine, those *enfants trouvés* discovered abandoned in Les Halles and brought up amidst the fruit and vegetables, wander gravely through the market-place on rainy days under an immense sunshade which they then turn into a shelter they call 'their house'.[110] Another of the market's children, Muche the son of a fishwife, would throw little dead fish into the gutter, in order to watch them swim, as he puts it.[111] While remaining external here, the narrative voice adopts a point of view on a level with that of the child.

As with Maupassant, the cruelty of which children are capable is captured in some remarkable passages, especially, perhaps, through the portrayal of Jeanlin in *Germinal*. Jeanlin's role as apprentice criminal is one we shall explore elsewhere, but the callousness with which he treats his younger accomplices, Lydie and Bébert, parallels the ferocity of the women who castrate the corpse of Maigrat and the unconscious barbarity of the bourgeoisie faced with the starving miners. Muche, in *Le Ventre*

[109] *Les Rougon-Macquart*, i. 638.   [110] Ibid., i. 765.
[111] Ibid., i. 815.

1. Greuze: The Dead Bird

2. Chardin: Boy with Spinning Top

3. Delacroix: Orphan Girl

4. Daumier: The Burden

5. Goya: Don Manuel Osorio de Zuñiga

6. Préault: Tuerie

7. Renoir: Mme Charpentier and her Children

8. M. Cassatt: Little Girl in a Blue Armchair

de Paris, reveals a hardly less calculating cruelty in his desire to reduce the beautifully starched and dressed-up Pauline to the same level of dirtiness and untidiness as himself. The child's cunning is emphasized, moreover, by the external viewpoint the novelist adopts here: Muche, we are told, 'doubtless nourished naughty plans to dirty Pauline. The latter, seeing him prepare to push her in the back, made as if to return indoors. At that he suddenly became very gentle.' (*devait nourrir l'idée mauvaise de salir Pauline. Celle-ci, en le voyant s'apprêter à lui donner une poussée dans le dos, recula davantage, fit mine de rentrer. Alors, il fut très doux.*)[112] The ease with which children ape the cruelty of their parents is also reflected in Pauline's own behaviour when Florent, whom she adored when he was in favour, loses her mother's esteem: 'little Pauline came out with the cruel expressions of an *enfant terrible* about the stains on his clothes and the holes in his linen.' (*la petite Pauline avait des mots cruels d'enfant terrible, sur les taches de ses habits et les trous de son linge.*)[113] But whereas the depiction of children's cruelty retains a salty realism, Zola tends to slip into an uncomfortable melodramatic intensity when he seeks to convey cruelty perpetrated against children. The most notable example is that of Lalie in *L'Assommoir*, brutally beaten by her father. Lalie's martyrdom transforms her into an allegory of suffering and brutalized woman, utterly incapable both physically and mentally of any form of revolt. What is disturbing here is the suspicion that the detail in which Zola indulges, the concentrated evocation of her sufferings in all their minutiae, reflects not merely indignation but also, and perhaps more so, a degree of sadistic pleasure, vicariously experienced through the act of writing.

Not merely cruelty, but also the animal drives Zola seeks to show dominating human behaviour, are very much present in his child as well as in his adult characters. The sexual experimentation of Marjolin and Cadine, and Jeanlin's exploitation of Lydie, are all part of a general world-view in which childhood sexual innocence has been swept out of existence. A far more brutal portrayal of childhood sexual awareness appears in *L'Argent* with its depiction of the 12-year-old Victor, already habitually sleeping with a 40-year-old woman:

---

[112] Ibid., i. 815.   [113] Ibid., i. 787.

In this late childhood, which still retained such purity of colour and in which certain aspects had the delicacy associated with girls, the virility that had flowered so suddenly was embarrassing and frightening, a kind of monstrosity.

Dans cette grande enfance, au teint si pur encore, avec certains coins délicats de fille, cette virilité, si brusquement épanouie, gênait et effrayait, ainsi qu'une monstruosité.[114]

Even the gentleness of the relationship between Jeanlin's two victims, Lydie and Bébert, yearns for a sexual expression:

A deep affection had slowly arisen between them, as they shared the same fear. He constantly thought of taking her, of hugging her very tight, as he had seen others do and she, too, would have been willing.

Lentement, une grande affection était née entre eux, dans leur commune terreur. Lui, toujours, songeait à la prendre, à la serrer très fort entre ses bras, comme il voyait faire aux autres et elle aussi aurait bien voulu.[115]

As the allusion to the behaviour of others suggests, however much emphasis Zola may place, particularly in his provocative and somewhat tongue-in-cheek *Roman expérimental*, on the importance of inherited characteristics, he is also interested in exploring the ways in which these are further shaped by the environment in which the individual grows up and the experiences he or she undergoes. Much of Nana's extraordinary career is adumbrated in the brief but telling scene in which she sees her mother Gervaise turn away from the vomit-stained bed in which her drunken husband Coupeau has collapsed and choose instead that of her former lover Lantier:

While Lantier pushed [Gervaise] into his bedroom, Nana's face appeared at the glass door, behind one of the panes. The child had just woken up and had climbed quietly out of bed, in her night shirt, her face pale with sleepiness. She looked at her father lying in his vomit; then, her face glued to the window, she stayed there waiting until her mother's skirt had disappeared into the other man's bedroom, opposite. She was very serious. She had the wide-open eyes of the depraved child, lit with sensual curiosity.

Pendant que Lantier la [Gervaise] poussait dans sa chambre, le visage de Nana apparut à la porte vitrée du cabinet, derrière un carreau. La petite venait de se réveiller et de se lever doucement, en chemise, pâle de sommeil.

---

[114] *Les Rougon-Macquart*, v. 151.   [115] Ibid., iii. 1366.

Elle regarda son père roulé dans son vomissement puis, la figure collée contre la vitre, elle resta là, à attendre que le jupon de sa mère eût disparu chez l'autre homme, en face. Elle était toute grave. Elle avait de grands yeux d'enfant vicieuse, allumés d'une curiosité sensuelle.[116]

Here, moreover, Zola's fascination with the gravity of children combines with what is becoming a traditional image of the child watching—through a window, from on high, across a balustrade, and so forth—the only partly comprehensible behaviour of the adults around them.

The presence of children in his novels offers Zola challenges not merely of a psychological but also of a stylistic nature. Florent, for instance, recounts his adventures in escaping from Devil's Island in the form of a child's story, narrated in the third person. Despite the horrors of the experience, it is clear that Zola relished the opportunity of evoking for the benefit of little Pauline the wild animals of Dutch Guyana, in terms redolent of an imaginative version of *Robinson Crusoe*:

great birds wheeled over his head, with a terrible sound of beating wings and sudden cries like a death rattle, the sounds of monkeys leaping and animals galloping came from the bushes in front of him, and he saw the boughs bend and leaves drop down in showers as if shaken by the wind, but what most froze him with fear were the snakes, when he stepped on the moving floor of dry leaves.

de grands oiseaux s'envolaient sur sa tête, avec un bruit d'ailes terribles et des cris subits qui ressemblaient à des râles de mort, des sauts de singes, des galops de bêtes traversaient les fourrés, devant lui, pliant des tiges, faisant tomber une pluie de feuilles, comme sous un coup de vent et c'était surtout les serpents qui le glaçaient, quand il posait sur le sol mouvant de feuilles sèches.[117]

Children can also provide the narrative focus, as Pauline does, for instance, in the opening passages of *La Joie de vivre*, where the strangeness of the coastal scenery, further transformed by the gradual coming of night, is conveyed through her gaze, to which all this is new.[118]

The advantages of focusing a text through a child's vision, as well as the technical demands imposed by such a choice, clearly spurred a wide variety of writers throughout the century, and that

---

[116] Ibid., ii. 632–3. [117] Ibid., i. 691.
[118] Ibid., iii. 816, 828–9.

challenge, together with the growing numbers of child readers, leads to a growth in the number of works in which children play a leading role. My next chapter, therefore, will concentrate on a selection of such works, to explore the techniques they employ and the archetypes they create.

3
Experiencing Childhood

More than any other figure the child-hero expresses the hopes
and fears of his age. In the nineteenth century the dominant
image of childhood seems to be that of the orphan, the loss of
family and of a sense of origins perhaps offering a parallel to
the intellectual uncertainty.

(P. Howe, 'The Child as Metaphor')

Until one looks back on one's own past one fails to realize
what an extraordinary view of the world a child has. The angle
of vision is entirely different from that of an adult, everything
is out of proportion.

(Agatha Christie, An Autobiography)

OUR reading of the ways in which childhood is captured in certain
autobiographies and those fictional works that give children a
secondary role has revealed some of the stylistic and narrative
problems associated with a literary representation of the child: in
this chapter, I plan to explore a selection of works where the child
appears as protagonist, in order to suggest some of the devices that
allowed writers to overcome the central problems of voice,
structure, and the re-creation of the child's space and time.
Moreover, since the kinds of problem encountered in autobiographies that concentrate exclusively on childhood do not differ
radically from those faced by novelists or poets promoting the child
to central position, and since the same kinds of solution are
attempted, the separation of the two modes is no longer necessary.
There can be little doubt that in attempting to resolve these
problems writers drew on familiar literary patterns, setting up for
their readers as well as for themselves a readily identifiable matrix.
Romanticism's image of the sensitive individual as outcast, the
world of the fairy-tale, the paradigm of the *Bildungsroman*, the
stories of adventurers, saints, and martyrs, the medieval accounts of
heroic children performing mighty deeds, are only some of the

threads drawn into the increasingly complex canvas that weaves the image of childhood as the century passes.[1]

ENFANT MAUDIT

The dark, brooding, tormented figures of what Baudelaire terms satantic romanticism—Maturin's Melmoth, Byron's Manfred and Childe Harold, Quinet's Ahasvérus, Borel's Champavert, and, in a different vein, Chateaubriand's René and Hoffmann's Nathanael, the hero of *Der Sandmann*—combine with images of the misunderstood genius—Hoffmann's Johannes Kreisler or Balzac's Louis Lambert—to form the mould from which the young Flaubert creates his first-person protagonist in *Mémoires d'un fou*. Written in 1838, but not published until 1900,[2] this ambitious exploration of the self offers a remarkably bleak image of childhood and the tormented passage of adolescence. Whether or not he had already read the evocations of unhappy childhood that appear in *Louis Lambert*, which was first published in 1832, or *Le Lys dans la vallée*, first published in 1836, the young Flaubert was certainly familiar with Mérimée's non-saccharine image of the child, since his own, even crisper, version of *Matteo Falcone* appears in his *Journal d'écolier*.[3] While the work's central image is undeniably that of the young mother nursing her infant, a sight that thrusts the protagonist into the sexual desires of adolescence, *Mémoires d'un fou* prepares for this event by a detailed exploration of the nature of childhood, in terms utterly alien to the world of Hugo's 'Lorsque l'enfant paraît'. It is this first half of Flaubert's tale that concerns us here.

Through its title, through the questions raised in the dedication, and through the position adopted in its opening paragraph, *Mémoires d'un fou* challenges the authority of the narrative voice, questions the very possibility of knowing the self—'[within these pages] you may find an entire soul. Is that soul mine? Is it some

---

[1] My purpose here is not, of course, to attempt a complete survey of those works that place childhood centre-stage, but rather to suggest some of the stratagems and solutions adopted.

[2] The work was first published in *La Revue blanche* from 15 December 1900 to 1 February 1901.

[3] On Flaubert's early reading see Bruneau, *Les Débuts littéraires de Gustave Flaubert*.

other person's?' (*[ces pages] renferment une âme tout entière. Est-ce la mienne? Est-ce celle d'un autre?*)[4]—and throws into doubt the position of both writer and reader:

Why write these pages? What is the use? What would I know? It's pretty stupid, in my view, to go round asking people why they act and why they write. Do you yourself know why you have opened the wretched pages a madman's hand is going to cover?

Pourquoi écrire ces pages?—A quoi sont-elles bonnes? Qu'en sçais-je moi-même? Cela est assez sot, à mon gré, d'aller demander aux hommes le motif de leurs actions et de leurs écrits.—Sçavez-vous vous-même pourquoi vous avez ouvert les misérables feuilles que la main d'un fou va tracer?[5]

The effect of this apparent abnegation of authority is to combine the Romantic image of the inspired madman with the child's perceptive ignorance in order to penetrate more deeply into an area of experience which, as we have seen, had, at the time Flaubert was writing, rarely been so directly approached. The unknowable nature of the subject also involves, or so the narrative voice insists, a rejection of any kind of set plan,[6] in favour of a random assortment of thoughts, dreams, and memories, capable of revealing all the more clearly the dichotomy between apparent surface calm and inner torment. The narrator also draws attention to the difficulty of finding a language capable of giving voice to the complexity and intensity of emotions without distorting them, the kind of problem, in fact, that so preoccupies Flaubert in writing *Madame Bovary* and to which so many autobiographers allude: 'how can one express in words things for which no language exists, those impressions of the heart, those mysteries of the soul of which the soul itself knows nothing?' (*comment rendre par des mots ces choses pour lesquelles il n'y a pas de langage, ces impressions du cœur, ces mystères de l'âme inconnus à elle-même?*)[7]

The narrative stance adopted in these *Mémoires* is that of a young man looking back at his younger self, with a mixture of cynicism and regret, but with no trace of judgemental patronizing, no sense of having achieved a degree of maturity where the emotions of childhood and adolescence seem unimportant, even if they can no longer be shared by a narrator whose experience of life

---

[4] *Œuvres de jeunesse*, i. 483.
[6] Ibid., i. 484.

[5] Ibid.
[7] Ibid., i. 512.

has, so he claims, dried up the well-springs of his heart. Indeed, where there is a conviction that such feelings can no longer be recaptured, this is accompanied by a regret bordering on despair. It may well be that the world-weariness of this presentation owes something to Musset's recently published *Confession d'un enfant du siècle*, and particularly its opening passages, with their insistence on the sense of hopelessness and cynicism among contemporary youth,[8] but the images through which that despair is conveyed are already quintessentially Flaubertian.

The narration suggests a tripartite division of the child's existence in the years before the encounter with Maria moves the memoirs into adolescence: a period of love for his mother, and of intense reveries associated with nature, the time of incarceration in college, and the realm of nightmare, in which the child's subconscious mind draws on the experience gleaned from books to work through a complex pattern of emotions based both on a sense that his parents have rejected him and on an implicit awareness of sexual jealousy and betrayal.[9] In fact, however, the reader feels increasingly, as the text progresses, that the narrator's prime concern in structural terms has been to keep in check the surges of jealousy that threaten not merely to disrupt the narration but also to destroy the narrator himself. By considering the dream sequences immediately after the evocation of early childhood, we can, I believe, see more clearly what the narrator is attempting to screen.

What dominates in the early evocations of the child's delight in nature is both beauty and transience—the changing clouds, the flowing water, the falling flowers, the shifting and fragile patterns of moonlight and shadows, the ephemeral patterns of sea-foam—and what marks the child's response is a participation in that beauty that entails a loss of personal identity, conveyed in the words '*extase*' (literally, standing outside oneself), '*s'abîmer*' (losing oneself in the abyss). Baudelaire evokes a similar sense of identification with the external world and loss of personal identity

---

[8] Cf. Flaubert's exclamation 'What a sad and strange age we live in' (*Triste et bizarre époque que la nôtre!*) *Œuvres de jeunesse*, i. 499.

[9] Marthe Robert would argue that all novels have as their basis this experience, when the child, formerly centre of the adult's world, finds its parents no longer so preoccupied with it. The child responds by forging a tale according to which its parents are not its real parents, the world in which it lives not the world in which it was destined to live, and so forth. See *Roman des origines*.

in his prose poem 'Le *Confiteor* de l'artiste' and in his study of hashish.[10] The links between the beach and Maria, whose cloak he is to rescue from the encroaching sea-foam, and between the sea and his mother, locked together in the frequently exploited homophony of *mer / mère*, are thrust under at this point by an affirmation of the difference between the present narrator and his younger self, and by a transposition from self to mother of the adjective '*pauvre*' (poor): 'I was happy and full of laughter, loving life, and my mother. Poor mother!' (*J'étais gai et riant, aimant la vie, et ma mère. Pauvre mère!*)[11]

In an attempt to find a firm footing again the narrative abruptly switches direction here, away from the implications of that exclamation, and towards an apparent source of childhood pleasure, watching horses. But the sharpness of vision, the curiosity and novelty of a child's perception, begin to disintegrate yet again, threatening to slip into the abyss when the horses' movement stops:

I loved the monotonous and rhythmic trot that made the carriage sway and then, when it stopped, everything fell silent in the fields. You could see the steam from their nostrils, the shaken carriage settled on its springs, the wind howled in the windows and that was all.

J'aimais le trot monotone et cadencé qui fait osciller les soupentes et puis, quand on s'arrêtait, tout se taisait dans les champs. On voyait la fumée sortir de leurs naseaux, la voiture ébranlée se raffermissait sur ses ressorts, le vent sifflait sur les vitres et c'était tout.[12]

What seems constantly to be threatening to surface in all these memories is the suppressed memory of the primal scene, the child catching sight of his parents making love, forming the strange shadows the moonlight throws on the walls, rocking the bed as though it were a moving carriage, breathing heavily like the horses, and then the silence, leading to the child's sense of abandonment and jealousy: 'And why so much bitterness in one so young?' (*Et pourquoi, si jeune, tant d'amertume?*)[13]

---

[10] See e.g. Baudelaire's *Œuvres complètes*, i. 420.
[11] *Œuvres de jeunesse*, i. 487.
[12] Ibid.
[13] Ibid. Marthe Robert also believes the primal scene to lie behind *Mémoires d'un fou*, but her reading is somewhat different from mine: see *Roman des origines*, 309. For Sartre's idiosyncratic and highly detailed reading see *L'Idiot de la famille*, ii. 1506 ff.

That sense of abandonment, that feeling of doubt about the relationship that had been central to his existence, is conveyed by the '*fou*' in terms of growing doubts concerning the possibility of knowledge, the existence of God, the value of virtue. The emptiness of all accepted values appears to him so evident that he can barely bring himself to sum them up as smoke and nothingness.[14] The desire to deny the existence of God, tantamount here to an expression of jealousy and disgust with his own father, boils up in one of the two nightmares the text recounts. The child is asleep in his father's house, on a night when snow fills his room with white light, the light, one might well assume, of the moon mentioned earlier. A sudden change takes place, altering the surrounding countryside so that it appears that a fire fills the windows with the red colour of rage and blood. One might suggest a link between this image of fire and the defiant statement made when the child expresses his sense of superiority over his schoolmates and teachers: 'I who felt myself as vast as the world, I who felt that a single one of my thoughts, if it were made of fire like lightning, could have reduced everything to dust' (*Moi qui me sentais grand comme le monde et qu'une seule de mes pensées, si elle eût été de feu comme la foudre, eût pu réduire en poussière*).[15] His room is invaded by bearded men, whose fingers leave traces of blood on everything they touch and who eat bread that drips blood. When they leave, the child hears an extended, vague, shrill cry,[16] a forerunner of the cry Emma is to hear after she has committed adultery for the first time. This curiously intense dream seems, therefore, to unite the theme of the death of God (the debased communion scene) with Flaubert's childhood memories of watching his father perform post-mortems. The father, identified in the dream by his beard, as a symbol of something he possesses and the child does not, is represented as powerful through his multiplication into seven or eight individuals. Through the kind of transference that Freud indicates as common in dreams, the attack on the dreamer can be read as a desire to destroy the father, a longing half-admitted in the confession: 'I had the impression that I had eaten flesh.' (*il me sembla que j'avais mangé de la chair.*)

This dream is immediately followed by one concerning the mother, separated from the first only by the word 'elsewhere', as

[14] *Œuvres de jeunesse*, i. 490.   [15] Ibid., i. 491.
[16] Ibid., i. 494.

though the child is insisting on a spatial gap between mother and father as an important factor in his revenge. Here nature is no longer surreal, as it was in the dream concerning the father, but of great, if treacherous, beauty. The speed with which the wish fulfilment operates is indicated by the breathless syntax: 'I was with my mother walking by the river, she fell.' (*J'étais avec ma mère qui marchait du côté de la rive, elle tomba.*)[17] Only after the body of his mother has disappeared, only, that is, when it is too late, does the child hear her cries for help, but when he lies down on the bank and peers into the river, although her cries continue, he can see nothing. Here, too, the child who has witnessed the primal scene seems to be trying to deny having seen anything at all, attempting to make sense of the sounds he has heard merely in terms of an effort made by the mother to communicate with him. This time, moreover, the adjective 'poor' is transferred from the drowning mother to the abandoned child: 'help! oh, my poor child, help me! help me!' (*au secours! ô mon pauvre enfant, au secours! à moi!*) Yet his jealous despair cannot be assuaged by the simple means of dream: the account of his nightmare ends with the words: 'The voice I heard from the depths of the river plunged me into despair and fury.' (*Cette voix que j'entendais du fond du fleuve m'abîmait de désespoir et de rage.*)[18] The sexual nature of water imagery in dreams and in imaginative fiction has, of course, been widely explored: what is, perhaps, most interesting in this work is the insistence on water as an extended metaphor connecting the child's love for his mother with his encounter with Maria.

Between the scenes of early childhood and these dream sequences Flaubert has placed the far more familiar theme of the college, that source of grief, suffering, and loss of innocence in so many nineteenth-century childhoods.[19] As Balzac had done in *Louis Lambert* and in *Le Lys dans la vallée*, and as Maupassant was to do in 'Le Papa de Simon', the young Flaubert emphasizes not the harmony and purity of children, but the cruelty that makes the boarding-school a microcosm of the outside world: 'the same injustice shown by the crowd, the same tyranny exerted by prejudice and power, the same selfishness, whatever people may have said about the disinterested and faithful nature of the young' (*même injustice de la foule, même tyrannie des préjugés et de la*

---

[17] Ibid., i. 495.   [18] Ibid., i. 495.
[19] This theme is explored in Chapter 4.

force, même égoïsme, quoi qu'on en ait dit sur le désintéressement et de la fidélité de la jeunesse).[20] This tyranny, which is also revealed in the opening pages of *Madame Bovary*, when Charles is so universally mocked for his failure to know what to do with his cap, is not, however, shown as directed in this instance at an innocent child. Indeed, the young narrator is depicted as possessing the same spirit of ironic mockery as that of his peers and teachers, just as the force of much of Flaubert's later writing stems from the fact that what he attacks in his protagonists is central to his own nature. Here, the balance of the sentence structure as well as the repetition of certain terms indicates the parallelism at issue:

So I lived there alone and bored, tormented by my teachers and mocked by my schoolmates. I was by nature mocking and independent, and my biting and cynical irony was no more sparing of an individual's whims than it was of the crowd's despotism.

J'y vécus donc seul et ennuyé, tracassé par mes maîtres et raillé par mes camarades. J'avais l'humeur railleuse et indépendante, et ma mordante et cynique ironie n'épargnait pas plus le caprice d'un seul que le despotisme de tous.[21]

The dreams of destruction that enable the child to deal with his sense that his parents have deserted him find a parallel here in day-dreams of glory that have little trace of childhood innocence about them, but reveal, rather, a remarkably mature imagination enriched by wide reading and capable of bringing brilliantly and concisely to life the Romantics' myth of the mystic East, which had become such a fertile source of inspiration to writers and artists alike since Napoleon's campaigns in Africa, the Greek war for independence from Turkey, Champollion's deciphering of the Rosetta stone in 1824, and the French colonization of Algeria in 1830:

I saw the East and its endless sands, its palaces through which wander camels with bronze bells; I saw horses bounding towards a horizon stained red by the sun; I saw blue waves, a cloudless sky, silver sand; I smelt the perfume of those warm southern oceans and then beside me, in my tent, shaded by an aloe with its broad leaves, a brown-skinned woman, eyes ablaze, holding me in her arms and talking to me in the tongue of the houris.

Je voyais l'Orient et ses sables immenses, ses palais que foulent les chameaux avec leurs clochettes d'airain; je voyais les cavales bondir vers

---

[20] *Œuvres de jeunesse*, i. 490.   [21] Ibid.

l'horizon rougi par le soleil; je voyais des vagues bleues, un ciel pur, un sable d'argent; je sentais le parfum de ces océans tièdes du Midi et puis, près de moi, sous une tente, à l'ombre d'un aloës aux larges feuilles, quelque femme à la peau brune, au regard ardent, qui m'entourait de ses deux bras et me parlait la langue des houris.[22]

Shakespeare, Goethe, Byron, 'and the most burning works of our age, all those works, in a word, that dissolve the soul in delight and burn it with enthusiasm' (*et les ouvrages les plus brûlants de notre époque, toutes ces œuvres enfin qui fondent l'âme en délices, qui la brûlent d'enthousiasme*)[23] combine therefore with a sense of deep irony and cynicism, and, no doubt, with the kind of rhetoric to be found in such meditational poems as Hugo's 'La Pente de la rêverie', to present the image of a mind on the point of falling into the bottomless pit of the infinite and constantly bruised by its encounters with a corrupt and materialistic society.

Escape from such anguish is provided, if only briefly, by a return to earliest childhood memories, but these in turn provoke the chain of images that again plunges the narrator into despair. Nevertheless, in building up to that moment of separation between younger and older narrators, Flaubert is able to seize on memories of the natural world that are general enough to spark off instant recognition in his reader, but that are saved from banality by the sharpness of the description: 'children's games played on the grassy meadow in the midst of daisies, behind a blossoming hedge, beside a vine with its golden bunches of grapes, on the brown and green moss, under broad leaves and cool shadows' (*jeux d'enfants sur l'herbe au milieu des marguerites dans les près derrière la haie fleurie, le long de la vigne aux grappes dorées, sur la mousse brune et verte, sous les larges feuilles, les frais ombrages*).[24] These generalized recollections lead into more specific memories, introduced by the now-familiar combination of joy leading to bitterness:

and I often fall into ecstasy at the memory of some pleasant day spent long ago, a mad and joyful day with shouts of laughter that still echo in my ears, and still tremble with gaiety, and bring a bitter smile to my lips. It would be some expedition on a horse that galloped along streaked with sweat, or a dreamy walk along a broad and shady pathway, with water flowing over pebbles, or an evening watching the beautiful, splendid sun set with its fireworks of flames and its red haloes. And I can still hear the horse's

---

[22] Ibid., i. 491.   [23] Ibid., i. 496.   [24] Ibid., i. 500–1.

galloping hooves, still see its steaming nostrils. I still hear the water flowing
by, the leaf trembling, the wind bending the wheat like a sea.

et je tombe souvent en extase devant le souvenir de quelque bonne journée
passée depuis bien longtemps, journée folle et joyeuse avec des éclats et des
rires qui vibrent encore à mes oreilles, et qui palpitent encore de gaieté, et
qui me font sourire d'amertume. C'était quelque course sur un cheval,
bondissant et couvert d'écume, quelque promenade bien rêveuse sous une
large allée couverte d'ombre, à regarder l'eau couler sur les cailloux ou une
contemplation d'un beau soleil resplendissant, avec ses gerbes de feu et ses
auréoles rouges. Et j'entends encore le galop du cheval, ses naseaux qui
fument. J'entends l'eau qui glisse, la feuille qui tremble, le vent qui courbe
les blés comme une mer.[25]

The sound of the horse, the steaming nostrils, the flowing water, the
image of the sea unite yet again in that compulsive repetition of the
scene in which childhood innocence is irreparably lost.

A significant claim that three weeks have passed between the
writing of these evocations and those that follow introduces the
meeting with Maria, emphasizing the difficulty encountered in
rendering memories that are presented as being at once the most
tender and the most painful in the narrator's experience. Again,
despite the opening statement concerning the unstructured nature
of these recollections, the initial meeting with Maria is carefully
separated from the scene in which she suckles her child by the older
narrator's digression stressing the grotesqueness of the act of love.
Attracted to each other by the mere hazard of one being a woman
and the other a man, two people, he tells us, stroll together in the
moonlight, getting wet with dew, breathe protestations of love, and
then 'soon they will be coupling grotesquely, flushed red and
heaving sighs, each eager to reproduce yet another imbecile, yet
another wretch who will do exactly the same!' (*les voilà bientôt
grotesquement accouplés, avec des rougissements et des soupirs,
soucieux l'un et l'autre pour reproduire un imbécile de plus sur la
terre, un malheureux qui les imitera!*)[26] Such cynicism does not,
however, prevent the young narrator, on the point of adolescence—
he tells us he is 15, and adds 'very young' (*bien jeune*)[27]—from
seeking to transfer to Maria the intensity of love he believes his
mother has rejected: 'how I would have gathered a single one of

[25] *Œuvres de jeunesse*, i. 501.   [26] Ibid., i. 509.
[27] Ibid., i. 504.

those kisses thrown like pearls in great profusion on the head of that babe in arms.' (*comme j'aurais recueilli un seul de ces baisers jetés, comme des perles, avec profusion sur la tête de cette enfant au maillot.*)[28] But it is, of course, the sight of Maria's bare breast that arouses in the child the combined ecstasy and rage that in turn awakens in him the longings and urges of adolescence. Yet the delight of this early love, however much it may have marked him, is nevertheless fleeting and leads again to the sense of the transience of things that has been so central to these *Mémoires*. It is summed up as a 'happiness of dusk falling in the night, a happiness that passes like the dying wave, like the shore' (*bonheur du crépuscule qui tombe dans la nuit, bonheur qui passe comme la vague expirée, comme le rivage*').[29]

The section of *Mémoires d'un fou* that explores the nature of childhood, as distinct from that of adolescence, is, therefore, a quite remarkably original projection of the experience of the child into the framework of the tormented, Romantic artist. Moreover, in ways which may or may not be fully conscious, it associates that sense of being an outcast not merely with the clash between the sensibilities of the artist and the materialism of the mass of men, but also with an intensely felt loss of childhood innocence faced with what the child sees as the obscenity of sexual love.

APPRENTICE ADULT

In an article focusing on *Histoire de ma vie*, Marilyn Yalom draws attention to the role played by George Sand in exploring the difficult passage from childhood to adulthood: 'when the history of female adolescence is written', she claims, 'it will be seen that the writing of George Sand offers a store of portraits and insights unparalleled in her time and place.'[30] While this may be true, it is nevertheless undeniable that George Sand depicts adolescence as part of childhood, using the term '*enfant*' (child) even for those of her heroes and heroines who are 16 or 17 years old, but who are

---

[28] Ibid., i. 509.
[29] Ibid., i. 513.
[30] 'Towards a History of Female Adolescence', p. 204. See for a different view Ariès, *L'Enfant et la vie familiale*, p. 19, who asserts that Wagner's Siegfried is the first European adolescent.

not yet married. Of course, this may have more to do with language than with concepts, but in *La Petite Fadette* she presents us not merely with a series of images of young children, but also with a study of the apprenticeship undergone, in reaching adulthood, by three protagonists, whom she refers to as children, and in doing so she also examines the way in which the acceptance of certain norms of behaviour is paralleled by the individual's acceptance of gender. Indeed, mère Barbeau's fears about the viability of twins—'each damages the other and, almost always, one of them must perish so that the other can thrive' (*ils se font tort l'un à l'autre, et presque toujours, il faut que l'un des deux périsse pour que l'autre se porte bien*)[31]—could serve as an introduction to the wider question of masculine and feminine tendencies within each individual.

The twins, Sylvinet and Landry, provide mirror images of each other, Landry having on his left cheek a more marked version of the sign his brother has on his right cheek. Moreover, in terms of personality, each is depicted as complementing the other, Landry's strength, gaiety, and courage being balanced by Sylvinet's intelligence, sensitivity, and deep friendliness. Summing them up on the morning of Landry's departure to begin work at La Priche, their mother emphasizes a further aspect of the way in which each supplements the other's character when she remarks:

'My Landry is a real boy. All he asks is to live, to move, to work, and to keep changing places. But [Sylvinet] has the heart of a girl; he's so tender and sweet you can't help loving him like the apple of your eye.'

'Mon Landry est un véritable garçon; ça ne demande qu'à vivre, à remuer, à travailler et à changer de place. Mais celui-ci [Sylvinet] a le cœur d'une fille; c'est si tendre et si doux qu'on ne peut pas s'empêcher d'aimer ça comme ses yeux.'[32]

Maternal tenderness is one thing: for the reader, however, it is clear that Sylvinet has not yet affirmed his own individuality, but has instead accepted his brother as the mirror image, that, in Lacan's well-known terms, should have allowed him to progress beyond the mirror stage to a realization of himself as separate entity. What he sees in the mirror is not himself but his brother, and while Landry's departure marks the start of that twin's entrance into manhood, it

[31] *La Petite Fadette*, 43. For a recent fictional exploration of this conviction see Tournier's *Les Météores*.
[32] *La Petite Fadette*, 58.

symmetrically precipitates Sylvinet back into infancy so that he clings to his mother's skirts like a small child.[33]

Sylvinet's desire to remain within the realm of childhood is further ironically exemplified by his discovery of the little mill that Landry had built and that Sylvinet now attempts to elevate into a symbol of permanence: Sylvinet

moved it a little further down where the stream no longer flowed, to watch it turn and to remember the delight Landry had felt when he first set it in motion. And then he left it, relishing the thought of coming back on the first Sunday with Landry to show him how the mill had survived because it was so solid and well built.

le porta un peu plus en bas, là où le riot s'était retiré, pour le voir tourner et se rappeler l'amusement que Landry avait eu à lui donner le premier branle. Et puis il le laissa, se faisant un plaisir d'y revenir au premier dimanche avec Landry, pour lui montrer comme leur moulin avait résisté, pour être solide et bien construit.[34]

Such fetishism is doomed to failure, for Sylvinet's refusal to acknowledge the passing of time and the changing of circumstances takes as its physical form an instrument that reveals that most changeable of physical phenomena, the wind. It is hardly surprising, therefore, that the little mill is crushed to smithereens by the cattle, for guarding cattle represents one of the duties of adulthood. As George Sand comments in her own autobiography,

Children's lives are like a magic mirror in which real objects become the laughing images of their dreams but a day comes when the talisman loses its strength, or the glass cracks and the splinters are scattered never to be reunited.

La vie des enfants est un miroir magique, où les objets réels deviennent les riantes images de leurs rêves mais un jour arrive où le talisman perd sa vertu, ou bien la glace se brise et les éclats sont dispersés pour ne jamais se réunir.[35]

Like many writers evoking the nature of childhood, George Sand delights in an evocation of the games that Sylvinet still enjoys and wishes to share with Landry, because such games create a space and

---

[33] Ibid., 63.
[34] Ibid., 66: cf. Clarétie, *Jouets de France*: '[in the 18th century] the little girl of humble birth is rarely represented in engravings without her habitual accessory, a windmill' (*la petite fille de condition modeste est rarement représentée dans les gravures sans son accessoire habituel, un moulin à vent*) (100).
[35] *Histoire de ma vie*, 728.

a time inaccessible to others,[36] while for his brother, who now accepts the space and time of adulthood, these games have been replaced by more serious pursuits. Sylvinet's tragedy is that, for him, Landry satisfies the emotional needs that should drive him to seek the company of women, and that, when he does at last go beyond this homosexual phase, it is to discover, inevitably enough, that he loves his brother's wife. His departure to become a soldier heralds the final separation of the twins, for whereas Landry's departure is part of an apprenticeship that leads to integration into society and the compensatory confirmation of his individuality, Sylvinet's decision is tantamount to a rejection of identity in preferring the mass uniformity of soldiers. Moreover, whereas Landry's future is that of fatherhood and creation, Sylvinet's, it is suggested, is one of destruction and sterile bachelorhood.

The exploration of gender definition in the twins prepares the ground for an analysis of Fadette's own discovery of identity. An orphan, abandoned by her mother, and therefore living somewhat outside the social circles that facilitate self-definition, the very young Fadette finds herself defined by others in terms of her mother's guilt. However much George Sand claims to portray reality, not as it is, but as it should be,[37] she makes no attempt to underplay the cruelty with which children can treat each other. Fadette explains to Landry that:

the world is so wicked that scarcely had my mother abandoned me, at a time when I was still weeping most bitterly for her, than, whenever the other children had the slightest bone of contention with me, for a game, for a mere trifle for which they would have forgiven each other, they would blame me for my mother's absence and try to make me blush for her.

le monde est si méchant, qu'à peine ma mère m'eut-elle délaissée, et comme je la pleurais encore bien amèrement, au moindre dépit que les autres enfants avaient contre moi, pour un jeu, pour un rien qu'ils se seraient pardonné entre eux, ils me reprochaient la faute de ma mère et voulaient me forcer à rouger d'elle.[38]

Her response is to reject society's demands, refusing to conform to the conventional image of girlhood and clinging both to the freedom of her tomboyish ways and to her reputation as sorceress.

[36] See Huizinga, *Homo ludens*, 28.
[37] See the preface to *La Mare au diable*.
[38] *La Petite Fadette*, 138.

The narrative voice maintains a strong degree of sympathy for this independent little heroine, presenting her as 'a very chatty and mocking child, as lively as a butterfly, as curious as a robin, and as black as a cricket' (*un enfant très causeur et très moqueur, vif comme un papillon, curieux comme un rouge-gorge et noir comme un grelet*)[39] and leaving to other voices the task of conveying society's judgements. This job is performed both by a chorus of the local gossips, affirming that 'it is high time that the cricket realized she is not a boy' (*il est bien temps que le grelet s'aperçoive qu'elle n'est point un garçon*),[40] and by Landry, who paints an undeniably attractive picture of her but adds contemporary society's gloss on what is demanded of girls:

'you climb trees like a real squirrel, and when you leap on a mare without bridle or saddle, you make her gallop as if she had the devil on her back. It's a good thing to be strong and agile, and it's good not to be afraid of anything. All those qualities are great advantages in a man. But for a woman too much is too much and you seem to want to have people notice you.'

'tu montes sur les arbres comme un vrai chat-écurieux, et quand tu sautes sur une jument, sans bride ni selle, tu la fais galoper comme si le diable était dessus. C'est bon d'être fort et leste, c'est bon aussi de n'avoir peu de rien, et c'est un avantage de nature pour un homme. Mais pour une femme trop est trop, et tu as l'air de vouloir te faire remarquer.'[41]

What the text is at pains to stress, however, is that while 'too much' might well be 'too much', Fadette's nature includes a rare degree of courage, friendship, fidelity, particularly to her mother, and kindness to other, younger children, as well as a refusal to accept society's evaluation of material riches.

Marthe Robert's imaginative theory[42] of the novel as genre, which draws both on Freud and on Lukàcs, is that it divides into two types: the pre-Oedipal child's conviction that he is a foundling and the post-Oedipal affirmation of the status of bastard who will punish his parents by succeeding despite them, through using women to rise to the top of society. If her study has a major flaw it

---

[39] Ibid., 83.
[40] Ibid., 168: cf. the judgement of an unspecified speaker that she lacks 'the pride a young girl should possess when she is already 15 years old' (*la fierté qui convient à une fillette lorsqu'elle prend déjà quinze ans*) (103).
[41] Ibid., 136.
[42] *Roman des origines*.

is that it is resolutely male-oriented, adopting the blinkers of phallocentric criticism to create a system in which the woman writer and the female protagonist have quite literally no place. *La Petite Fadette*, however, provides a further dimension to such a theory in showing a girl who, when her mother abandons her, chooses to reject society's criticism of that act, and forge her own world, as Robinson Crusoe created his, on her own terms. Yet the text implies that such a world cannot continue to exist within the dominant world of social conventions. For Fadette to achieve happiness, she must conform, but the very strength of her vision of an alternative world nevertheless empowers her to alter society. If Landry is presented as right in urging Fadette to abandon her boyish ways, therefore, she in turn is seen as correct in her chastisement of him for his empty pride:

I don't respect you . . . either you or your twin, or your father and mother who are proud because they are rich, and who think that anyone who helps them is merely carrying out their duty. They have taught you to be ungrateful, Landry, and that's the worst fault a man can have, after that of being fearful.

Je ne vous estime point . . . ni vous, ni votre besson, ni vos père et mère qui sont fiers parce qu'ils sont riches, et qui croient qu'on ne fait que son devoir en leur rendant service. Ils vous ont appris à être ingrat, Landry, et c'est le plus vilain défaut pour un homme après celui d'être peureux.[43]

Moreover, Fadette's knowledge of the natural world, which accords her powers contemporary society attempts to reject as witchcraft, throws into question a system of values that sees as beautiful only that which is obviously useful, and allows her an understanding of psychological illnesses beyond the grasp of other healers. 'Now, I know,' she tells Landry, 'without being a witch for all that, the uses of the slightest herbs you crush under foot, and when I know their uses I look at them and I don't despise either their perfume or their appearance.' (*Moi je sais, sans être sorcière, à quoi sont bonnes les moindres herbes que tu écrases sous tes pieds et quand je sais leur usage, je les regarde et ne méprise ni leur odeur ni leur figure.*)[44] The lesson Landry reads her, in other words, is balanced by the lesson she reads him, and leads him to greater maturity by showing him that looking at individuals without the

---

[43] *La Petite Fadette*, 114.
[44] Ibid., 137.

prejudices he has hitherto accepted as natural will enable him to understand them and not despise them.

Through this joint apprenticeship both Landry and Fadette pass from childhood to maturity. The novel suggests the painful nature of such a transition and carries, one might think too obviously, the message that, if some degree of rebellion has to be abandoned, conforming brings certain benefits. Fadette, moreover, is forced to conform only in regard to accepting the conventional view of female behaviour: in terms of making herself accepted for her merits, rather than her riches, no compromise is necessary. Indeed, the discovery of the pot of gold is very much a placing of the novel in the genre of the fairy tale, with its magical happy ending, rather than an integral part of the argument.

The central message here, as in many of George Sand's works, is that love is the transforming force, changing Fadette from ugly and despised to pretty and respected, and altering her little brother, Jeannet, beyond recognition. Indeed, it is her love for this lame and unprepossessing child, left in her care when their mother abandons them, that is the most remarkable feature of the young girl's character and that reveals the other side to her apprenticeship. As in *Les Maîtres-Sonneurs*, the initiation into a vicarious maternity is a central episode in forming the young girl's nature and indicates the way in which society demanded greater responsibility and greater sacrifices of girls than of boys, as of course the autobiographical record confirms. The extent to which he is a cross to bear is firmly indicated in the first description of him:

Her little brother, the grasshopper, who was even skinnier and more cunning than she was, was always clinging to her side, losing his temper when she ran off without waiting for him, trying to throw stones at her when she mocked him, flying into a fury bigger than he himself was.

Son petit frère, le sauteriot, qui était encore plus sec et plus malin qu'elle, et qui était toujours pendu à son côté, se fâchant quand elle courait sans l'attendre, essayant de lui jeter des pierres quand elle se moquait de lui, enrageant plus qu'il n'était gros.[45]

This aspect of the novel, moreover, allows George Sand to reveal further images of childhood and the ways in which children were treated. Two depictions are particularly vivid, suggesting a sharply observing eye. At the dance on the feast of Saint-Andoche, for

[45] Ibid., 84.

instance, the child is all the noisier and more ill-behaved because his cap is embellished by a peacock's feather and a false-gold tassel, while after Fadette's departure, when he is being nursed by Fanchette, the latter's godmother, he dashes off after Landry, escaping from Fanchette's embrace, at the risk of leaving one of his feet behind.[46] Nor is the vision of the sometimes brutal way in which children were treated in any way glossed over. Landry, for instance, hears 'the voice of the grasshopper bellowing because his grandmother had whipped him, something that happened to him every evening, whether or not he deserved it' (*la voix du sauteriot qui beuglait parce que sa grand'mère l'avait fouaillé, ce qui lui arrivait tous les soirs, qu'il l'eût mérité ou non*).[47] Nevertheless, three differing attitudes to children are incorporated in the text, that of the narrative voice suggesting that it is unpleasant to go against the wishes of children you love, even when it is for their own good,[48] that of the firmly disciplinarian grandmother, and that of Fadette herself, who as an adult welcomes into her house all the unhappy children who live nearby.

A novel of apprenticeship, therefore, *La Petite Fadette* sets the exploration of the passage from childhood to adulthood, the acceptance of individuality and of society's view of what is fitting for each sex, within the familiar context of the *Bildungsroman*, fused with elements of fairy story. One could well argue that Hoffmann, whose *Nußknacker und Mausekönig* George Sand so admired as an accurate portrait of the child's intellectual life,[49] may also have played a role in this work, since several of his own works, notably *Prinzessin Brambilla* and *Der gold'ne Topf*, chart in similar ways the development of immature heroes and heroines to maturity and fulfilment, though they do so in the mode of the fantastic, whereas Sand's approach is resolutely set in the territory of the real. That reality is above all social, and her central interest here is not in exploring the results of any of the physical changes that mark the end of childhood, but in analysing the psychological acceptance of social demands. Most importantly, perhaps, Sand's text enters the mind of children without patronizing, suggests a degree of

---

[46] *La Petite Fadette*, 197.
[47] Ibid., 95.   [48] Ibid., 50.
[49] *Histoire de ma vie*, 556. E. Boney's article on the influence of Hoffmann on Sand, published in Glasgow, *George Sand*, offers only a brief and superficial view of a topic that cannot be expanded here but that would be worth closer attention.

sympathy rare at the time, and conveys negative judgements of them through a series of different voices all of which are revealed to be blinkered by convention. Both for the exploration of twinship and for its evocation of the tomboy, *La Petite Fadette*, for all its apparent simplicity, is undeniably a landmark in studies of childhood.

THE CHILD AS EXPLORER

The 1870s saw a much wider acceptance of the pedagogical ideas of Rousseau and Comte, and particularly of their insistence on the need to teach children not just through abstract theory but primarily through practical experience. This pedagogical conviction combined with a variety of literary models to produce tales in which children, abandoned to their own devices, acquire knowledge through the need to make their way in the world. *Robinson Crusoe*, the only novel Rousseau allows Émile to read, and one of those most frequently mentioned by autobiographers as having marked their childhoods,[50] combines with Fénelon's *Télémaque*, in which the young hero sets out to find his lost father and in doing so finds an understanding of life, and the traditions of the picaresque and the *Bildungsroman*—invigorated, perhaps, by the recent publications of Verne's *Vingt mille lieues sous les mers* in 1870 and *Le Tour du monde en quatre-vingts jours* in 1873—to provide the pattern of the novel in which the child hero appears as explorer, both of France and, more importantly, of him or herself. The loss of Alsace in the Franco-Prussian War gives a particular urgency to Augustine Fouillée's *Le Tour de la France par deux enfants*, published in 1877, under the pseudonym G. Bruno, and destined to sell three million copies in the first decade of its existence.[51] This eminently practical story of two children, orphaned and dispossessed of their nationality by the war, seeking their family and their fortunes in France, is a veritable encyclopedia of the towns, famous men, industries, and occupations of the country that is constantly presented as the greatest on earth. The high moral tone of the work, the undeviating perfection of the two heroes, the elevated language,

---

[50] See Chapter 4.
[51] See J.-P. Bardos's 'postface' in the facsimile edition of 1977, 312, and J. and M. Ozouf's article, 'Le Tour de la France', 291.

both spoken and written, adopted by the children—' "Oh!" said Julien, "How active people are in Paris, how much they exert themselves in order to learn! I recall that the young Dupuytren studied medicine in Paris and that Monge taught at the École polytechnique." ' (*'Oh! dit Julien, que de mouvement on se donne à Paris, que de peine on prend pour s'instruire! Je me rappelle que le petit Dupuytren avait étudié la médecine à Paris et que Monge a professé à l'École polytechnique'*)[52]—leave little sense that the acquiring of information is paralleled by any getting of wisdom, which the two boys seem to have possessed in full measure from the outset. As J.-P. Bardos argues:

This mingling of object lesson and moral lesson (and within the same field of reference, that of France) leads to a confusion of notions and values; . . . in this book, learning that Dijon is the capital of the Côte d'Or and that modesty is the flower of virtue demands the same mental action.

À mêler ainsi leçon de choses et leçon de morale (et dans un même champ de référence, la France), notions et valeurs se confondent; . . . apprendre que Dijon est le chef-lieu de la Côte d'Or et que la modéstie est la fleur de la vertu relèvent dans ce livre d'une même opération de l'esprit.)[53]

Nevertheless, because it is in itself an exciting and moving tale and because it responded to a longing for security, the work not only became for decades the book *par excellence* for large numbers of French readers, but also inspired a considerable progeny, the most famous of which is probably Selma Lagerlöf's adventures of Nils Holgersson in Sweden.[54]

In France, the nineteenth-century novel that seems to have combined the possibilities of *Le Tour de la France* most successfully with a discovery of the self is Hector Malot's *Sans famille*. Malot, who claims in his dedication to have written the novel with his daughter constantly in mind, chooses as his protagonist a foundling whose adventures include considerable physical and moral suffering before he is eventually rewarded by the discovery of his true identity. Through a series of false recognitions and failures to recognize, paralleled by a complex pattern of doubles, Malot finds literary expression in his child hero for the nineteenth-century

[52] *Le Tour de la France par deux enfants*, 287.
[53] Ibid., 328.
[54] Despite *Le Tour de la France*'s immense popularity, it does not rate even a passing mention in Carpenter and Pritchard's *Oxford Companion to Children's Literature*.

individual's sense of loss of identity. T. Cave, in a wide-ranging study of recognition, claims that the failures of recognition in Dickens's *Hard Times* reflect an uncertainty that 'has to do with an endemic—even epidemic—fear of social and personal anonymity in an age of mass organization':[55] Malot, it could be argued, reveals the foundling child as metonymic of a rapidly changing society in which the individual can assert personal continuity and presence only by an exploration of his or her childhood. He is also, however, drawing on a social reality of the age, the actual presence of abandoned and vagabond children whose predicament had become a central political and moral preoccupation brought into focus by the polemics of Terme and Maufaulcon, by the speeches in Parliament of Lamartine, and by the studies of Haussonville, among many others.[56]

A work of constant redefinition of the central character, *Sans famille* begins with a definition of the narrative voice which at the same time suggests a complete identification of narrator and protagonist: 'I am a foundling.' (*Je suis un enfant trouvé.*)[57] At the age of 8, Rémi is thrust out into the world in a form of second birth, in which the relative comfort and security of his life so far are shown to be based on illusion. The woman he believed was his mother is merely a foster-mother and the safety of their house offers no protection against his foster-father's decision to sell him to a strolling player. The trauma of this sudden awareness of uncertainty is conveyed both by the generalized definition—Rémi presents himself to the reader not as possessing a name and an identity but as belonging to the category of 'foundling children'— and by a feeling of placelessness in which the child no longer has any sense of belonging: 'I have had no village of my own, no place of birth, no more than I have had a father and mother.' (*Je n'ai pas eu de village à moi, pas de lieu de naissance, pas plus que je n'ai eu de père et de mère.*)[58] From this position Rémi goes through an apprenticeship whose mid-point is marked by yet another expulsion into the world, when the family that had given him protection

---

[55] *Recognitions*, 416.
[56] See Haussonville, 'L'Enfance à Paris', and Terme and Monfaulcon's *Histoire statistique et morale des enfants trouvés* and *Nouvelles considérations sur les enfants trouvés*. For a comparison with the situation in England see Walvin's *A Child's World*.
[57] *Sans famille*, i. 1.
[58] Ibid., i. 2.

is forced to separate, but this second expulsion is one that he is able to greet with a robust sense of adventure and freedom that allows a greater self-definition: 'Forward! The world lay before me, and I could turn my face to the North or the South, to East or West, according to my whims. I was a mere child but I was my own master.' (*En avant! Le monde était devant moi, et je pouvais tourner mes pas du côté du nord ou du sud, de l'ouest ou de l'est, selon mon caprice. Je n'étais qu'un enfant, et j'étais mon maître.*)[59] Though still a child, the hero is now free to discover and to forge his true identity. The rootlessness and instability of contemporary society becomes, therefore, a source not of despair and destruction but of freedom and creation. The courage and loyalty with which Rémi faces a series of moral dilemmas and physical dangers are rewarded by the discovery of a family, a history, and a place that are legally his, but, perhaps more importantly, by the moral creation of his own family in the form of two friends, Mattia and Lise. From foundling child, one might say, he becomes the child who finds. While there is some slippage, as these quotations reveal, between *Erzählzeit* and *erzählte Zeit*,[60] between the time at which the story is told and the time at which the story takes place, the narrative position is always that of an internal focalization, where the narrator tells only what the protagonist can know at any particular time.[61] This not only lends the text a sense of immediacy, but also avoids the temptation of an older narrator to look down on his younger self.

The adoption of such a position does not, however, preclude the insertion both of passages that have a clear pedagogical purpose and of pleas for a more just society. In the course of self-discovery, Rémi is also discovering the country in which he lives, at first by passively following his master Vitalis, and then by learning to read a map that will take him to the various friends he has made. Practical experience, in other words, feeds into theoretical knowledge, the written word has meaning only in relation to a previously acquired understanding. Moreover, the child's curiosity leads him to reject as unsatisfactory certain answers given him by adults: although throughout the work adults are the child's guide and source of truth, Rémi learns that only some adults have the key to

---

[59] *Sans famille*, ii. 1.
[60] On these terms see Müller, *Morphologische Poetik*, 269–86.
[61] These terms are taken from Genette's *Figures III*.

understanding, and that these are often those whom their peers reject or who seem on first sight to be unlikely repositories of knowledge. Thus, the strange little barber, who appears such a clown, is revealed to have musical knowledge far beyond Rémi's expectations, while the question what is earth coal, which provokes from the miner: 'it's coal found under the earth' (*c'est du charbon qu'on trouve dans la terre*), finds a more satisfactory answer from a man whom other adults find laughable.[62] The main point here is that the established patterns and traditional hierarchies have to give way before the discoveries of the modern world.

As well as being a pedagogical novel, not just in the sense that it conveys knowledge to its child readers, but also in that it suggests ways of learning to read and shows Rémi himself attempting to teach his friend to read,[63] *Sans famille* pleads a series of social messages that are only partly obscured in the firmly bourgeois nature of the novel's conclusion. The plight of foundling children, particularly those sent to hospices, is conveyed with the intensity of the 8-year-old Rémi's imagination and in a list-like syntax that attempts to capture the child's patterns of speech:

In the village there were two children who were called 'hospice children'; they wore a lead plaque around their necks with a number on it; they were poorly dressed and dirty, they were mocked and beaten. The other children were often cruel enough to run after them, as you run after a lost dog, for fun, and because a lost dog has no one to stick up for it.

Il y avait au village deux enfants qu'on appelait 'les enfants de l'hospice'; ils avaient une plaque de plomb au cou et un numéro; ils étaient mal habillés et sales; on se moquait d'eux; on les battait. Les autres enfants avaient la méchanceté de les poursuivre souvent comme on poursuit un chien perdu pour s'amuser, et aussi parce qu'un chien perdu n'a personne pour le défendre.[64]

The horror of the hospice is also evident in George Sand's *François le champi*. There, the child, suspecting that he is to be sent away by his adoptive mother, hysterically begs her to keep him:

and too, the world *hospice*, that had several times been uttered in his presence, came back to him. He didn't know what a hospice was, but it

[62] *Sans famille*, ii. 141 ff. and 56 ff.

[63] Malot is here drawing on the example of many working-class groups in which knowledge was shared in this way: for a first-hand account of such self-help groups see Nadaud's *Mémoires de Léonard*.

[64] *Sans famille*, i. 23.

struck him as even more frightening than the coach, and he cried out, with a shudder: 'You want to put me in a hospice!'

puis le mot d'hospice, qu'on avait plus d'une fois lâché devant lui, lui revint à la mémoire. Il ne savait ce que c'était que l'hospice, mais cela lui parut encore plus épouvantant que la diligence, et il s'écria, en frissonnant: 'Tu veux me mettre dans l'hospice!'[65]

Equally, Malot's novel attacks the Second Empire's failure to provide adequate village schools, and laments the fate of an eldest daughter in a motherless family: 'instead of going to school, she had been obliged to stay home, prepare the meals, sew a button or a patch on her father's clothes or those of her brothers, and carry Lise in her arms.' (*au lieu d'aller à l'école, elle avait dû rester à la maison, préparer la nourriture, coudre un bouton ou une pièce aux vêtements de son père ou de ses frères, et porter Lise dans ses bras.*)[66] She, too, therefore, loses her identity, as Rémi has lost his, to become a mere servant to her siblings.

These social pleas are closely linked within the text to Rémi's search for true values, values based on friendship and equality, and the discovery of these values is part of a wider understanding of education than that traditionally provided. Education, in this sense, is something acquired only as a result of effort, beginning with a public recognition that in terms of what he is learning—initially, the art of acting—Rémi is not only more ignorant but also 'more stupid' (*plus bête*) than the monkey, Joli-Cœur.[67] Moreover, *Sans famille* does not pull its punches in the depiction of this kind of practical education: because he falls asleep when he should be on guard, two of the performing dogs are devoured by wolves, and the little monkey dies of cold. The child's guilt is not glossed over, the dogs are not miraculously discovered safe and sound, the doctor's efforts fail to save the monkey: while Malot is writing for children, therefore, and while we are left in little doubt that Rémi will eventually find happiness, the text in no way glosses over the harshness of the foundling's lot.

The general educational pattern of *Sans famille*, the gradual recognition of true values, true friends, true relations, depends on two major factors: a motif of doubling, which is used both to strengthen the structure and to add depth to the presentation of

---

[65] *François le champi*, 69.
[66] *Sans famille*, i. 298.
[67] Ibid., i. 68.

character, and a series of false recognitions, and of failures to recognize, leading at length to true recognitions. Thus, mère Barberin, the woman who has cared for Rémi from infancy, perceives him as her real child replacing her own son who dies very young. At the end of the book, she finds a new child in Rémi's own son, Mattia. There is a further parallel here in that Lise, after her father's imprisonment, discovers a new family in her aunt and uncle who themselves have lost their own child. The imprisonment of Vitalis, which causes the first unrecognized meeting between Rémi and his real family, is paralleled by the imprisonment of Acquin, which separates Rémi's surrogate family and leads him to travel in search of them, as later he is to travel in search of his actual family, the Milligans. Finally, Rémi chooses to show his affection for mère Barberin by replacing the cow her husband forced her to sell with one he has been able to earn himself: in this case the child, like a latter-day Petit Poucet, sets to rights a household thrown into despair and confusion by the very person who should have protected it, and thus, by offering himself as double of the husband, claims the substitute mother's undivided love. The point is driven home even more clearly by the fact that Barberin's disruptive arrival destroys the planned meal of pancakes, while Rémi's return is celebrated, precisely, by a meal of pancakes.

The theme of doubling is closely linked to that of false and true recognitions, both of individuals and of values. In order to choose between a range of images of the father, for example, the child has to establish his own moral values. While he initially fears Vitalis as the man who has taken him from mère Barberin and as a master who has total power over him, he comes to recognize him as a potential father, worthy of his love and esteem, for all he has no recognized social status. Driscoll, however, who claims to be Rémi's true father, fills him with a revulsion he struggles to overcome as he faces the moral question of whether this revulsion does not simply result from the overturning of his expectations that his true family would be rich. Barberin and Acquin also provide potential models of the child's father in an increasingly confusing plethora of potential relations. Indeed, he encounters two false families before he is discovered by his true family, whom, in a somewhat melodramatic failure of recognition, he meets early in the novel, but without recognizing them. Countering the kindness of the Acquin family, who welcome him into their midst after the death of Vitalis and who offer an example of deserving but ill-starred workers, the Driscolls, whom Rémi's upbringing encourages him to honour and obey merely because they are presented as his parents, are thieves and drunkards. The political implications of such a situation are clear enough, if never made explicit. This series of false recognitions is paralleled by a series of true recognitions. Setting out on his travels again after the imprisonment of Acquin, Rémi discovers the little hunchback boy he had met on his first arrival in Paris, and accepts him as an equal partner. His reunion with mère Barberin, played over many times in imagination, does indeed take place, as does the rediscovery of Lise and the final acceptance of Rémi as Mrs Milligan's elder son.

Although *Sans famille* is above all a straightforward, swiftly moving narration, in which representation is privileged over narration, and where the plot frequently moves forward mainly by conversation, Malot does make some attempt to vary his techniques. A series of inserted tales gradually allows us to piece together the story of the infant Rémi's theft from his family and his discovery by père Barberin. Mattia tells his own tale, on the excellent pedagogical grounds that if Garofoli becomes Rémi's master, this story may serve as a fruitful example, and as he contemplates a possible separation from Vitalis once they reach Paris, Rémi creates a kind of free-verse poem that sums up the child's experience of life so far:

After my wet-nurse, Vitalis.
After Vitalis, another.
Will it always be like this? Will I ever find someone to love for always?
Little by little I had grown attached to Vitalis, as if he were my father.
So I will never have a father:
Never a family:
Always alone in the world:
Always lost on this vast earth, where I can never settle anywhere!

Après ma nourrice, Vitalis.
Après Vitalis, un autre.
Est-ce que ce serait toujours ainsi? Est-ce que je trouverais jamais personne à aimer pour toujours?
Peu à peu, j'en étais venu à m'attacher à Vitalis, comme à un père.
Je n'aurais donc jamais de père;
Jamais de famille;

Toujours seul au monde;
Toujours perdu sur cette vaste terre, où je ne pouvais me fixer nulle
part![68]

In *Sans famille*, therefore, Malot forges his own myth of modern
man expelled from Eden and forced to create his own society by
making use of newly developed talents. Failures to do so result in
imprisonment, suffering, separation, death: success, which allows
Lise to recover her voice, Mattia to develop his talents as a
musician, and Rémi to find a place where he is at last at home on
this 'vast earth', is achieved only by integrity, hard work, and the
acquisition of practical knowledge. Without making any great
claims for the novel as an aesthetic or psychological masterpiece,
one can nevertheless see in it a satisfactory fusion of the adventure
novel and the *Bildungsroman*, a work directed at children that
neither patronizes nor panders to them, that neither thrusts moral
questions aside nor discounts its central character's weaknesses and
failings. Above all, however, it presents a clear symbol of the search
for self in a world whose values had rapidly and radically altered.

APPRENTICE REVOLUTIONARY

Being bereft of family is only one nineteenth-century image of
unhappiness and rootlessness: the way in which families, and
through them the State, invade the individual's privacy to the extent
of denying his or her personality provides a further theme for
studies of childhood in the last decades of the century. From its
dedication—'to all those who died of boredom at school and who
were made to cry in the bosom of their families, to those who
during their childhoods were tyrannized by their teachers or beaten
by their parents' (*à tous ceux qui crevèrent d'ennui au collège ou
qu'on fit pleurer dans la famille, qui pendant leur enfance, furent
tyrannisés par leurs maîtres ou rossés par leurs parents*)—to its
closing assertion that 'this is no time for tears, it's time to live' (*il ne
s'agit plus de pleurer! Il faut vivre*),[69] Jules Vallès's *L'Enfant*
affirms itself as an irate rejection of accepted ideas concerning the
nature and education of children. First published in 1879 through
the assistance of Hector Malot, this largely autobiographical and

[68] Ibid., i. 247.   [69] *L'Enfant*, 404.

highly comic novel attacks, with considerable verve and originality, two central convictions of the bourgeoisie: the value of a classical education and the purity of parental love. The intensity of the imagery and language reveals clearly enough, moreover, that this is no late-adolescent desire to shock, to *épater le bourgeois*, but part of the visceral imperative to change society that dominates both Vallès's political writing and his active participation in the Commune of 1870–71.[70] Inevitably, he was, to some extent, drawing on ideas others had already expressed, although less virulently. In various different ways the power of parental love or at least the ideal nature of child–parent relationships had been questioned in, for example, the confessional novels of Chateaubriand and Constant, while George Sand had argued that not all women have an instinctive maternal urge, and Baudelaire had not only suggested in 'La Corde' that greed can be a more natural instinct but also pointed elsewhere to the explosion of revolt provoked in children by paternal repression.[71] Equally, the value of current methods of education had been a source of energetic debate throughout the century, with the Jesuits' belief in the value of a purely classical curriculum combating the pleas for a more practical and pragmatic training, inspired by Locke, Rousseau, and Jean-Paul Richter. The poet Laprade, who also wrote a series of rather sugary poems about children and childhood, is typical of many, for while he argues for more physical exercise in the school programme, he continues to insist that 'the Greeks' entire intellectual production will always provide humanity with the best object of study and the finest model' (*toute l'œuvre intellectuelle des Grecs seront toujours pour l'humanité le meilleur sujet d'étude et le meilleur modèle*).[72] Michelet, while not rejecting such a view of the subjects to be taught, nevertheless queries contemporary methods of teaching:

school ought to give the young mind . . . some lofty and generous idea that will come back to him in those long empty days, an idea to support him in the long hours of boredom. In the present state of affairs, schools, which are organized for boredom, do little other than pile weariness on weariness.

l'école doit donner au jeune esprit . . . quelque haute et généreuse idée qui lui revienne dans ces grandes journées vides, le soutiene dans l'ennui des

[70] For a study of Vallès as political journalist and activist see R. Bellet's *Jules Vallès journaliste*.
[71] See Chapter 1, 55–6.
[72] *L'Education homicide*, 86–7.

longues heures. Dans le présent état des choses, les écoles, organisées pour l'ennui, ne font guère qu'ajouter la fatigue à la fatigue.[73]

Moreover, as Donzelot points out, in his *Police des familles*, this was an age in which the State began to consolidate its power over the individual by increasing its control of matters previously considered the private domain of the family, and in particular to inculcate a specific view of parental duty, through the writings of Jules Simon and Paul Janet, among others. Janet even justified the barbarity of contemporary education by arguing that it forced the child to attempt to earn the right to return to the comparative gentleness of the family.[74] And he insists: 'school life is laborious and disagreeable, and that is precisely what is good about it.' (*la vie de collège est laborieuse, désagréable, et c'est par là qu'elle est bonne.*)[75] The horrors of college life are of course a staple theme in nineteenth-century autobiography, but the intensity of Vallès's anger suggests that his attack on it has little to do with the need to include a standard topos, and his subsequent, lifelong support for children's rights attests the depth of his convictions.[76] One final element should be mentioned in considering what forms the matrix from which Vallès forges his novel: the use of fiction to plead a social cause, exemplified in the nineteenth century by Dickens, Balzac, and Hugo.[77] What makes *L'Enfant* unique is the way in which it combines an attack on the substance and methods of teaching, in the widest sense of the word, with a political awareness of the State's encroachment on individual and family liberty, and above all presents its indictment through the experience of the child rather than the reasoning of an adult.

Frequently adopting the limited focus of the child's understanding, *L'Enfant* offers the kind of disingenuous and burlesque naïvety that we find in Swift's *Gulliver's Travels* or Montesquieu's *Les Lettres persanes*. This enables him to include, notably in the early stages of the novel, wonderfully sharp and exaggeratedly comical descriptions of the curious behaviour and appearance of adults.

---

[73] J. Michelet, *Le Peuple*, 66.
[74] *La Famille*, 156.
[75] Ibid., 154.
[76] On this see Moores, *Vallès: L'Enfant*, 57–8.
[77] On Vallès's appreciation of these writers, and more generally on his view of the role of literature in changing society, see his *Littérature et révolution*.

Jacques's paternal aunt, for instance, is both dumb and eager to communicate:

Her eyes, her brow, her lips, her hands, her feet, her nerves, her muscles, her flesh, her skin, everything she possesses moves, chats, questions, replies, she harasses you with questions, she demands replies, her pupils dilate and shrink, her cheeks swell and sink, her nose leaps!

Ses yeux, son front, ses lèvres, ses mains, ses pieds, ses nerfs, ses muscles, sa chair, sa peau, tout chez elle remue, jase, interroge, répond; elle vous harcèle de questions, elle demande des repliques; ses prunelles se dilatent, s'éteignent; ses joues se gonflent, se rentrent, son nez saute![78]

Occasionally the child's limited horizon is briefly opened up by an overheard conversation revealing how outsiders see the Vingtras family, allowing Jacques to understand relationships that have hitherto perplexed him.[79] In general, however, Vallès prefers to emphasize the child's mental and physical suffering by refusing to suggest adult interpretations and thereby forcing his reader to play an active recuperative and interpretative role. This is particularly clear in the episode in which Jacques's father is tempted by the seductive Mme Brignolin. Here, the challenge, which the very fervency of Vallès's anger prevents him from meeting entirely, consists in suggesting the reasons behind the father's longing for someone so different from his wife, while at the same time depicting the mother's distress, and the ways in which each parent works out his or her frustration on the distressed and uncomprehending child:

There was no one I could ask; moreover, the very memory of that time obsessed me like a pain and I drove it away rather than attempting to find anything out! What was there to find out? What was done was done! I am perhaps the one most deeply affected, I, the innocent young child!

Je ne pouvais questionner personne; d'ailleurs, le souvenir seul de ce moment m'obsédait comme un mal, et je le chassais au lieu d'essayer de le savoir! Savoir quoi? Ce qui était fait était fait! Je suis peut-être le plus atteint, moi, l'innocent, le jeune, l'enfant![80]

The final sentence of this quotation indicates both the difficulty of maintaining the internal focus, and the multiplicity of individual voices Vallès encompasses in the first-person pronoun. Indeed, throughout the novel a considerable slippage takes place between

---

[78] *L'Enfant*, 15.
[79] See e.g. *L'Enfant*, 211–12.
[80] Ibid., 207.

'I' (usually the experiencing child, but occasionally, as we have seen, the observing adult), 'he' (referring to the little boy), and 'Jacques'. Although the third person frequently indicates a form of free indirect discourse presenting adult speech, it is also on occasion a further attempt at a realistic portrayal of the child's mentality, recalling the tendency of small children to refer to themselves in the third person and to tell themselves stories in which they play a role that another aspect of their personality passively observes. An example of this technique occurs when Jacques's mother unwittingly humiliates him by tricking him out in a top hat and concocting for him a quite preposterous jacket embellished with a complete row of olive-green buttons, *à la polonaise*:

Oh! it's hardly surprising if later on he was hard on the Poles! The name of that nation, you see, was for him always tied to a terrible memory . . . the prize-day jacket, the jacket with fruit stones, with oval buttons the shape of olives and the colour of gherkins. Add to that the fact that I had been decked out with a top hat that I'd brushed against the grain and that rose up like a threat on my head.

Ah! quand, plus tard, il fut dur pour les Polonais, quoi d'étonnant! Le nom de cette nation, voyez-vous, resta chez lui cousu à un souvenir terrible . . . la redingote de la distribution des prix, la redingote à noyaux, aux boutons ovales commes des olives et verts comme des cornichons. Joignez à cela qu'on m'avait affublé d'un chapeau haut de forme que j'avais brossé à rebrousse-poil et qui se dressait comme une menace sur ma tête.[81]

The kind of slippage that operates between narrator and child also marks the use of tenses in the novel, which slides between present and past, action and judgement, what is experienced and what is remembered, to suggest the power of memory to restore the past to the present. As an example one might take the following passage, with its refusal to adhere to a grammatical logic of tense that does not correspond to an inner and more important logic of emotion:

I do not recall ever seeing a flower in the house. According to Mother they are a nuisance and after a couple of days they smell bad. I pricked myself on a rose the other evening, and she shouted at me: 'That'll teach you!'

Je ne me rappelle pas avoir vu une fleur à la maison. Maman dit que ça gène et qu'au bout de deux jours ça sent mauvais. Je m'étais piqué à une rose l'autre soir, elle m'a crié: 'ça t'apprendra!'[82]

[81] Ibid., 48. Original ellipses.
[82] Ibid., 7.

Moving between burlesque comedy and the sharp, bleak tones of black humour barely covering repressed anger, *L'Enfant* further intensifies this attempt to enter the child's mind by employing a language that increases in lexical and syntactical complexity as the boy grows older. From the onomatopoeias of the early paragraphs to the concision of such expressions as the following when Jacques's father learns that his new headmaster disapproves of publicly chastising children: 'the news reached my father's ears and protected mine' (*la nouvelle est arrivée aux oreilles de mon père et a protégé les miennes*),[83] *L'Enfant* reveals a delighted fascination in the evocative powers of language and its related ability to suggest what is not stated. It is this delight that makes bearable a vision of human relationships that is almost unrelievedly grim, inflating and exaggerating the punishments meted out to the child to the point of buffoonery while yet retaining a bitter kernel of realism. Thus, Jacques refers to the beatings inflicted on him in the following hyperbolic terms:

up to that time I was the drum on which my mother played her rat-tat-tats, trying out on me rolls and flourishes, working me in all directions, pinching me, slashing me, ramming me, cramming me, slapping me, rubbing me, carding me, and tanning me.

j'ai été jusqu'ici le tambour sur lequel ma mère a battu des *rrra* et des *fla*, elle a essayé sur moi des roulées et des étoffes, elle m'a travaillé dans tous les sens, pincé, balafré, tamponné, bourré, souffleté, frotté, cardé et tanné.[84]

But when he refers to the death of a little girl at the hands of her brutal father, his style is completely sober, allowing a line of dots to suggest that the unpunished crime is so appalling that no amount of verbal manipulation can convey its horror.

L'Enfant is also remarkable both for the ease with which Vallès captures the rhythms and vocabulary of conversation, frequently moving his episodes forward mainly by direct and uncommented speech, and for the delight it reflects in lists, a device frequently encountered in literature written for children and used here to convey a sense of half-fascinated, half-repelled amazement at the multiplicity of objects the world presents to the child's astonished eyes:

[83] *L'Enfant*, 251.   [84] Ibid., 194.

those bright spots, those patches of joyful colour, the sounds the toys made, the penny trumpets, the sweets with their lace corsets, the pralines made like a drunkard's nose, those crude tones and subtle tastes, the soldier that melted, the sugar that dissolved, those feasts for the eye and banquets for the tongue, the smell of paste, the perfume of vanilla, the debauchery of the nose and the audacity of the ear drum, that little bit of madness, that little bit of fever, oh! what a good thing they are, once a year!

ces points vifs, ces taches de couleur joyeuse, ces bruits de jouet, ces trompettes d'un sou, ces bonbons à corset de dentelle, ces pralines comme des nez d'ivrognes, ces tons crus et ces goûts fins, ce soldat qui coule, ce sucre qui fond, ces gloutonneries de l'œil, ces gourmandises de la langue, ces odeurs de colle, ces parfums de vanille, ce libertinage du nez et cette audace du tympan, ce brin de folie, ce petit coup de fièvre, ah! comme c'est bon, une fois l'an![85]

While this is not the vocabulary of childhood, the adoption of a list formula instead of a suggestion of logical links between the elements certainly communicates the freshness of the child's view expressed through the voice of the adult narrator.

Structurally, *L'Enfant* adopts a broad chronological development, within which memories cluster around such central topics as the family and the school, later presented as though the slightly older child were writing classroom essays on set subjects: 'my teacher', 'my house'.[86] This, like the slippage of tenses, suggests the child's gradual awareness of the complexity of time and of memory, a complexity increased in the brief forward glimpse that is provided, in the form of a *mise en abyme* of *Le Bachelier*, the second novel in the trilogy, when Jacques spots a *répétiteur* (crammer) forced to live as a tramp, sleeping under bridges and washing his linen in the river. The awareness that this, or at best the unrelieved drudgery of his father's life, is all that awaits him casts an even bleaker light over the despairing view of childhood Vallès paints, grimly subverting the Romantic vision of the child's insouciant anticipation of the future.

Subversion, indeed, is a central structuring feature of the novel as a whole. The received wisdom of the bourgeoisie, and particularly its encapsulation in the form of clichés, is a constant butt of Vallès's sardonic humour. Variants of the old saw 'spare the rod and spoil the child' are used to justify much of the ill-treatment of

---

[85] Ibid., 73–4.   [86] Ibid., 248–9.

the children and underlie Vallès's ironic affirmation in the following reference to the way Mme Vingtras beats Jacques: 'it's for my good so the more she pulls my hair out, the more she thumps me, the more convinced I am that she is a good mother and that I am an ungrateful child.' (*c'est pour mon bien aussi, plus elle m'arrache de cheveux, plus elle me donne de taloches, et plus je suis persuadé qu'elle est une bonne mère et que je suis un enfant ingrat.*)[87] Béatrice Didier, in her preface to the Folio edition of the novel, and Pamela Moores, in her analysis of the text, both seem to me to be perversely wide of the mark when they present Jacques as masochist: Vallès is surely much more concerned with an ironic depiction of the ways in which the received wisdom about sparing the rod and spoiling the child promotes sadism in the adult. Choosing to see as masochism Jacques's indictment of parental brutality is tantamount to choosing to ignore Vallès's potent political message. Moreover, it suggests a more straightforward failure to respond to his irony. But then, if being found out is the failure of the liar, the ironist's failure is not being found out. Yet more bitter, given the racism of Louis-Philippe's France, is his affirmation that he would have liked to be a Negro: 'firstly, Negro women love their little ones. I would have had a mother who loved me.' (*d'abord, les Négresses aiment leurs petits.—J'aurais eu une mère aimante.*)[88] Even the consecrated patriotic tag '*liberté, égalité, fraternité*' is not spared: Vallès gives one chapter the parodic title 'Frottage—Gourmandise—Propreté' (Scrubbing—Greed—Cleanliness), to suggest middle-class debasing and sanitizing of revolutionary values.

Traditional aspects of autobiography are also subjected to ironic treatment in *L'Enfant*. The opening lines of the work, for instance, gain even more power if they are set in the context of the search for a beginning that, as we have seen, marks so many autobiographies. Vallès's narrator opens by asserting the impossibility of complete knowledge and the doubtful nature of maternal love: 'Was I breast-fed by my mother? Was it a peasant who gave me her milk? I know nothing about it.' (*Ai-je été nourri par ma mère? Est-ce une paysanne qui m'a donné son lait? Je n'en sais rien.*)[89] And when he offers his earliest memories, he makes no attempt to transform them from trivial into significant: 'so my first memory goes back to

---

[87] Ibid., 12.   [88] Ibid., 175.   [89] Ibid., 3.

a spanking. My second is full of astonishment and tears.' (*mon premier souvenir date donc d'une fessée. Mon second est plein d'étonnement et de larmes.*)[90] Where a Cellini or a George Sand would have tied that early pain to an image of great clarity or beauty, suggesting its link with the awakening of the child's intelligence, for Vallès it merely marks the start of an almost endless series of repetitions. And where Cellini and George Sand are exonerated from any guilt concerning the pain they have suffered, Vallès's hero is always, apparently by definition, guilty, reflecting the power of Jansenist and Calvinist teachings on the innate evil of children. Nevertheless, however ironically he may treat certain aspects of the autobiographical form, the search for the central formative moment escapes that irony, standing out from the general mocking nature of the text in a passage of exceptional power. Here Vallès's parodic voice is briefly stilled as he sets out to convince us that the roots of Jacques's subsequent revolutionary activity lie deep in early childhood and derive from a statement in which the child is, for once, treated as the adult's intellectual and moral equal:

I respect bread.

One day I threw a crust away and my father went and picked it up. He did not speak to me harshly as he usually did.

'My child,' he said to me, 'You mustn't throw bread away; it is hard to earn. We don't have too much of it ourselves, but if we did, we would have to give it to the poor. You may not have enough of it one day and then you'll know what it's worth. Remember my words, Jacques.'

I have not forgotten that.

This remark, spoken, perhaps for the first time in my childhood, without anger but with dignity, went to the very depths of my being. And I have respected bread ever since.

J'ai le respect du pain.

Un jour je jetais une croûte, mon père est allé la ramasser. Il ne m'a pas parlé durement comme il le fait toujours.

'Mon enfant, m'a-t-il dit, il ne faut pas jeter le pain; c'est dur à gagner. Nous n'en avons pas trop pour nous, mais si nous en avions trop, il faudrait le donner aux pauvres. Tu en manqueras peut-être un jour, et tu verras ce qu'il vaut. Rappelle-toi ce que je te dis là, mon enfant!'

Je ne l'ai pas oublié.

[90] Ibid., 4.

Cette observation, qui, pour la première fois peut-être dans ma vie de jeunesse, me fut faite sans colère, mais avec dignité, me pénétra jusqu'au fond de l'âme et j'ai eu le respect du pain depuis lors.[91]

In sharp contrast with the tone and even vocabulary of the rest of the novel, this passage allows a fleeting, naked view of Vallès's moral purpose, and while it is easy to mock it both for its simplicity and for its intensity, the quiet insistence on the child's ability to respond to a calmly expressed explanation stands in clear contra-distinction to the pomposity of, say, Janet, whose study on the family includes the condescending affirmation: 'however base this little being may appear, however slight the difference between it, when it first comes into the world, and an animal, philosophy must not despise this first sketch of humanity.' (*quelle que soit la bassesse apparente de ce petit être qui, lorsqu'il vient au monde, est à peine différent de l'animal, la philosophie ne doit point dédaigner cette première ébauche de l'humanité.*)[92]

Overturning accepted ideas concerning parental dignity and filial love is also central to *L'Enfant*, part of Vallès's general political purpose of throwing into doubt the received beliefs concerning the right of one group to make decisions on behalf of another. The child's-eye viewpoint adopted in the text reveals the arbitrary nature of adult behaviour, but also stresses the complexity of the child's response to his parents. This is no misogynistic or misanthropic attack, as one could argue is the case in Renard's *Poil de carotte* or, even more so, Bazin's *Vipère au poing*. On the contrary, the very naïvety of Jacques's view throws into sharp relief the pressures on a father who is seen as *déclassé*, a peasant who has succeeded in getting a toehold in the territory of the bourgeoisie but who, as a result, is subjected to humiliating treatment both from his superiors in the school and from pupils and their parents. Indeed, Gerbod, in his study of daily life in nineteenth-century *lycées*, argues that teachers, by their very profession, were *déracinés*, torn from their roots, forced, moreover, into an increasingly restrictive mould of behaviour by administrators eager to insist on obedience to the slightest aspect of the Napoleonic vision of education.[93] Taken along to his father's school when his mother is too ill to look after him at home, Jacques cannot but overhear what the pupils say

[91] *L'Enfant*, 37–8.
[92] *La Famille*, 128.
[93] *La Vie quotidienne dans les lycées*, 43, 50.

about the teacher they describe as dog: 'they mock his large nose, his old jacket, they make him appear ridiculous in the eyes of his child, and, unbeknown to him, I am suffering.' (*ils se moquent de son grand nez, de son vieux paletot, ils le rendent ridicule aux yeux de son enfant, et je souffre sans qu'il le sache.*)[94] Equally clear, and even more moving, is the unhappiness of the mother, torn between loyalty to her peasant, Auvergnat roots, with their convictions about how to dress, behave, and speak, and her muddle-headed desire to support her husband and prepare her son for life as one of the middle classes. The embarrassments she unwittingly inflicts on her menfolk are expressed in terms that make the reader cringe in sympathy but there is frequently also an indication of the unhappiness of the woman herself, inserted in a world that is not merely alien, but hostile, to her.[95] While it is acceptable for the German teacher's wife to sing an Alsatian song and dance one of the region's waltzes, there can be nothing but ridicule for the whole family when Jacques's mother leaps on to the stage with a spirited offering from the Auvergne.[96] This sense of displacement, of having lost contact with physical, linguistic, and social roots, is even more strongly experienced by the child, who is made to feel an outsider in his parents' house and whose moves from Le Puy to Saint-Étienne, Nantes, and then Paris leave him with a collection of fragmentary, melancholy memories but with no feeling of belonging to any of these towns. Indeed, the short-lived happiness he enjoys on visiting relatives who work as farmers, and his ephemeral project of becoming a farm-worker himself, can be seen both as a longing for a place where stability rather than mobility is the norm, and as a reaction against the demands made on him by his parents, with their unexamined expectations that he will follow his father into the thankless career of teaching.

That sense of being forced into an alien environment finds a physical correlative both in the frequent references to the appalling clothes Jacques is obliged to wear and in the depictions of the pressures of school. Descriptions of these clothes, created by a mother whose sense of economy far outweighs any aesthetic or

---

[94] *L'Enfant*, 31.

[95] B. Didier's assertion of Mme Vingtras's *conscious* desire to humiliate Jacques seems to me an extension of misogyny which is unjustified by the text itself and denies Vallès's insight into the way in which social repressions force individuals into particular patterns of behaviour.

[96] *L'Enfant*, 273–5.

even practical considerations, punctuate the whole text, a source of constant discomfort and embarrassment and a burlesque image of Jacques's difficulty in fitting into the class in which he finds himself. In a passage that blends humour and pathos, self-mockery and self-pity, exaggeration and understatement, a sardonic rejection of clichés and an apparent acceptance of them, Jacques describes some of these outfits:

I am often dressed in black, 'nothing dresses like black', and in evening dress and tails, with a top hat, I look like a stove.

But because I wear things out quickly, they have bought for me, in the country, a yellow, hairy material in which they envelop me. I ape the Lap ambassador. Foreigners salute me, professors stare at me.

But the material of which my trousers have been made dries out and shrivels up, flays me and makes me bleed.

Alas! From now on I will not live but merely drag myself around.

All childhood games are prohibited for me. I cannot play prisoners' base, I cannot leap or run or fight. I crawl about, all alone, calumniated by some, pitied by others, useless to everyone! And in the heart of my home town, at the age of 12, isolated in my trousers, I am granted the knowledge of what it is like to suffer the dull grief of exile.

Je suis en noir souvent, 'rien n'habille comme le noir', et en habit, en frac, avec un chapeau haut de forme j'ai l'air d'un poêle.

Cependant comme j'use beaucoup, on m'a acheté, dans la campagne, une étoffe jaune et velue dont je suis enveloppé. Je joue l'ambassadeur lapon. Les étrangers me saluent, les savants me regardent.

Mais l'étoffe dans laquelle on a taillé mon pantalon se sèche et se racornit, m'écorche et m'ensanglante.

Hélàs! Je vais non plus vivre, mais me traîner.

Tous les jeux d'enfance me sont interdits. Je ne puis jouer aux barres, sauter, courir, me battre. Je rampe, seul, calomnié des uns, plaints par les autres, inutile! Et il m'est donné, au sein même de ma ville natale, à douze ans, de connaître, isolé dans ce pantalon, les douleurs sourdes de l'exil.[97]

Just as clothes offer a comic image of Jacques's nature as a misfit, so also does the depiction of school life. Although the social historian H. J. Graff argues that 'the school as microcosm . . . forms a mechanism of socialization frequently neglected by scholars',[98] Vallès, like many nineteenth-century autobiographers, shows himself to be only too aware of that mechanism. Jacques is made to see

[97] *L'Enfant*, 44–5. No empty final phrase this: Vallès was driven into exile for years as a result of his involvement with the Commune.

[98] *Literacy in History*, 47.

how low is the rank assigned to him as a mere teacher's son by the position he is allotted in the classroom:

That classroom was near the toilets, and they were the little boys' toilets! For a whole year I swallowed that foul air. I had been placed near the door because that was the worst spot, and as a teacher's son it was my duty to be in the vanguard, in the place of sacrifice, in the danger zone . . .
Cette classe était près des latrines, et ces latrines étaient les latrines des petits!
Pendant une année j'ai avalé cet air empesté. On m'avait mis près de la porte parce que c'était la plus mauvaise place, et en ma qualité de fils de professeur, je devais être à l'avant-garde, au poste de sacrifice, au lieu de danger . . .[99]

The triple use of the word 'latrines', an object whose very existence polite society affected to ignore, the sense of a faceless power encapsulated in the indeterminate passive, and the ironic choice of such militaristic expressions as 'danger zone' all indicate the frequency and firmness with which the child's attention was drawn, by both superiors and peers, to his inferior social position.

The child's view of the school conveys not merely this unspoken criticism of its social prejudices but also an outspoken attack on the inadequacy and empty pretentiousness of what, and how, it taught. The ridiculous Hellenisms and Latinisms of the injunction: 'do not extend your digital extremities to your *cothurnus*' (*ne portez pas vos extrémités digitales à vos* cothurnes)[100] and the idiocy of the insistence that the child should imagine himself in Themistocles' place and write a speech taken piecemeal from his reading (one thinks of Proust's parodic evocation of a similar exercise in which Gisèle writes an essay on the following: 'Sophocles writes from Hades to Racine in order to console him for his lack of success with *Athalie*' (*Sophocle écrit des Enfers à Racine pour le consoler de l'insuccès d'*Athalie))[101] are sharpened by the brief introduction of the Italian exile whose practical pedagogical methods at last give Jacques an insight into geometry:

They want to teach children what a cone is, how it can be cut, the volume of a sphere, and all they show them is lines, lines! Give them a wooden cone, a shape in plaster, teach them how you cut an orange! Their old system is nothing more than theology.

---

[99] *L'Enfant*, 113. Original ellipses.   [100] Ibid., 291.
[101] *A la recherche*, i. 911–12.

On veut enseigner aux enfants ce que c'est qu'un cône, comment on le coupe, le volume de la sphère, et on leur montre des lignes, des lignes! Donnez-leur le cône en bois, la figure en plâtre, apprenez-leur cela, comme on découpe une orange! De la théologie, tout leur vieux système.[102]

What makes Vallès's text most remarkable, however, is the way in which these symbols of oppression combine with the black humour of his style to produce an unforgettable image of the child as underling, oppressed and mistreated by those who are judged to know better than he does, as the working class was oppressed and abused by the middle classes, on the justification that peasants and workers were too ignorant to decide their own futures. In the other works in the trilogy, *Le Bachelier* and *L'Insurgé*, the anger becomes more corrosive, the attacks on the political status quo more explicit, the humour more caricatural: in *L'Enfant* Vallès achieves the remarkable feat of transforming childhood into a political metaphor while at the same time forcing his readers to acknowledge a very different image of actual childhood from anything that had been produced so far.

THE CHILD AS PUPPET MASTER

With its central symbol of the puppet theatre as microcosm, Pierre Loti's *Le Roman d'un enfant* may well be the first French autobiographical novel that not only acknowledges fully the central role of childhood in the formation of the adult, but also consistently attempts to find images, a language, and a structure adequate to capturing the fluctuations of the child's personality.[103] The polyvalence of the book's very title is an indication of the work's complexity and of the concomitant intricacy accorded to the child's developing intelligence. The indefinite article had, by the time Loti published his book in May 1890, become a fairly common means of apparently shifting attention from the individual to the general

[102] *L'Enfant*, 303. By the time Vallès was writing, it should be said, educational thinkers like Jean Macé were indeed producing far more practical teaching methods: see e.g. his *L'Arithmétique de grand-papa* and Mme Pape-Carpentier's *Le Secret des grains de sable*.
[103] R. Coe's argument that Stendhal's *Vie de Henry Brulard* is the first French 'Childhood' ('Stendhal, Rousseau and the Search for Self') may be convincing in terms of Stendhal's vision of his work's thematic content, but Loti's work appears to me far more ambitious in terms of structure and language in addition to theme.

nature of childhood experiences, even if the work itself is concerned above all with revealing what was unique to the particular child involved: Mme Michelet's *Mémoires d'une enfant* of 1867, Alphonse Daudet's *Le Petit Chose: Histoire d'un enfant* of 1868, and Mme Daudet's *L'Enfance d'une parisienne* of 1883 are just three earlier works using the same device.[104] Loti's decision to call his work a *roman* can be seen as part of the same desire to justify what Stendhal had called 'the terrible quantity of "I"s and "me"s',[105] but there remains the ambiguity of the question of whether this is a story about a child or by a child, and part of Loti's purpose is to draw on that ambivalence to suggest the extent to which this child creates himself and the world around him from the shadows and the void from which he comes. Revolving around the unshakeable conviction of the intensity of childhood sensations, *Le Roman d'un enfant* draws both on the aesthetics of Impressionism to build up its image of childhood, not in any simple linear fashion but by the gradual accretion in the reader of layers of memory, and on certain aspects of autobiography that, as we have seen, had by this stage acquired the status of tradition, notably the belief in the organizing importance of the first memory and the conviction of the writer's ability to locate decisive moments in his or her development.

The text is explicitly presented as determined by the child's point of view: 'I hope', the narrator comments at one point, 'that if [my teachers] were to read this, they would understand the child's-eye view I am adopting in order to write it. Were I to come across them today, I would of course shake them by the hand, apologizing for having been such an intractable pupil.' (*J'espère que s'ils [mes professeurs] lisaient ceci, ils comprendraient à quel point de vue enfantin je me replace pour l'écrire. Si je les retrouvais aujourd'hui, j'irais sans nul doute à eux la main tendue, en m'excusant d'avoir été leur élève très indocile.*)[106] Obviously, the desire to give expression to the boy's resentment at treatment meted out to him by his teachers, while acknowledging the impossibility that the adult could behave towards them with anything other than

---

[104] B. Vercier, in his preface to the Garnier-Flammarion edition of 1988, struggles unnecessarily to explain Loti's decision to use the phrase 'un enfant' because he neglects to see the work in its context at this point, although elsewhere he places Loti among a rather heteroclite assortment of '*mémorialistes*' and authors of '*enfances*': see *Le Roman d'un enfant*, 12 and 14.

[105] *Vie de Henry Brulard*, 15.   [106] *Le Roman d'un enfant*, 187.

apologetic cordiality, may well be what provokes this particular assertion of the standpoint adopted. Nevertheless, there is in Loti's writing a determination to re-enter the world of childhood that is so patent that ulterior motives such as this can have played only a minor role. However much the child's view may be privileged, there is none the less a series of external judgements on him, which have both a psychological and a structural function. The older narrator not only elucidates the boy's individual sense of beauty but also places it in a more general perspective, for instance, when he affirms:

> moreover my feelings about beauty have greatly changed since then, and I would have been greatly astonished in those days if anyone had told me what kind of faces I would eventually find charming in the unforeseen path my life was to take. But all children have the same ideal in this regard, an ideal which then changes as soon as they reach adulthood.

> du reste mon sentiment sur la beauté s'est beaucoup modifié depuis cette époque, et on m'eût beaucoup étonné alors en m'apprenant quelles sortes de visages j'arriverais à trouver charmants dans la suite imprévue de ma vie. Mais tous les enfants ont sous ce rapport le même idéal, qui change ensuite dès qu'ils se font hommes.[107]

(It is both typical and significant that the French text here expresses the idea of reaching adulthood through the phrase: '*se font hommes*' (literally: 'make men of themselves'), instead of any one of the various synonyms that could have appeared: *Le Roman d'un enfant* presents itself very much as the novel of a child creating himself as individual.) Structurally, between the initial evocation of the first memory, which heralds the child's self-creation as thinking individual, and the self-expulsion from childhood that results from his decision to choose a career in the navy, Loti places, almost symmetrically, two external judgements on the child. The first of these is conveyed by the sister, in her diary, during one of their visits to the Île d'Oléron; the second, in reported speech, is that of the brother on his return from the islands of the Pacific. The diary entry acts as a private confirmation of the child's own early reading of his character: the mania for collecting, the close attachment to a special little girl, the deep sense of sorrow at the thought of separation.[108]

---

[107] *Le Roman d'un enfant*, 116.
[108] *Le Roman d'un enfant*, 100–2: cf. the version reproduced in annex 4, ibid., 270–3, written by Loti's sister.

The brother's public remarks signal the beginning of the child's passage away from the emotionality he attributes to the female side of his personality to the more active, practical activities associated with the male side:

he realized that I was enduring a real overdose of intellectual work, in regard to art, I mean; that Chopin and Peau-d'Ane were each equally dangerous for me and that I was becoming excessively refined . . . So one day he decreed, to my great delight, that I should be allowed to go riding.

il comprenait que je subissais un réel surmenage intellectuel, en fait d'art s'entend; que Chopin et Peau-d'Ane m'étaient aussi dangereux l'un que l'autre; que je devenais d'un raffinement excessif . . . Un jour donc, il décréta, à ma grande joie, qu'il fallait me faire monter à cheval.[109]

In a text dominated by overlapping time-sequences and frequent returns of basic themes—the museum, the butterfly called the '*citron-aurore*', the puppet theatre—three other structural features demand attention for the way in which they shape the creation of self. The first of these is the contrast between the initial affirmation of the child's gradual awareness of identity through a series of 'sudden flashes of light' (*jets de clartés brusques*),[110] and his sense of giving birth to a second, social self when he starts attending school:

during this time a certain superficial 'I', created for purposes of social relationships, was already forming like a thin envelope and was beginning to succeed in remaining more or less on good terms with everyone, while the real 'I' of my deep self continued to elude them completely.

cependant un certain moi superficiel, pour le besoin des relations sociales, se formait déjà comme une mince enveloppe, et commençait à savoir se maintenir à peu près en bons termes avec tous, tandis que le vrai moi du fond continuait de leur échapper absolument.[111]

A similar sense of symmetry pervades a second structural feature, which crystallizes around the ambiguous word '*berceau*', here meaning 'arbour' but carrying with it, as do so many of the images in this text, associations with birth through its other meaning of cradle. The arbour in which he writes the letter asking for his brother's help in enlisting in the navy, an act he refers to elsewhere as 'the most important fact of my childhood life' (*le fait capital de*

---

[109] Ibid., 234.   [110] Ibid., 43.   [111] Ibid., 238.

ma vie d'enfant),[112] is foreshadowed in a story that deeply affects him as a little boy, a story of a prodigal son returning home to find all in ruins:

> in the abandoned garden, in an arbour of stripped branches, the prodigal child, bending down to the damp earth, recognized among all the autumn leaves a blue pearl which had remained there since the days when he used to come and play there with his sister . . .

> dans le jardin abandonné, sous un berceau aux branches dégarnies, l'enfant prodigue, en se baissant vers la terre mouillée, reconnut parmi toutes les feuilles d'automne, une perle bleue qui était restée à cette place depuis le temps où il venait s'amuser là, avec sa sœur . . . [113]

The pivot of these careful symmetrical structures is the chapter that immediately follows the account of the discovery of relations with whom Pierre and his sister will spend holidays in the mountains of the south. The child's delight in at last being in a position to see real mountains[114] leads with no transition into the evocation of an immense melancholy, described as one of the strangest in this rather cheerless child's existence.[115] The voyage to the mountains, it would appear, included an episode that caused the child such despair that not only was the specific incident itself suppressed from his 'novel' but the organizing conscience was also driven to situate precisely here an emotion that replaces it, shifting the source of sorrow from something definite to something incomprehensible, even if this is in itself so different from the adult's experience that he adds:

> In my adult life I have scarcely ever felt again that distress that had no known cause and that was intensified by the worry of not being able to understand, of constantly losing my footing in the same immeasurable depths; I have hardly ever suffered again without at least knowing the reason why.

> Dans ma vie d'homme, je n'ai guère retrouvé ces angoisses sans cause connue et doublées de cette anxiété de ne pas comprendre, de se sentir perdre pied toujours dans les mêmes insondables dessous; je n'ai plus guère souffert sans savoir au moins pourquoi.[116]

---

[112] *Le Roman d'un enfant*, 168.
    [113] Ibid., 77. Original ellipses, in more ways than one. Loti's relationship with his sister and his suppression in *Le Roman d'un enfant* of any mention of her engagement to their cousin is explored in B. Vercier's preface to his edition.
    [114] Ibid., 146.   [115] Ibid., 150.   [116] Ibid.

It hardly matters whether we wish to interpret this moment biographically (Loti's sister was subsequently to marry the cousin met for the first time on this holiday) or see in it the first clear awareness of the yawning gap between image and reality, the discovery that Baudelaire expresses in 'Le Voyage':

> Oh! how vast is the world in the light of the lamps!
> In memory's eyes, how small is the world!
>
> Ah! que le monde est grand à la clarté des lampes!
> Aux yeux du souvenir, que le monde est petit![117]

What is important is that this careful structural patterning, balanced by a desire to convey the ephemeral, the impalpable, the void, can be seen as a means both of suggesting, and of keeping at bay, the immeasurable depths.

The search for a suitable structure also predominates in the depiction of the child's gradual awareness of the world and his place in it. On the one hand, the narrative voice locates a series of traces of his presence, captured in the form of a pressed flower, an engraving in a book first seen in childhood, and, most originally and memorably, the tracks left by snails on his history book after he had absent-mindedly left it outside. Testaments to the child's passage, these objects or others like them can precipitate the adult back into childhood by the power of affective memory: 'I have never been able to watch that ray of light fall without thinking again of that other ray, the one that fell on that Sunday in the past, and without feeling the same, precisely the *same* melancholy impression.' (*je n'ai jamais pu voir descendre ce rayon sans repenser à l'autre, celui de ce dimanche d'autrefois, et sans éprouver la même, précisément la* même *impression triste.*)[118] On the other hand, the child is presented as creating his world from the hazy contours of his earliest perceptions. Thought is seen as being produced by the child's physical exertions when he first realizes he can run and jump: 'at the same time as my little legs, my mind awoke.' (*en même temps que mes petites jambes, mon esprit s'était éveillé.*)[119] The giving of names allows the child to gain a further degree of control over the world, to put it into some kind of order: from the naming of the cat (*La Suprématie*), to the choice of a masculine

---

[117] *Œuvres complètes*, i. 129.
[118] *Le Roman d'un enfant*, 61.
[119] Ibid., 46.

name for Lucette (*Luçon*) or the classification of shells or butterflies, words are a means of taking possession of the world. They can, of course, also take possession of the child, as they do when he discovers the old ship's logbook which tells him that

From *noon to four in the afternoon on the 20 June 1813, at longitude 110 degrees and latitude 15 degrees south,* . . . *the weather was fair, the sea smooth, and a pleasant south-east breeze blew,* . . . and swimming beside the ship were a school of golden-heads.

De *midi à quatre heures du soir, le 20 juin 1813, par 110 degrés de longitude et 15 degrés de latitude australe,* . . . *il faisait beau temps, belle mer, jolie brise de sud-est* . . . *et que, le long du navire, des dorades passaient.*[120]

The desire to impose order is reflected in the fascination the child feels for two childhood entertainments, his museum and the puppet theatre. The museum acts as a storehouse of images, a collection of triggers to the imagination that can prompt daydreams of far-flung places, conjuring the beauties of the colonies out of the flat landscape of Rochefort.[121] The controlled and ordered world of the museum is, however, only a stage in the child's development, a means of briefly keeping at bay, through these strictly delimited representations of the world's multiplicity, the temptations to participate in it. Hence the child's despair when he hears the sailors celebrating Mardi Gras, for, while he may have no conscious desire to join them, wanting instead to 'put in order the multicoloured family of the Purpuriferae' (*mettre en ordre la famille multicolore des Purpurifères*),[122] he is nevertheless filled with a longing that leads him to request his mother to come and sit with him, as a charm counteracting their attraction. Later, when his older brother sets off again for the Orient, the mother's conviction that Pierre, at least, will stay at home no longer offers the same sense of security, but rather serves to sharpen his determination to leave. Indeed, if the museum is initially a source of imaginative departures, it gradually loses its ability to curb the longing for a physical departure and becomes in itself a source of nostalgic yearning, opening up vistas into the past where initially it projected the child into a possible future:

---

[120] *Le Roman d'un enfant,* 216.   [121] Ibid., 117.
[122] Ibid., 132.

What nostalgic impressions the museum held for me now, when I climbed up there on winter Thursdays, after I had finished my homework or my impositions, always somewhat late; the light was already fading, the vista over the great plains was already acquiring a pinkish grey haze which I found extremely sad. Nostalgia for the summer, nostalgia for the sun and the south, induced by all those butterflies from my uncle's garden which were lined up under glass, by all those mountain fossils that I had gathered there together with the little Peyral boys.

This was the foretaste of my longings to return to *other lands*, longings which later, after long journeys to the warm countries, were to spoil my winter homecomings.

Très nostalgiques à présent, les impressions que me causait mon musée, quand j'y montais les jeudis d'hiver, après avoir fini mes devoirs ou mes pensums, et toujours un peu tard; la lumière baissant déjà, l'échappée de vue sur les grandes plaines s'embrumant en un gris rosé extrêmement triste. Nostalgie du soleil et du Midi, amenée par tous ces papillons du jardin de mon oncle, qui étaient rangés là sous des verres, par tous ces fossiles des montagnes, qui avaient été ramassés là-bas en compagnie des petits Peyral.

C'était l'avant-goût de ces regrets *d'ailleurs*, qui plus tard, après les longs voyages aux pays chauds, devaient me gâter mes retours au foyer, mes retours d'hiver.[123]

Like the museum, the puppet theatre offers a *mise en abyme* of the external world, but a world that remains largely within Pierre's control. It, too, is a repeated motif in the text, returning at significant points as a means of charting the child's emotional and intellectual development. Moreover, this little theatre serves as a crucible for Pierre's future projects, to such an extent that it is presented as emblematic of what he terms 'the entire fantasy of [his] life' (*toute la chimère de [sa] vie*).[124] The most remarkable experiment with this '*théâtre de Peau-d'Ane*' occurs when Pierre and his friend Jeanne use it to create an impression of the void, but in the very elevation of their ambitions lies the germ of failure, or, at least, non-completion, for, as he claims: 'every time we had new ideas about it, always there were more astonishing projects, and the dress rehearsal was postponed month after month, put off until some unlikely future date.' (*c'étaient chaque fois des conceptions nouvelles, toujours de plus étonnants projets, et la répétition générale était reculée de mois en mois, jusque dans un avenir improbable.*) And the adult narrator adds: 'all my life's enterprises

---

[123] Ibid., 198.   [124] Ibid., 145.

will have or have already had the same fate as this toy theatre . . . '
(*toutes les entreprises de ma vie auront, ou ont eu déjà, le sort de
cette Peau-d'Ane* . . .)[125] Through the narrative voice and the
structures he adopts, and above all by never denying the evocative
power of childhood experience, Loti is, therefore, able to reveal the
child's games as encapsulations of the future, convex mirrors in
which everything is already contained but has still to be interpreted.

One particular series of icons demands attention in the image it
provides of childhood, and perhaps more specifically of the
relationship between the child and the world. While one of the
earliest related memories is of the child perceived but not
perceiving, when Lucette, from her vantage-point hidden in a tree,
sees him hiding in the grass, it is more common for him to be
depicted looking out at, or down on, the surrounding world.
Watching the cake-seller from the doorway, gazing down on
passers-by from the upper windows of the house, looking out from
the battlements of Castelnau, Pierre observes a world in which he
cannot yet participate, in what is to become a classic image of the
child's vision of reality. The view from on high, from stairways,
through half-drawn curtains, from under tables, a view always
slightly distorted or restricted, comes to offer a physical representation of the child's limited understanding of adult behaviour, not
merely in books such as *L'Enfant à la balustrade* but also and
perhaps most potently in films such as *Fallen Idol, Cria Cuervos*,
and *Shane*.

Loti's fascination with the idea of the emblematic image, with
increasingly powerful and nostalgic icons, is also evident in the
series of special places that are evoked in the text in such a way as
to become inextricably linked with each other. Early memories of
the Île d'Oléron fuse with recollections that cluster around La
Limoise, and feed into the strongly contrasted associations of the
feudal castle of Castelnau, lost in its blue mountains. All of them,
moreover, are connected to the world of imagination and dream,
particularly dreams associated with the 'delicious island', Tahiti.
This link becomes especially evident in a dream sparked off by a
letter Pierre receives from his brother, which conjures up the image
of a corridor allowing instant access between home and the exotic
islands. Here, too, the impossibility of ever possessing the dream,
even if it eventually becomes a physical reality, is adumbrated in the

---

[125] *Le Roman d'un enfant*, 186. Original ellipses.

child's awareness that he is only dreaming, and his awakening with his hand clutching in vain at 'the impalpable nothingness of dream' (*l'impalpable rien du rêve*).[126] There is a counterpart to such pessimism, however, in the episode when the child awakens on the day after his brother's return to find his room transformed into a miniature Polynesia:

necklaces of shells threaded on human hair, feather head-dresses, ornaments that were primitive and sombre in their savagery, hung more or less everywhere, as if far-off Polynesia had come to me while I slept.

des colliers en coquilles enfilés de cheveux humains, des coiffures de plumes, des ornements d'une sauvagerie primitive et sombre, accrochés un peu partout, comme si la lointaine Polynésie fût venue à moi pendant mon sommeil.[127]

Yet the experience of the museum tells us that this representation of reality will also, in time, lose its power to satisfy the child's longings.

The description of these special places also allows, moreover, for the creation of a physical correlative for emotion, such that the monotonous charm of La Limoise, with its tranquillity, its unbroken lines, its gentle melancholy, becomes an externalization of Pierre's schoolboy mentality. Such a realization leads to a generalization, a truth discovered, so the narrative voice informs us, too late:

The total charm that the outside world seems to us to possess resides within us; it is we ourselves who exude that charm—for ourselves alone, of course—and all that is happening is that the charm then returns to us.

La somme de charme que le monde extérieur nous fait l'effet d'avoir, réside en nous-mêmes; c'est nous qui la répandons,—pour nous seuls, bien entendu,—et elle ne fait que nous revenir.[128]

Throughout *Le Roman d'un enfant,* indeed, places are less important for themselves, however detailed and apparently mimetic the descriptions of them may be (as is the case with La Limoise, for instance), than for their ability to represent emotion. Perhaps the most successful example of the way in which mood is produced by objects occurs immediately after the second departure of Pierre's brother, at the point when the child knows that he, too, wants to travel. In a passage that unites the emotive power of objects and

[126] Ibid., 175.   [127] Ibid., 233.   [128] Ibid., 138.

that of the written word, Loti expresses with remarkable concision the intensity of the child's response:

And in that empty living-room, where the armchairs had been disarranged and a chair had fallen over, leaving the melancholy impression of departures, while I stood there close to my mother, clinging to her, but with my eyes already turned away from her and distress in my soul, I suddenly remembered the shipboard log of those sailors of yore, that I had read in the setting sun last spring at La Limoise; the short sentences, written in yellowing ink on the old paper, slowly came back to me one after the other with the soothing and perfidious charm that must come from magical incantations: 'Fine weather . . . smooth sea . . . light south-east breeze . . . shoals of golden-heads . . . passing to port.'

Et dans ce salon vide, où les fauteuils dérangés, une chaise tombée, laissaient l'impression triste des départs, tandis que j'étais là, tout près de ma mère, serré contre elle, mais les yeux toujours détournés et l'âme en détresse, je repensais tout à coup au journal du bord de ces marins d'autrefois, lu au soleil couchant, le printemps dernier à la Limoise; les petites phrases écrites d'une encre jaunie sur le papier ancien, me revinrent lentement l'une après l'autre, avec un charme berceur et perfide comme doit être celui des incantations de magie: 'Beau temps . . . belle mer . . . légère brise de sud-est . . . Des bancs de dorades . . . passent par bâbord.'[129]

A magical charm, indeed, but one whose magic lies less in any external reality than in the clusters of sounds and imaginative associations that build up around it. This is the moment that establishes Pierre's identity as a continual oscillation between nostalgia for the bright summers of childhood and expectation of 'the improbable improvement of the future' (*l'improbable mieux de l'avenir*).[130]

Loti's *Roman d'un enfant*, therefore, offers a particularly rich and suggestive myth of childhood, an evocation heavy with melancholy for all its beauty, and above all a language and a structure whose density conveys the complexity of the child's formation.

Hitherto, this study has concentrated on ways in which nineteenth-century texts exploit a wide variety of narrative devices in their attempts to convey children and the world of childhood, exploring the potential of various narrative voices, of time and of vocabulary. But an understanding of the vision of the child afforded by

[129] *Le Roman d'un enfant*, 236. Original ellipses.   [130] Ibid., 200.

nineteenth-century literature also depends on an awareness both of the thematic elements that constitute the world of childhood, as these texts perceive it or at least convey it, and of the metaphorical uses to which the topos is put. It is to these subjects that I now wish to turn.

4
Deciphering Childhood

I love in childhood's little book
To read its lessons through
& o'er each pictured page to look
Because they read so true
& there my heart creates anew
Love for each trifling thing.

(John Clare, 'Childhood')

For us the book, do you hear me, the book, whatever its nature, is the fundamental and irresistible means of freeing the intelligence.

Pour nous le livre, entendez-vous, le livre, quel qu'il soit, est l'instrument fondamental, irrésistible, de l'affranchissement de l'intelligence.

(Jules Ferry, speech in Parliament, 20 December 1880)

FIGURES of children abound in Impressionist paintings: children gazing at us with frank curiosity as they bowl hoops or play on swings or peer under umbrellas; children turning their backs on us to look through railings or windows at a world they cannot yet enter; sisters embracing sisters, sons sitting on their father's knee as the artist delights in the subtle differences and inescapable similarities that run through families. Yet perhaps one of the most significant images is that of the child reading. No doubt one of the advantages to the painter in choosing this subject is that the child can more easily be kept still, but for us looking at such a painting the image is rich in historical and metaphorical suggestions: the imbrication of the physical world and the world of imagination, the indication of further dimensions of space and time as the reading child explores different lands and past or future eras, above all, perhaps, the sense of the simultaneous presence and absence of the child, who is bodily present in the painting but whose mind is in a world we can never completely share, since even if we know the book the child reads, our response to it will be subtly different. The subject of the child reading, therefore, can act as an icon of the difficulties of recapturing the lost content of childhood. I will argue in what follows that when the image is used in nineteenth-century autobiographies and fiction it becomes metonymical for the interpretation of life and the world more generally, suggesting both the child's decoding of the semiotics of existence and our interpretation of the child-figure in literature, the transformation of chaos into cosmos.

READING

The experience of reading, both the physical experience of holding the book in one's hands, and the intellectual discovery of the connection between sign and sound, is one of the experiences of childhood most frequently evoked in nineteenth-century texts, already sanctioned as it is in Rousseau's *Confessions*. There, the intoxicating, addictive pleasure of reading is conveyed with an intensity few later writers will surpass, perhaps above all because it more than anything else dissolves the barriers between adult and child, father and son, living and dead:

My mother had left some Novels. My father and I set about reading them after supper. At first it was only a question of practising my reading skills on some interesting books but soon we grew so interested in them that we read them turn and turn about without stopping and spent whole nights thus occupied. We could never leave a book until we had finished it. Sometimes my father, on hearing the swallows in the morning would say in deep shame: 'Let's go to bed, I'm more of a child than you are.'

Ma mère avait laissé des Romans. Nous mîmes à les lire après soupé mon père et moi. Il n'était question d'abord que de m'exercer à la lecture par des livres amusans mais bientôt l'intérêt devint si vif que nous lisions tour à tour sans relâche, et passions les nuits à cette occupation. Nous ne pouvions jamais quitter qu'à la fin du volume. Quelquefois mon père, entendant le matin les hirondelles, disait tout honteux: allons nous coucher; je suis plus enfant que toi.[1]

Whether the experience of reading is shared, as here, or one in which the isolated child delights in a different society from that of daily life, many writers share with Vallès the desire to convey the unfading memory of the colour, feel, and smell of books read in

---

[1] *Œuvres complètes*, i. 8.

childhood: 'I can still see the green cardboard cover, a marbled green which turned white under the fingers and stained the hands, with its spine of white calf-skin, which opened only with difficulty.' (*Je vois encore le volume cartonné de vert, d'un vert marbré qui blanchissait sous le pouce et poissait le mains, avec un dos de peau blanche, s'ouvrant mal.*)[2] Pierre Loti's image of the child choosing to recite Xenophon or Homer while lying on the stairs, his feet higher than his head,[3] Jules Simon recalling his own favourite reading spot hidden under his father's desk,[4] Goncourt depicting reading as an escape from illness—'each of the illnesses [Chérie] had suffered in those days remained in her memory only as a delightful experience of sinking deliciously into a book' (*chacune de ses maladies de ce temps se représentait seulement à sa mémoire par le souvenir d'un délicieux enfoncement dans un livre*)[5]—Marie d'Agoult's memories of abstracting Cazotte's *Le Diable amoureux* and Mrs Radcliffe's novels from a bookcase she felt sure should have been locked,[6] are all attempts to recreate the association of the physical and the imaginary, to symbolize the book's double existence in the sensory world and in that of the mind. The joy of locking oneself away with a book, of closing out the external world and escaping to an alternative world of illicit pleasure, is expressed with particular intensity by Stendhal in his *Vie de Henry Brulard*:

Soon I managed to get hold of *La Nouvelle Héloïse*, I think I took it from the top shelf of my father's library at Claix. I read it lying in my trapeze at Grenoble, having taken care to lock myself in, and in transports of happiness and pleasure that words cannot describe . . . From that moment, stealing books became the great affair of my life.

Bientôt je me procurais la *Nouvelle Héloïse*, je crois que je la pris au rayon le plus élevé de la bibliothèque de mon père à Claix. Je la lus couché dans mon trapèze à Grenoble, après avoir eu soin de m'enfermer à clef, et dans des transports de bonheur et de volupté impossibles à décrire . . . Dès lors voler des livres devint ma grande affaire.[7]

Numerous images convey the way in which the book's ability to conjure up its own space encourages the child to seek out a special place for reading, a place perceived as uniquely suitable for the

[2] *L'Enfant*, 34.
[3] *Le Roman d'un enfant*, 152.
[4] *Premières années*, 46–7.
[5] *Chérie*, 110.
[6] *Mes souvenirs*, 138–40.
[7] *Vie de Henry Brulard*, 200.

magic nature of the operation. Marouzeau locates that ideal place in the loft, adopting a syntax that makes it impossible to determine whether he is discussing the space or the book:

in the loft I discovered 'the book', the one that teaches you nothing, that contains nothing that is useful or even comprehensible, with the result that its natural place is where you never go. A door opening into a foreign world, beyond life, access to something whose prestige I vaguely sensed and which I did not know as the Spirit.

au grenier je découvrais 'le livre', celui dans lequel on n'apprend pas, qui ne contient rien d'utile ou même de compréhensible, si bien que sa place toute naturelle est là où l'on ne va jamais. Porte ouverte sur un monde étranger, hors de la vie, accès à quelque chose dont je sentais confusément le prestige, et que je ne savais pas être l'Esprit.[8]

Loti attempts to find a physical correlative for the images of Greece he extracts from *Télémaque* by reading the book either in the dark and dusty warmth of the loft, or in the double-locked security of his uncle's old orchard with its space and its silence.[9] Rimbaud's 7-year-old poet also chooses special places to read:

> And as he savoured above all those things that are sombre,
> When, in his bare bedroom with its closed shutters,
> High and blue and smelling sharply of damp,
> He read his novel, the novel he thought about constantly,
> Full of heavy ochre skies and drowned forests,
> Flowers of flesh spread out in the sidereal woods,
> Vertigo, collapses, routs and pity!
> —While the noise of the quarter rose from
> Below—alone, and lying on pieces of unbleached
> Linen, with a violent foretaste of sails!

> Et comme il savourait surtout les sombres choses,
> Quand, dans la chambre nue aux persiennes closes,
> Haute et bleue, âcrement prise d'humidité,
> Il lisait son roman sans cesse médité,
> Plein de lourds ciels ocreux et de forêts noyées,
> De fleurs de chair aux bois sidérals déployées,
> Vertige, écroulements, déroutes et pitié!
> —Tandis que se faisait la rumeur du quartier,

---

[8] *Une enfance*, 43–4.
[9] *Le Roman d'un enfant*, 166–8.

En bas,—seul, et couché sur des pièces de toile
Ecrue, et pressentant violemment la voile![10]

The transformation of the dank, dark room into heavy skies and tropical forests, or of scraps of linen into sails, in short the metamorphosis of the surrounding world into the diegetic world, is paralleled by the alchemy that alters the reading child's awareness of the passage of time. Nowhere, perhaps, is this so powerfully evoked as in Vallès's *L'Enfant*. Here, Jacques, locked in an empty classroom as punishment, comes across a book that instantly abolishes all his awareness of chronological time:

in a crack, a book: I can see its spine, I crush my nails trying to get it out. At last, with the help of a ruler, and breaking a desk in the process, I succeed; I hold the volume and look at the title: ROBINSON CRUSOE.
  I suddenly realize that it is night. How many hours have I spent in the book? What's the time?

dans une fente, un livre: j'en vois le dos, je m'écorche les ongles à essayer de le retirer. Enfin, avec l'aide de la règle, en cassant un pupitre, j'y arrive; je tiens le volume et je regarde le titre: ROBINSON CRUSOE.
  Il est nuit.
  Je m'en aperçois tout d'un coup. Combien y a-t-il de temps que je suis dans ce livre—quelle heure est-il?[11]

Moreover, for adults looking back to childhood, the book as physical object, like a magic carpet allowing travel through space and time, also serves to abolish the years that have passed since they first read it: Champfleury is exemplary here (even if he no doubt deludes himself) in his assertion that he could not reread *Gil Blas* as an adult without feeling exactly the same emotions as when he first read it.[12]

The alteration of ambient space and time through the focusing power of the book's own inner world finds a parallel in the way in which the child discovers the connection between the black marks on the white page and the words of the spoken language with which it is already familiar. The general nineteenth-century embarrassment about evoking the apparently trivial memories of early childhood seems to have erased this breakthrough from most evocations of reading, and even twentieth-century works make

---

[10] *Œuvres complètes*, 45.
[11] *L'Enfant*, 117. Compare Vallès's comment on the importance of *Robinson Crusoe* in *Œuvres*, i. 232. [12] *Souvenirs*, 30.

somewhat heavy weather of it. Michelet is unusual in his ability to suggest the way in which he felt himself to be not so much reading Thomas Aquinas as hearing him speak.[13] Bosco attempts to suggest the emotion of the discovery in the following, disappointingly flat, terms: 'What is wonderful in this is to find oneself at first in front of signs that say nothing and that little by little—and this is the mystery—start telling you something.' (*Le merveilleux dans cette affaire, c'est de se trouver au début devant des signes qui ne disent rien et qui peu à peu—c'est là le mystère—se mettent à vous dire quelque chose.*)[14] Francis Jammes, writing in 1921, is far more successful in conveying the child's excitement on comprehending the function of poetry, no doubt because the abstract terminology of Bosco is replaced by the sharply etched evocation of the physical surroundings:

and this is where the initiation into poetry begins, in that primary school, on that bench, towards the left as you look at the doorway. A book lies open before me. And suddenly, without anyone having warned me, I can see and hear that its lines are alive, that they answer each other two by two through the rhyme, like birds or grape-pickers, and that what they tell us enchants us in the way of beings and things that have no need of translation.

et c'est ici que commence l'initiation poètique, dans cette école primaire, sur ce banc, vers la gauche, en regardant la porte d'entrée. Un livre est ouvert devant moi. Et soudain, sans qu'on m'en ait prévenu, je vois et j'entends que ses lignes sont vivantes, que deux à deux elles se répondent par la rime comme des oiseaux ou des vendangeurs, et que ce qu'elles racontent nous enchante à la manière des êtres et des choses qui n'ont pas besoin qu'on les traduise.[15]

And while many earlier writers refer to the avidity with which they seized on books, and to the sense of feverish, ecstatic, intoxicated delight these books produced,[16] few succeed in expressing as well as Agatha Christie the child's sense both of the triumph and of the normality of the achievement:

---

[13] J. Michelet, *Ma jeunesse*, 37.
[14] *Un oubli moins profond*, 259.
[15] *De l'âge divin*, 116–17.
[16] See Ackerman, *Œuvres*, p. iii; Green, *Partir avant le jour*, 128; Gide, *Si le grain ne meurt*, 58; Lavisse, *Souvenirs*, 30; etc.

[My mother believed] no child should be allowed to read until it was eight years old: better for the eyes and for the brain.
Here, however, things did not go according to plan. When a story had been read to me and I liked it, I would ask for the book and study the pages which, at first meaningless, gradually began to make sense. When out with Nursie, I would ask her what the words written up over shops or on hoardings were. As a result, one day I found myself reading *The Angel of Love* quite successfully to myself. I proceeded to do so out loud to Nursie. 'I'm afraid, Ma'am', said Nursie apologetically to mother the next day, '*Miss Agatha can read*'.[17]

And it is another English writer, Augustus Hare, who provides the most remarkable image of the way in which reading allows the child to piece together the multiple and complex images the world provides and forge them into some kind of understanding of life:

My mother's 'religion' made her think reading any novel or any kind of work of fiction, absolutely wicked at this time, but Grannie took in *Pickwick*, which was coming out in numbers. She read it by her dressing-room fire with closed doors, and her maid, Cowbourne, well on the watch against intruders and I used to pick the fragments out of the waste-paper basket, piece them together, and read them too.[18]

Indeed, for most children evoked in nineteenth-century texts, the 'magic of literature',[19] as Gosse terms it, seems to derive above all from the fragmentary and kaleidoscopic nature of the books they came across. Very few found their greatest pleasure in reading books written specifically for them: certainly, as Anatole France argues, 'children show, in most cases, an extreme repugnance to read the books written for them' (*les enfants montrent, la plupart du temps, une extrême répugnance à lire les livres qui sont faits pour eux*),[20] and not just because so few suitable books were produced for them before the arrival on the scene of the far-sighted and energetic Hetzel. Despite recent attempts to rehabilitate Berquin, his constant moralizing and the patronizing tone he adopts make Adèle Esquiros almost alone in singing his praises: 'I carried off under my arm some dusty old book/And found delight in Berquin's dreams' (*J'emportais sous le bras quelque poudreux*

---

[17] *An Autobiography*, 24. This book is also a rich source of information on the kinds of works Victorian parents gave their children.
[18] *The Story of my Life*, 31.
[19] *Father and Son*, 65.
[20] *Le Livre de mon ami*, 258.

bouquin/Alors, je m'égayais aux rêves de Berquin).[21] Even here, one suspects that the reference to Berquin is less a sharp memory than a product of the rhyme. Baudelaire's view of Berquin expresses with characteristic vigour a more commonly held conviction:

One day when my brain was curdled with the fashionable question of the role of morality in art, the writer's guardian angel slipped a volume of Berquin into my hand. The first thing I saw was that the children in this book spoke like grown-ups, like books, and that they lectured their parents. Now that's a false sort of art, I said to myself. But as I continued I realized that in this book good behaviour was constantly showered with sweets and bad behaviour constantly ridiculed with punishments. If you are good, you'll get something scrumptious, that's the basis of that morality. Virtue is the *sine qua non* of success. It's enough to make you doubt that Berquin was a Christian.

Un jour que j'avais le cerveau embarbouillé de ce problème à la mode: la morale dans l'art, la providence des écrivains me mit sous la main un volume de Berquin. Tout d'abord je vis que les enfants y parlaient comme de grandes personnes, comme des livres, et qu'ils moralisaient leurs parents. Voilà un art faux, me dis-je. Mais voilà qu'en poursuivant je m'aperçus que la sagesse y était incessamment abreuvée de sucreries, la méchanceté invariablement ridiculisée par le châtiment. Si vous êtes sage, vous aurez du nanan, telle est la base de cette morale. La vertu est la condition *sine qua non* du succès. C'est à douter si Berquin état chrétien.[22]

Indeed, the works most frequently associated with child readers suggest that, like the Australian writer Miles Franklin, who 'early grew superior to gaudily apparelled books designed to lure young minds, and despised pompous pretentious ones for old dullards',[23] such readers found their greatest delight in weighty adult books.[24] Balzac's placing of the Old and New Testaments in the hands of the 5-year-old Louis Lambert, and his evocation of the boundless delights his young hero experiences on reading dictionaries,[25] make him seem less of a prodigy and more of a dullard if we compare the Comtesse de Boigne's throw-away affirmation that she had learnt

---

[21] 'Souvenirs d'enfance'; see also Lamartine, *Confidences*, 82.
[22] *Œuvres complètes*, ii. 42. Compare George Sand, *Historie de ma vie*, 627, and P. Hazard's pithy comment on Berquin: 'he was an ass of the saccharine and pathetic sort' (*Les Livres, les enfants et les hommes*, 39), but for an attempt at rehabilitation see Bravo-Villasante, 'Le Vice et la vertu'.
[23] *Childhood at Brindabella*, 64.
[24] The expression is Baudelaire's: see *Œuvres complètes*, ii. 42.
[25] *Louis Lambert*, 351 and 354.

to read so easily that at 3 she perused and recited for her own pleasure the tragedies of Racine.[26] Nerval, in *Promenades et Souvenirs*, makes his first-person narrator assert that at the age of 8 he was studying Greek, Italian and Latin, German, Arabic, and Persian, and that his favourite poems and poets included *Pastor fido* and *Faust*, Ovid and Anacreon,[27] while the 7-year-old Benjamin Constant 'used to spend eight or ten hours a day reading everything that [his] hand fell on, from the works of La Mettrie to Crébillon's novels' (*lisai[t] huit à dix heures par jour tout ce qui [lui] tombait sous la main, depuis les ouvrages de la Mettrie jusqu'aux romans de Crébillon*).[28] (Whatever doubts we may have about whether these books were actually read, their titles nevertheless contribute to the image of childhood conveyed in nineteenth-century literature.) One could well argue that the talismanic nature of the book is so strong that for many writers evoking childhood—it little matters whether that childhood is ostensibly their own or an imaginary one—the book's title alone serves to reproduce the magic of the world it created. Furthermore, the function of the accumulation of titles produced by writers such as Boucher, Chastenay, and Simon,[29] to mention only these three, seems to be less to give an accurate account of what was read, than to recreate metonymically the atmosphere of childhood through a device common to children's books, that of the list. The enumeration of the fish swimming past the Nautilus as it lies trapped under ice, or of the food Ratty prepares for his first picnic with Mole—' "There's cold chicken inside it", replied the Rat briefly: "coldtonguecold-hamcoldbeefpickledgerkhinssaladfrenchrollscresssandwidgespotted-meatgingerbeerlemonadesoda-water" '[30]—the Mock Turtle's list of school subjects—'Reeling and Writhing, . . . and then the different branches of Arithmetic—Ambition, Distraction, Uglification, and Derision'[31]—both reflect and stimulate the child's simultaneous delight in the multiplicity of objects in the world and the corresponding multiplicity of words in the language.

Certain works, however, are repeatedly mentioned throughout the century in ways suggesting that they, rather than the mere act of

[26] *Mémoires*, i. 71.
[27] *Œuvres complètes*, 467.
[28] *Le Cahier rouge*, in *Œuvres*, 112.
[29] *Souvenirs*, 35–6; *Mémoires*, i. 19–20; *Premières années*, 46–7.
[30] *The Wind in the Willows*, 14.
[31] Carroll, *The Annotated Alice*, 129.

reading itself, did play a significant role in shaping the imaginations of those who read them. Among these, no doubt read in abridged form, was *Don Quixote*. This is the first novel Flaubert remembers having read to him and it is the engravings in a copy of the novel that Frédéric Moreau and little Louise Roque colour in together. Nodier read it in a Spanish version, or rather, as he says: 'I divined what I could not understand.' (*je devinais à défaut de comprendre.*)[32] Stendhal salutes it as a breath of fresh air in the repressive and deeply unhappy atmosphere in which he lived after the death of his mother: 'so I was very deceitful, very wicked, when in the beautiful Claix library I discovered a copy of *Don Quixote* in French. . . . Don Quixote made me die of laughter.' (*j'étais donc fort sournois, fort méchant, lorsque dans la belle bibliothèque de Claix je fis la découverte d'un* Don Quichotte *français. . . .* Don Quichotte *me fit mourir de rire.*)[33] Delécluze, in an autobiography written in the third person, refers to it as the first book placed in his hands and adds: 'it would be hard to put into words the pleasure and intensity of emotions the three young readers experienced on discovering the story of the Knight of the Sorrowful Countenance.' (*il serait difficile d'exprimer le plaisir et la vivacité des émotions que causa aux trois jeunes lecteurs l'histoire du chevalier de la Triste Figure.*)[34] And Anatole France announces, somewhat sententiously, that 'provided one makes large excisions, *Don Quixote* is the most agreeable book into which a 12-year-old mind can plunge' (*est, moyennant de larges coupures, la lecture la plus agréable où puisse se plonger une âme de douze ans*).[35]

Even more frequently referred to is *Robinson Crusoe*. Jules Sandeau, in his children's book, *La Roche aux mouettes*, evokes it as an 'immortal book, the delight of childhood, an education for people of all ages, one of the human mind's rare blessings' (*livre immortel, délice de l'enfance, enseignement de tous les âges, rare bienfait de l'esprit humain*).[36] Daudet's 'Petit Chose' reads and rereads it: 'in the evenings I used to learn it by heart; during the day I had an absolute mania for acting it out.' (*le soir, je l'apprenais par cœur; le jour, je le jouais, je le jouais avec rage.*)[37] The serious-minded Cournot manages to fit it in between his readings of Laplace's *Exposition du système du monde* and the correspondence

---

[32] *Souvenirs de jeunesse*, 12.
[33] *Vie de Henry Brulard*, 108.
[34] *Souvenirs*, 12–13.
[35] *Le Livre de mon ami*, 260.
[36] *La Roche aux mouettes*, 35.
[37] *Le Petit Chose*, 103.

of Leibnitz and Clarke, together with 'other philosophical opuscules' (*d'autres opuscules philosophiques*).[38] And Jules Simon,
despite his isolated childhood in a Brittany village, still manages to
get his hands on a copy and to find in it a source of delight, even if
he subsequently comes to prefer—*horribile dictu*—*Le Robinson
suisse*.[39] Both in the prose poem 'La Solitude' and in 'Le Cygne', the
adult Baudelaire pays passing tribute to Defoe, whose novel he had,
somewhat dramatically, ordered should be handed on to a young
cousin as he himself set sail for Réunion.[40] Rimbaud transforms the
proper name into a verb in his poem 'Roman' and writes his own
intensely imaginative version of the novel in 'Le Bateau ivre'.
Indeed, its popularity and the multiple versions it has continued to
spawn have made it so much a part of the mythology of childhood
reading that R. André seems to speak for many writers in denoting
it as 'a book . . . that clings so closely to my dreams that I felt I knew
it before I read it' (*un livre . . . qui colle si bien à mes rêveries qu'il
me sembla le connaître avant de l'avoir lu*).[41]

A third work is also frequently mentioned: Fénelon's *Télémaque*.
Marie Audoux, in the autobiographical novel *Maire-Clare*, evokes
it as a 'young prisoner [she] would go and visit in secret' (*jeune
prisonnier que j'allais visiter en cachette*),[42] and Louise Chastenay,
having listed Mme de Genlis's comedies, Mme d'Aulnoy's fairy
tales, and several volumes of the *Thousand and One Nights*, adds
rather coyly: 'Will I say that the fables of La Fontaine, will I say
that *Télémaque* added variety to these delights? Nevertheless, it is
the truth and yet I do not boast about it.' (*Dirai-je que les fables de
La Fontaine, dirai-je que Télémaque en variaient les plaisirs? Cela
est vrai et pourtant je ne m'en vante pas.*)[43]

Very few writers, however, explore what it was that these three
works offered their child readers, choosing rather to invoke their
titles in the expectation of touching a cord of recognition so strong
as to need no further explanation. Nevertheless, it would seem that
their prime seduction lay in providing their reader with excitement,

---

[38] *Souvenirs*, 35.
[39] *Premières années*, 46–7.
[40] See Baudelaire's *Correspondance*, i. 88.
[41] *L'Enfant miroir*, 226. The presence of M. Tournier's version, *Vendredi ou les
limbes du pacifique*, confirms the continuing popularity and inspirational power of
the novel.
[42] *Marie-Claire*, 126.
[43] *Mémoires*, i. 20.

in the days before the existence of adventure stories written specifically with children in mind. Moreover, they succeed in combining the attraction of the exotic with the rejection and reforging of the conditions of existence: Telemachus sets out to discover his lost father and thus restore the social balance; Don Quixote refuses to live in a world in which romance and adventure are not everyday occurrences, and therefore systematically replaces the banal with the extraordinary; Robinson's rebellion against his father's demands leads to the shipwreck that obliges him to impose on his new world the conditions of civilized existence. As such they provide the child with both a pattern and a springboard for creating its own, compensatory society,[44] particularly in an age where, as we have seen, so many adults were seeking their places in a rapidly changing world.

If books are frequently a source of seductive pleasure, they can also be a cause of considerable emotional disturbance. Chateaubriand is representative in recording that when he was about 12 years old he came across two works that profoundly shook his vision of existence:

Chance placed in my hands two very different books, an unexpurgated version of *Horace* and a story of *Confessions mal faites*. The disorder into which these two books threw my thoughts is beyond belief: a strange world arose around me. . . . Shaken both physically and morally, I still went on struggling to protect my innocence against the storms of premature passion and the terrors of superstition.

Le hasard fit tomber entre mes mains deux livres bien divers, un *Horace* non châtié et une histoire des *Confessions mal faites*. Le bouleversement d'idées que ces deux livres me causèrent est incroyable: un monde étrange s'éleva autour de moi. . . . Frappé à la fois au moral et au physique, je luttais encore avec mon innocence contre les orages d'une passion prématurée et les terreurs de la superstition.[45]

Michelet recalls a similar experience:

When I was alone in the workshop I used to snatch up the books that had

---

[44] Marthe Robert sees *Robinson Crusoe* and *Don Quixote* as offering the basic models of the two types of novel, that of the pre-Oedipal foundling and that of the post-Oedipal bastard, justifying her argument by reference to Freud's concept of the 'family novel' the child tells himself. Obviously this is too vast a subject to embark on here, but the role of these works in shaping the 19th-century child's imagination cannot be overlooked.

[45] *Mémoires d'outre-tombe*, 78–9.

been left lying about on the floor; they were not always good books. The
fear of being caught may have added to my pleasure. I used to read standing
up, ears pricked; my blood boiled to fever pitch.

Lorsque j'étais seul à l'atelier, je m'emparais des livres qu'on laissait traîner
sur les planches; ils n'étaient pas toujours bons. La crainte d'être surpris
ajoutait peut-être au plaisir. Je lisais debout, l'oreille au guet; mon sang
s'enflammait jusqu'à la fièvre.[46]

And Stendhal's already passionate nature was thrown into a
torment of longing by the discovery of the erotic novel, *Félicia ou
mes fredaines*: 'I went completely mad; possessing a real mistress,
which at that time was my burning desire, could not have plunged
me in such a torrent of pleasure.' (*je devins fou absolument, la
possession d'une maîtresse réelle, alors l'objet de tous mes voeux,
ne m'eût plongé dans un tel torrent de volupté.*)[47] While explicit
scenes of sexuality or violence may propel the child into a world of
terror rather than delight—one thinks of Louise's nightmares when
Frédéric Moreau reads *Macbeth* to her—the work that seems most
strongly to have stirred its youthful readers' feelings is Bernardin de
Saint-Pierre's apparently innocent tale of two children growing to
adolescence in the tropical paradise of Mauritius, *Paul et Virginie*.
While it may strike modern readers as somewhat dull and
melodramatic, there is a splendour in its descriptions of natural
beauty, a great warmth in the relationship between the two
children, and an intensity in its depiction of Virginie's awareness of
herself no longer as a child but as an adolescent verging on
womanhood, and it is presented throughout the century as exerting
considerable power over the imaginations of the children who read
it. If, for Lamartine's Jocelyn, it is merely a 'touching tale/of love
and misfortune' (*touchante histoire/ D'amour et de malheur*),[48] for
Flaubert's Emma it provides the first outline of an image of ideal
love which constantly alters with the works she reads. Here it is 'the
sweet friendship of some good little brother' (*l'amitié douce de
quelque bon petit frère*).[49] Judith Gautier, who had earlier
delighted in 'Little Red Riding Hood', 'because of the wolf' (*à cause
du loup*),[50] is encouraged by her father to read widely but told, in

[46] J. Michelet, *Ma jeunesse*, 66.   [47] *Vie de Henry Brulard*, 197.
[48] *Jocelyn*, quatrième époque, 91.   [49] *Madame Bovary*, 33.
[50] *Le Collier des jours*, 81.

the kind of formulation that can only have encouraged a self-respecting child to read it straightaway, that *Paul et Virginie*

struck him as the most dangerous book in the world for young imaginations. He could remember the burning emotions he himself had experienced on reading it, emotions that had not been equalled by any subsequent impressions caused by reading.

lui paraissait être le livre le plus dangereux qui fût au monde, pour de jeunes imaginations. Il se souvenait de l'émotion brûlante qu'il avait éprouvée, lui-même, en le lisant, et qui n'avait été égalée, plus tard, par aucune impression de lecture.[51]

Goncourt spells out the same opinion in *Chérie*:

the obscene book and the erotic book have no effect on the young French girl. When it happens that a girl is led astray by her reading, it comes about through a sentimental book. . . . The book in which [Chérie] found everything [she needed to be corrupted] was *Paul et Virginie*.

le livre obscène, le livre érotique n'ont aucune action sur la jeune fille française. Quand elle arrive à se perdre par la lecture, elle se perd par un livre sentimental . . . Le livre où [Chérie] trouvait tout [ce qu'il fallait pour la perdre] c'était dans [sic] *Paul et Virginie*.[52]

Paul Adam claims to have experienced an enormous emotion on discovering it,[53] Bosco recalls having been overwhelmed when a neighbour read the novel to him,[54] and Rémusat comments portentously: '[*Paul et Virginie*] may well be the first novel I read and my reading of it did not leave me as it found me.' (*pouvaient bien être le premier roman que j'eusse lu, et cette lecture ne me laissa pas tel qu'elle m'avait trouvé.*)[55]

The book as means of interpretation of the mysterious world in which the child finds itself, the book as coded message, becomes an even more powerful source of delight or disturbance when it is written in a foreign language. For many children, principally boys, given the difference in the education provided for the two sexes, reading works in Latin or Greek was an occasion of powerful pleasure, a pleasure that is only partly connected with the substance of what was read and that derives to a large extent from the sense of

---

[51] Ibid., 248.
[53] *Les Images sentimentales*, 94.
[55] *Mémoires*, 95.

[52] *Chérie*, 149.
[54] *Un oubli moins profond*, 173–4.

a code successfully interpreted. Benjamin Constant provides a remarkable image for this sense of deciphering, in claiming to have learnt Greek at the age of 5 when his tutor encouraged him to invent it as a code: 'all this engraved itself into my head in a wonderful way because I believed I had invented it myself.' (*tout cela se gravait merveilleusement dans ma tête, parce que je m'en croyais l'inventeur.*)[56] Rémusat asserts that nothing amused him more than the *Iliad* and that he read it incessantly up to the age of 10, adding: 'it is frequently through this old master of all poetry [Homer] that children are initiated not only into their first awareness of the feelings, passions, and interests that fill our lives, but even into war and politics.' (*c'est par ce vieux maître de toute poésie que l'enfance est souvent initiée à une première connaissance des sentiments, des passions, des intérêts qui remplissent l'existence et même de la guerre et de la politique.*)[57] The precocious Juliette Adam, who insists that from early childhood she was as familiar with the stories of Homer (in translation) as she was with 'Le Petit Chaperon rouge' and 'Peau-d'Ane', gradually comes to add a passion for Virgil (read in Latin) to her two initial passions: ancient Greece and ancient Gaul.[58] George Sand, however, sounds a warning note in this regard, a note taken up with particular anger by Vallès:

but the French, Latin, and Greek that children are taught take up too much time, whether because they are taught by poor methods or because these are the most difficult languages in the world, or because the study of any language is the driest of exercises for a child.

mais le français, le latin et le grec qu'on apprend aux enfants prennent trop de temps, soit qu'on les enseigne par de mauvais procédés, ou que ce soient les langues les plus difficiles du monde, ou encore que l'étude d'une langue quelconque soit ce qu'il y a de plus aride pour les enfants.[59]

Yet, however powerful the pedagogical or pragmatic arguments, the joy of decoding a foreign language, the seductive entrance into

---

[56] *Le Cahier rouge*, 111.
[57] *Mémoires*, 27.
[58] *Le Roman de mon enfance*, 89. Growing up in a family of widely differing and intensely held beliefs, Juliette Adam presents herself as the target of continual arguments about literature, ranging from Balzac to Goethe, Eugène Suë to Toussenel, Fourier to Mme de Staël.
[59] Sand, *Histoire de ma vie*, i. 710.

an alien existence, remains one of the frequently mentioned joys of nineteenth-century childhood.

Books are often, moreover, associated with the visual arts in providing access to an imaginary or exotic world. Francis Jammes seizes on the power of illustrations to open up what is opaque in the written word, and highlights the way in which great illustrators— one thinks perhaps above all of the combination of Doré and both Dante and Rabelais—can seduce the child into accepting a work whose unembellished written message may otherwise have been too advanced or too dry:

At this time I became acquainted with a book called *Don Quixote* ... that I understood through Tony Johannot who penetrated Cervantes' mind in the same way that Cervantes penetrated the mind of his hero. . . . Two of the most profound geniuses, whose genius is revealed in the smallest fragments of their landscapes, were two Romantics disdainfully abandoned to children, Tony Johannot and Grandville.

Je fis connaissance à cette époque avec un livre qui s'intitule *Don Quichotte* . . . et que j'ai compris à travers Tony Johannot qui a pénétré Cervantes comme Cervantes s'est assimilé son héros. . . . Deux des génies les plus profonds, dans le moindre bout de paysage, furent deux romantiques dédaigneusement abandonnés aux enfants, Tony Johannot et Grandville.[60]

Paul Arène, in his novel *Jean-des-figues*, suggests the way in which a decorated surface, in this case a screen, can encourage the same sorts of day-dreams as can books:

yet one memory floats up above all these forgotten things: M. Antoine's screen. . . . For it was the first to open the world of dream and poetry for me . . . This screen represented a vague landscape in faded colours, littered with fountains, terraced palaces, and great stags.

un souvenir pourtant surnage entre toutes ces choses oubliées: le paravent de M. Antoine. . . . Car lui, le premier, m'ouvrit le monde du rêve et de la poésie . . . Il représentait, ce paravent, un flottant paysage aux couleurs ternies, encombré de jets d'eau, de châteaux en terrasse, de grands cerfs.[61]

Emma Bovary, too, as a young girl, is profoundly influenced by the engravings she comes across in novels and keepsakes lent to her

---

[60] *De l'âge divin*, 142–3. See also Judith Gautier, who discovers both Nodier's tales and Goethe's *Werther* through works illustrated by Tony Johannot (*Le Collier des jours*, 210), and Pierre Loti's evocation of illustrated travel books in *Prime jeunesse*, 24–5.

[61] *Jean-des-figues*, 14.

while she is in the convent. In describing her discovery of these engravings, Flaubert combines the physical and the sentimental, locking together, with characteristic and consummate skill, parody and sympathy in order to convey both the power of the experience and the paltry nature of its cause:

She used to tremble as she blew on the silk paper of the engravings to lift them, and watched them rise up, half folded, and then fall back softly on the page. Behind the balustrade on a balcony would be a young man in a short cloak enfolding in his arms a girl in a white dress.

Elle frémissait, en soulevant de son haleine le papier de soie des gravures, qui se levait à demi plié et retombait doucement contre la page. C'était, derrière la balustrade d'un balcon, un jeune homme en court manteau qui serrait dans ses bras une jeune fille en robe blanche.[62]

Anatole France, in *Le Livre de mon ami*, suggests how rich a source Callot's engravings were for the imagination of his young protagonist: 'I would feast my eyes on these monsters and when I was in my little galleried bed I used to see them again without having the wits to recognize them. Oh the magic of Jacques Callot.' *(Je nourrissais mes yeux de ces monstres, et, quand j'étais couché dans mon petit lit à galerie, je les revoyais sans avoir l'esprit de les reconnaître. O magie de Jacques Callot.)*[63] Yet, as so often with France, the emotional exclamation is made to replace any analysis or even any real evocation. We are left with an affirmation and the sense that a late-Romantic *attendrissement*, which may well have its roots in unacknowledged embarrassment, has prevented the depiction of childhood here from being anything but skin deep.

Two further examples of a child's delight in the visual might be briefly noted, although one occurs in an English childhood and the other was not recounted until the 1960s. The first appears in Ruskin:

the carpet, and what patterns I could find in bed covers, dresses or wallpapers to be examined, were my chief resources and my attention to the particulars in these was soon so accurate, that when at three and a half I was taken to have my portrait painted by Mr Northcote, I had not been ten minutes alone with him before I asked him why there were holes in his carpet.[64]

---

[62] *Madame Bovary*, 35.   [63] *Le Livre de mon ami*, 11.
[64] *Praeterita*, 14.

Julien Green, who had been so moved by an illustration in a Bible of a priest performing a sacrifice that he himself sacrificed his father's top hat, was deeply affected by a painting of a Pharaoh who had killed two slaves for bringing bad news:

The Devil lent my eyes a terrible lucidity for looking at that canvas . . . After the age of 11 I never saw it again, but from 6 to 11 I was often taken to see it and it devastated me. The expression is not too strong. My life may well not have been what it was had it not been for that painting.

Cette toile, l'ennemi me prêtait pour la voir un regard d'une lucidité terrible . . . Après onze ans je ne la revis plus, mais de six à onze ans, je fus mené devant elle à bien de reprises, et elle me ravagea. Le mot n'est pas trop fort. Ma vie n'eût peut-être pas été ce qu'elle fut sans cette toile.[65]

Berlioz poring over maps of the world, Baudelaire's child-figure in in 'Le Voyage' eagerly gazing at prints in the lamplight, or Rimbaud's deliberately naïve view of the distortions produced by conveying three dimensions on the two-dimensional canvas[66] are all unforgettable icons of the child decoding the world of literature and art, but they are also symbols evoking the deciphering of the natural world: Nodier, who claims to have been aware at the age of 12 that his schooling had taught him nothing, attempts to teach himself foreign languages, but, he adds, 'of all the written or rational alphabets I attempted to decipher, none inspired in me such fervour as that of nature' (*de tous les alphabets écrits ou rationnels que j'essayais de déchiffrer, il n'y en avait point qui m'inspirât autant de ferveur que celui de la nature*).[67]

THE WORLD

The child's relationship with the world in which it finds itself, its sense of insertion into a particular physical or social space, and the ways in which it makes meaning of that space are central to the nineteenth-century image of childhood, from the Romantics' vision of the fusion of the child and nature to the Naturalists' depiction of the union of the child and the city.

The child's delight in natural beauty is a central tenet of

[65] *Partir avant le jour*, 49.   [66] *Œuvres complètes*, 121.
[67] *Souvenirs*, 3.

Lamartine's poetry, exemplified by his portrayal of the young Jocelyn spending entire days 'In the garden, in the meadows, in a few green pathways/Worn into the hillsides by the village cattle,/All veiled in hawthorn and wild brambles'. (*Au jardin, dans les près, dans quelques verts sentiers/Creusés sur les coteaux par les bœufs du village,/Tout voilés d'aubépine et de mûre sauvage*).[68] Equally, Chateaubriand's depiction of René and Amélie as children focuses on images of them sharing a love of nature that parallels his own boyhood delight in the seashore at Saint-Malo: 'one of the first pleasures I experienced', René remarks, 'was that of wrestling with the storms, playing with the waves that retreated from me or rushed towards me on the shore.' (*un des premiers plaisirs que j'aie goûtés était de lutter contre les orages, de me jouer avec les vagues qui se retiraient devant moi, ou couraient après moi sur la rive.*)[69] The sense of being at one with nature, and particularly with the kind of landscape that the child first sees, is also a deeply held conviction in the autobiographies of the Provençal writers Bonnet and Mistral, and in Mme de Genlis's mémoires. Stendhal, typically, introduces into this somewhat suspect depiction of the child's untutored appreciation of natural beauty a note of refreshing cynicism: 'one of my father's and M. de Raillane's *literary* failings was to exaggerate constantly the beauties of nature (which these fine souls can have felt but little, they thought only of earning money).' (*un des défauts* littéraires *de mon père et de M. de Raillane était d'exagérer sans cesse les beautés de la nature (que ces belles âmes devaient peu sentir, ils ne pensaient qu'à gagner de l'argent).*)[70] The questions of the extent to which the child intuitively appreciates nature and to what degree beauty is an acquired taste, the product, as Stendhal suggests, of reading in adulthood, or perhaps of a nostalgic re-creation of childhood, are at most only partially answerable, part of the sense we have that the past, even our own, is another country.

For other writers, on the contrary, it is through nature that the child discovers humanity's problematic insertion in a world with which it is rarely in harmony. Central to the depiction Rimbaud gives us in the prose poem 'L'Aube' of the affiliation of child and nature is the poignant sense that the other—human or not—will

---

[68] *Jocelyn*, 90.   [69] *René*, 45.
[70] *Vie de Henry Brulard*, 99.

always elude our grasp. While in 'Sensation', the poet explores a
sense of delightful if future union between nature and child—

> Through the blue evenings of summer, I shall walk along the paths,
> Pricked by the wheat, crushing the fragile grass:
> Dreaming, I shall feel the coolness at my feet.
> I shall let the wind bathe my bare head

> Par les soirs bleus d'été, j'irai dans les sentiers,
> Picoté par les blés, fouler l'herbe menu:
> Rêveur, j'en sentirai la fraîcheur à mes pieds.
> Je laisserai le vent baigner ma tête nue[71]

—the prose poem moves from the triumphant opening declara-
tion—'I have embraced the summer dawn' (*j'ai embrassé l'aube
d'été*)—to the enigmatic, impersonal conclusion: 'on awakening it
was noon' (*au réveil il était midi*).[72] Like Mallarmé's faun, the child
is forced to acknowledge that the sense of harmony with a world in
which stones watch and flowers speak, a world in which it is
possible to touch, however fleetingly, the vast body of dawn, may
belong merely to the domain of dream.

It is the destructive violence of the untamed natural world that
dominates the vision of the foundling Rémi, in Malot's *Sans
famille*, even if this vision can be seen as partly metaphorical and
partly determined by the needs of the plot. During the period when
he is cared for by his foster-mother, nature is reduced to that
clichéd *locus amoenus*, the garden that he cultivates, just as the
reunion with his real family brings with it the corresponding
discovery of a natural space belonging to him, the vast but tamed
family park he inherits. Yet, in the period during which he
undergoes the apprenticeship that culminates in these rich rewards,
his lack of social place is exemplified by the violence of the natural
world in which he finds himself, a world whose howling gales,
freezing temperatures, and blinding snowstorms lead to the deaths
not only of his animal companions but also of Vitalis. Indeed, the
child subjected to the unpredictable vehemence of nature is a
frequent and potentially melodramatic nineteenth-century topic:
Hugo's intensely imaginative depiction of Cosette's fears in the
dark and threatening forest, or Daudet's evocation of Jack's terror
in the unknown woods on his flight from college, are only two

---

[71] *Œuvres complètes*, 6.   [72] Ibid., 140.

examples of the ambivalence of nature and above all of the ways in which the child is seen as fragile victim in a world where beauty itself can appear hostile.

Nature can also be presented as a means of escape from reality. Balzac's character Félix de Vandenesse turns to the beauties of nature when he is refused the love of his family, but whatever the power with which the novelist conveys the child's delight in the evening star, there is always the underlying suggestion that such admiration is merely a *pis-aller*, the substitution of something that will not reject him for someone who has rejected him. Similarly, Vallès's Jacques finds in the countryside a calm, warmth, and love in stark contrast with the quarrelsome, violent, and uncertain emotional atmosphere to which he is accustomed, and Daudet's downtrodden, lonely hero Jack, having escaped from the horrors of the college, enjoys a brief respite of profound happiness in the forest around his mother's home in the country before the jealousy of his surrogate father drives him off to apprenticeship in the infernal forges of Indret.

If delight in the natural world is frequently a substitute for human company, it can also be linked to intellectual pleasures. Two writers in particular indicate the intricate relationship between the child's response to nature and the delight experienced in exploring language.[73] For both Loti and Nodier the child's attempt to understand and assimilate the complexity of the natural world introduces it not merely into a world of sensory beauty but, more importantly, into a lexical treasure-house. For both, the collection of butterflies entails the pleasure of colour and shape, the search for rarity, and the constant hope of discovery, but it also brings the intoxication of a rich and varied nomenclature. Nodier's attempted self-irony merely alerts us here to the intensity of his feelings, an intensity so great as to demand protection, in the form of self-mockery, from potential readerly mockery. He describes his younger self as 'rich and proud because of a few scraps of a fortuitous nomenclature which at least initiated [him] into the language of another universe' (*riche et fier de quelques lambeaux d'une nomenclature hasardée qui [l]'initiait du moins au langage d'un autre univers*).[74] The hypnotic power of this memory is such

[73] In the English-speaking world, the most outstanding example of such a response is provided by Anne in L. M. Montgomery's novel *Anne of Green Gables*.
[74] *Souvenirs de jeunesse*, 24.

that later he returns to it, expanding and embellishing his first reference:

There is something marvellously sweet in this study of nature, which attaches a name to all creatures, a thought to all names, and affection and memories to all thoughts, and he who has not penetrated into the grace of these mysteries may perhaps lack a sense that will allow him to enjoy life. The nomenclatures themselves, the work of an entirely poetic genius and probably humanity's last poetry, have an inexpressible charm when our imaginations are still young enough to feel the prestige of fables and stories.

Il y a quelque chose de merveilleusement doux dans cette étude de la nature, qui attache un nom à tous les êtres, une pensée à tous les noms, une affection et des souvenirs à toutes les pensées et l'homme qui n'a pas pénétré dans la grâce de ces mystères a peut-être manqué d'un sens pour goûter la vie. Les nomenclatures elles-mêmes, œuvre d'un génie tout poétique, et qui sont probablement la dernière poésie du genre humain, ont un charme inexprimable, à cet âge d'imagination où la fable et l'histoire n'ont pas encore perdu leur prestige.[75]

The adult narrative voice in Loti's *Roman d'un enfant* also professes surprise at his childhood passion for 'the learned classifications of Cuvier, Linnaeus, Lamarck, or Brugières' (*les savantes classifications de Cuvier, Linné, Lamarck ou Brugières*), but goes on to recapture the joy of exploring them: 'with what emotion I used to copy out into my notebook opposite the name of a Spirifera or a Terebratula enchanted and sun-drenched words like these: "East coast of Africa, coast of Guinea, Indian Ocean"!' (*avec quelle émotion je transcrivais sur mon cahier, en face du nom d'une Spirifère ou d'un Térébratule, des mots comme ceux-ci, enchantés et pleins de soleil: 'Côte orientale d'Afrique, côte de Guinée, mer des Indes!'*)[76] Reading nature, therefore, offers a pleasure analogous to that experienced in reading literature.

While much of this pleasure derives from the future writer's joy in words, part of the delight in naming the elements of nature stems from a sense that the act of conferring a name allows the child to exert some degree of control over the external world. Fadette easily masters the will-o'-the wisp that had reduced Landry to cowering fear, because she is able to encapsulate it in her little jingle:

[75] Ibid., 40–1.
[76] *Le Roman d'un enfant*, 131.

Fadet, Fadet, little fairy,
Take your candle and your cornet
I have taken my cape and my cloak
Every will-o'-the-wisp has his mate.

Fadet, Fadet, petit fadet,
Prends ta chandelle et ton cornet
J'ai pris ma cape et mon capet
Toute follette a son follet.[77]

Wielding authority over the natural world, taking possession of it
and stamping it, to some extent, with one's own identity, is also one
of the satisfactions the child experiences in a garden.[78] Boylesve, in
an evocation of childhood that deserves to be better known, evokes
the sense of unthreatening mystery a garden can offer a child. Here,
he describes the path to his favourite object, the sundial:

It was situated in the second garden. One reached it by a dozen worn and
shaky stairs in which the daily passage had worn a double path through the
moss. When you put your foot on a certain step, you felt it wobble and you
thought you could hear the faint sound of a mine exploding far away.

Il était situé dans le second jardin. On y accédait par une douzaine de
marches dégradées et branlantes où le passage quotidien avait créé un
double sentier parmi la mousse. Lorsqu'on posait le pied sur une certaine
marche, on la sentait osciller, et l'on croyait entendre le bruit sourd de
l'éclat lointain d'une mine.[79]

Juliette Adam, whose knowledge of the natural world was largely a
product of close observation inspired by her father's reading of
Toussenel's Fourierist study *L'Esprit des bêtes*, affirms that she was
only 9 when she assumed responsibility for her grandparents'
neglected garden, transforming it, with the aid of a gardener, into a
fine fruit and vegetable orchard. Here, as with Malot's Rémi, the
garden affords the child the possibility of providing for the adult
who has hitherto done all the providing, a rare source of gifts
within the child's power to bestow. But the garden has a further
function in *Le Roman de mon enfance*: a privileged space that
opens the child's eyes to what she terms the poetry of snow—'it
was like fairyland, when at sunset these stalactites lit up, gleaming

---

[77] Sand, *La Petite Fadette*, 110.
[78] Access to a garden was, however, largely a matter of class in 19th-century
France.
[79] *L'Enfant à la balustrade*, 35–6.

in the last rays of the sun, and when diamond-like droplets slid down to the very end of their sharp tips' (*c'était féerique, lorsqu'au coucher du soleil ces stalactites s'éclairaient, luisaient sous les derniers rayons du soleil et que glissaient jusqu'à leurs pointes fines des gouttes de diamant*)[80]—it symbolizes the lost paradise of childhood when Juliette's grandmother sells it in order to provide her with a dowry. A further turn to the screw is supplied by the fact that the garden is destroyed to make room for a school Juliette herself will subsequently attend. The passage of child to adult is here epitomized through a series of images revealing the transposition from natural world to artificial space, the substitution of pragmatic values for aesthetic criteria, the metamorphosis from a space the little girl shapes and controls to one that will mould her into marriageable woman.

The garden, therefore, supplies a sense of both beauty and safety which is all the more poignant for being shown as transient. For many nineteenth-century adults, indeed, childhood itself is represented as an enclosed space acting as a safe storehouse of memories. Alexandre Dumas, evoking the cloister of Saint-Rémy, formulates this conviction with imagery fusing the world of literature and that of nature:

What childhood memories lie forgotten by me in the paths and meadows of that enclosure, memories I would rediscover at every step if I were to return there today, like the unfading flowers of diamonds, rubies, and sapphires plucked in the gardens of the *Thousand and One Nights*!

Quels souvenirs d'enfance gisent, oubliés par moi, dans les chemins et les prés de cet enclos, souvenirs que je rédécouvrirais à chaque pas, si j'y retournais aujourd'hui, comme les fleurs inflétries de diamants, de rubies et de sapphires cueillies dans les jardins des *Mille et une nuits*![81]

Lamartine, looking back at the garden at Milly in which he grew up, argues that the space of childhood permanently shapes the individual, forming a secret chamber within the adult rather than remaining attached to any physical structure: 'there is not a tree, not a carnation, not a patch of moss in that garden that has not become encrusted in our souls as if it were part of it.' (*il n'y a pas un arbre, un œillet, une mousse de ce jardin, qui ne soit incrusté dans notre âme comme s'il en faisait partie.*)[82] No one, perhaps, creates a

---

[80] *Le Roman de mon enfance*, 196.
[81] *Mes mémoires*, 69.
[82] *Confidences*, 76.

more elaborate mythology of the effect of outer world on inner world than does George Sand in *Les Maîtres Sonneurs*, the novel in which she attempts to come to terms with the destructive violence and repressive backlash that seemed to be the culmination of the utopian hopes of the 1840s. Given a peasantry either too placid to precipitate change or too violent to impose any new form of stability, she forges from the natural landscapes of the Bourbonnais and the Berrichon an extended metaphor in which permanent social change can result only from uniting the calm and cheerful temperament of those who live in the fertile plains with the melancholy, imaginative, but frequently wild characteristics of those who live in the wooded hills.

For others, the essential shaping space is neither garden nor house but some other structure central to their childhood. Renan, for instance, partly in self-mockery, partly in self-justification, establishes a parallel between the nature of his intellect and the architecture of the cathedral at Tréguier:

That cathedral, a masterpiece of lightness, a mad attempt to give granitic form to an impossible ideal, led me astray first of all. The long hours I spent there are to blame for my complete inability in all things practical.

Cette cathédrale, chef-d'œuvre de légèreté, fol essai pour réaliser en granit un idéal impossible, me faussa tout d'abord. Les longues heures que j'y passais ont été cause de ma complète incapacité pratique.[83]

For Champfleury the determining space is the loft, with its row upon row of cardboard masks, while Paul Arène reveals a close correspondence between the mentality of his hero, Jean-des-figues, and the urban landscape formed by the 'quartier du Rocher' with its 'score of stairway streets, plunging, narrow, spread with a thick bed of box and lavender without which our feet would have slipped, streets that clambered one above the other as in Arab villages' (*vingtaine de rues en escaliers, taillés à pic, étroites, jonchées d'une épaisse litière de buis et de lavande, sans laquelle le pied aurait glissé, et dégringolant les unes par-dessus les autres, comme dans un village arabe*).[84] Both Hugo, in his exploration of the gamin, and Zola, in portraying the foundlings brought up in the city's central market, indicate the relationship between the child's

---

[83] *Souvenirs*, 7.
[84] *Jean-des-figues*, 15.

personality and the urban milieu in which it grows up.

The interplay between the individual and the natural or urban world is further ramified and intensified by the transforming power of the child's imagination. Hugo, in depicting Cosette creating a doll from a sabre, and Edmond de Goncourt describing Chérie telling herself stories that she simultaneously acts out, present from the somewhat lofty vantage-point of adult narration the way in which external space shows itself almost infinitely malleable for the purposes of make-believe. Anatole France, in *Jean Servien*, uses a similar focus to evoke 'that power of illusion that allows children to live in a perpetual miracle and which [in his imagination] transformed a handful of earth and wood into marvellous galleries and fairy-tale castles' (*cette puissance d'illusion qui fait vivre les enfants dans un miracle perpétuel [et qui] fit changer pour lui une poignée de terre et de bois en de merveilleuses galeries, en de châteaux féeriques*).[85] Few writers in the nineteenth century attempt to show this miracle from the child's own viewpoint, either in autobiography or in fiction. France, in *Le Livre de mon ami*, succeeds momentarily in offering us a child's-eye view, only to spoil it by a patronizingly adult comment:

That dining-room offered me a very good representation of a village square. My imagination easily transformed the mahogany dresser, where I changed horses, into the White Horse inn. . . . Confined in this small, dark space, I enjoyed a vast horizon and experienced within these well-known walls the surprises that constitute the charm of travel. This was because in those days I was a great magician. . . . Since then I have had the misfortune to lose this precious gift.

Cette salle à manger me représentait très bien une place de village. Le buffet d'acajou où je relayais me semblait sans difficulté l'auberge du Cheval-Blanc. . . . Confiné dans un petit espace sombre, je jouissais d'un vaste horizon et j'éprouvais, entre des murs connus, ces surpris qui font le charme des voyages. C'est que j'étais alors un grand magicien. . . . J'ai eu, depuis, le malheur de perdre ce don précieux.[86]

Perhaps only Rimbaud, in 'Le Bateau ivre', succeeds in suggesting how what an adult might perceive as merely a toy ship, 'as fragile as a May butterfly' (*frêle comme un papillon de mai*), floating in the

---

[85] *Jean Servien*, 9.
[86] *Le Livre de mon ami*, 103.

cold and dirty water of a puddle, can offer a child direct access to
the Poem of the Sea, steeped in stars, and allow him to perceive
what men have only thought they have perceived.[87]

FOOD

If there is one aspect of the external world more than any other that
symbolizes the child's awareness both of being inserted in a context
and of being able through the power of imagination to transcend
that context, albeit briefly, it is surely food. John Clare's brilliant
evocation of childhood can provide us with a link between the
power of the imagination and the delight and pain of food:

> The mallow seed became a cheese
> The henbanes loaves of bread
> A burdock leaf our table cloth
> On a table stone was spread
> The bind weed flower that climbs the hedge
> Made us a drinking glass
> & there we spread our merry feast
> Upon the summer grass.[88]

A source of intense pleasure or profound repugnance, a means of
self-assertion for the child or of discipline for the adult in charge of
the child, food is one of the clearest ways in which the child
becomes aware of its individuality, of its relationship with the
external world, and of the rules and conventions of adult society, as
a passage from *Alice in Wonderland* illustrates:

> 'I like the Walrus best,' said Alice: 'because he was a little sorry for the
> poor oysters.'
> 'He ate more than the Carpenter, though,' said Tweedledee. 'You see he
> held his handkerchief in front, so that the Carpenter couldn't count how
> many he took: contrariwise.'
> 'That was mean!' Alice said indignantly. 'Then I like the Carpenter
> best—if he didn't eat so many as the Walrus.'
> 'But he ate as many as he could get,' said Tweedledum.
> This was a puzzler. After a pause, Alice began, 'Well! They were both
> very unpleasant characters—.'[89]

[87] *Œuvres complètes*, 66–9.
[88] 'Childhood', in *Poetry*.
[89] Carroll, *The Annotated Alice*, 236–7.

Alice, as naive reader responding instantly to the tale of the Walrus and the Carpenter by attempting to apportion sympathy and blame, finds herself confronted with a series of moral dilemmas, among which is the uncomfortable awareness that the pleasure of eating oysters is obtained only at the expense of the oyster's life: death, as so often in Carroll's rich broth, bubbles briefly to the surface. Small wonder that Alice, caught between gluttony and pretence, action and intention, should respond by condemning both parties, and with them adult values.

Food, as a means by which one group emphasizes its power over another, as the Walrus and the Carpenter overpower the oysters, is frequently reflected in the eyes of French fictional children, in an age when literature both recorded, and attempted to influence, social change. For some of the autobiographers, in particular, the description of the kinds of meals they ate in childhood is presented as serving above all a documentary purpose, a means of anchoring a form of life on the point of disappearing for ever. The peasant Guillaumin's *Vie d'un simple* etches a kind of existence he claims to be utterly different from that experienced by 'today's spoiled and coddled children' (*les petits d'aujourd'hui qu'on dorlote et qu'on choie*), and lingers over the eternal soup that peasants of his day used to eat: 'soup was our main fare; onion soup in the morning and evening, and at noon, potato soup, bean soup, or pumpkin soup, with the tiniest knob of butter.' (*la soupe était notre pitance principale; soupe à l'oignon le matin et le soir, et, dans le jour, soupe aux pommes de terre, aux haricots et à la citrouille, avec gros comme rien de beurre.*)[90] Marmontel, in mémoires which rush over childhood with a speed indicative of embarrassment, nevertheless lingers longingly over an idyllic pastoral evocation of food:

the small farm's grain harvest provided for our basic needs: the wax and honey, from bees carefully cultivated by one of my aunts, was an inexpensive bonus; oil crushed from our own walnuts while they were fresh had a taste and smell that we preferred to those of olive oil. Our buckwheat cakes, moistened, while still hot, with good Mont d'Or butter, were for us a most delicious feast. I cannot imagine what dishes we would have preferred to our own turnips and chestnuts . . . I remember, too, the smell that wafted from a fine quince which had been roasted under the ashes.

---

[90] *La Vie d'un simple*, 24, 7.

la récolte des grains de la petite métairie assuraient notre subsistance: la cire et le miel des abeilles, que l'une de mes tantes cultivait avec soin, étaient un revenu qui coûtait peu de frais; l'huile exprimée de nos noix encore fraîches, avait une saveur, une odeur que nous préférions au goût et au parfum de celle de l'olive. Nos galettes de sarrasin, humectées, toutes brûlantes, de ce bon beurre du Mont d'Or, étaient pour nous le plus friand régal. Je ne sais pas quel mets nous eût paru meilleur que nos raves et nos châtaignes . . . Je me souviens aussi du parfum qu'exhalait un beau coing rôti sous la cendre.[91]

For other writers the documentary value seems a far less pressing concern: their interest centres more on capturing, however briefly, the sense of delight provoked by certain kinds of food. One thinks, for instance, of Marie d'Agoult's affirmation that the true food of children and school pupils is that produced by Germany, or Rimbaud's miraculous formulation: 'sweeter to children than the flesh of sour apples' (*plus douce qu'aux enfants la chair des pommes sures*).[92] For others, predictably, certain types of food could be a source of disgust, making the child suddenly aware both of its vulnerability and of its powerlessness to prevent the world's incursions.[93] Food therefore comes to carry a moral weight, as the child is deprived of what it likes and forced to eat what it dislikes. Chateaubriand speaks briefly of his parents' severity: 'certain foods disgusted me: I was forced to eat them. . . . There is a great difference between those severe parents and today's child-spoilers.' (*j'avais une répugnance pour certains mets: on me forçait d'en manger. . . . Il y a loin de ces parents sévères aux gâte-enfants d'aujourd'hui.*)[94] Vallès's Jacques is far less restrained. Indeed, no nineteenth-century writer explores more vehemently the link between children and the oppressed through the ways in which food is used as a means of asserting power. The chapter 'Frottage— Gourmandise—Propreté', whose parodic title, as we have seen, insists on a political dimension to the domestic situation, provides brilliant examples of his narrative technique and the way in which it slips from the voice of the child to that of the adult:

A curse on onions . . .

[91] *Mémoires*, 6.
[92] *Œuvres complètes*, 66.
[93] See e.g. Jeanne Bouvier's account of her reaction to soup in *Mes mémoires*, 39, and compare Marie Cardinal's evocation in *Les Mots pour le dire*, 214 ff.
[94] *Mémoires d'outre-tombe*, 47.

Every Tuesday and Friday, it was mashed onions and for seven years I could not eat mashed onions without feeling sick.
That vegetable disgusts me.
Like a rich child! Yes, indeed!—Stuck-up little thing, I allowed myself to dislike this and that, to turn up my nose when I was given something I did not like. *I would listen to myself* and above all focus on my feelings, and the smell of onion turned my stomach—what I called my stomach, of course, for I am not sure that the poor are allowed stomachs.
'You've got to *force yourself*!' my mother would cry. 'You do it on purpose', she used to add, 'just as you always do.'

Je maudis l'oignon . . .
Tous les mardis et vendredis, on mange du hachis aux oignons, et pendant sept ans je n'ai pas pu manger de hachis aux oignons sans être malade.
J'ai le dégoût de ce légume.
Comme un riche! mon Dieu, oui!—Espèce de petit orgueilleux, je me permettrais de ne pas aimer ceci, cela, de rechigner quand on donnait quelque chose qui ne me plaisait pas. *Je m'écoutais*, je me sentais surtout, et l'odeur de l'oignon me soulevait le cœur,—ce que j'appellais mon cœur, comprenons-nous bien; car je ne sais pas si les pauvres ont le droit d'avoir un cœur.
'Il faut *se forcer*, criait ma mère. Tu le fais exprès, ajoutait-elle, comme toujours.'[95]

The child's individuality, its right to have likes and dislikes, are thrust under here, firstly in the indeterminate 'it was mashed onions', which subsumes Jacques into the family, then by the phrase 'the poor', which defines him in terms of class and denies him the right to differentiate himself from that class. The polyphonic device of the intertwining voices joins with the slippage of tenses, from present, to iterative past, to past historic, in revealing the permanence of memory, the ineradicability of childhood in the adult personality. But the moral the child draws has nothing to do with tailoring one's passions to suit one's cloth:

I loved leeks.
What of it?—I hated onions and loved leeks. They would be snatched from my mouth, as a gun is snatched from a criminal's hands, as a cup of poison is snatched from a wretch who wants to commit suicide.
'Why can't I eat leeks?' I would ask, in tears.

[95] *L'Enfant*, 128. Original ellipses.

'Because you like them,' would reply that woman of good sense who did not want her son to have passions.

Thou wilst eat of the onion because it makes thee ill, thou wilst not eat of the leek, because thou lovest it.

'Do you like lentils?'

'I don't know . . . '

J'aimais les poireaux.

Que voulez-vous?—Je haïssais l'oignon, j'aimais les poireaux. On me les arracha de la bouche, comme on arrache un pistolet des mains d'un criminel, comme on enlève la coupe de poison d'un malheureux qui veut se suicider.

'Pourquoi ne pourrai-je pas en manger? demandais-je en pleurant.

—Parce que tu les aimes', répondait cette femme pleine de bon sens, et qui ne voulait pas que son fils eût des passions.

Tu mangeras de l'oignon parce qu'il te fait mal, tu ne mangeras pas de poireaux, parce que tu les adores.

'Aimes-tu les lentilles?'

—Je ne sais pas . . . '[96]

Professing ignorance of individual preference is by far the safer option.

Similarly, food can be the means through which the child discovers its place in a hierarchical society. However much Baudelaire, for example, might reject the saccharine image of the child that dominates early Romantic writing, particularly in regard to its sexual awareness, in 'Les Yeux des pauvres', he nevertheless uses children to symbolize the working-class poor, dazzled by the conspicuous consumption of France's Second Empire. Faced with the glittering new café in which 'all of history and mythology [are] placed at the service of gluttony' (*toute l'histoire et toute la mythologie [sont] mises au service de la goinfrerie*),[97] Baudelaire's examples of urban poverty, the middle-aged father and his two young children, respond with a carefully differentiated admiration, the adult aware that 'all the gold of the poor has settled on these walls' (*tout l'or du pauvre monde est venu se porter sur ces murs*) while the older child recognizes that 'it is a house you can enter only if you are not like us' (*c'est une maison où peuvent seuls entrer les gens qui ne sont pas comme nous*) and the younger merely conveys 'a mindless and profound joy' (*une joie stupide et profonde*) which

---

[96] *L'Enfant*, 129–30. Original ellipses.
[97] *Œuvres complètes*, i. 318.

his command of language cannot yet put into words. However contrived Baudelaire's allegory may be here, the image offers an unforgettable indication of how gluttony, alimentary or otherwise, is seen as a confirmation of class status, and how that confirmation is registered as such as soon as the individual proceeds beyond the stage of finding pleasure in merely looking on at a ceremony from which that individual is excluded by his or her very nature.

While Baudelaire's prose poem may seem to border on the precious, with its over-evident symbols and its petulant rejection of the poet's mistress for refusing to provide the poet with a mirror of his own thoughts, nevertheless, in his counterpart piece to 'Les Yeux des pauvres' he offers a far more ferocious exploration of the nexus of childhood, food, and social class. In 'Le Gâteau' the narrative voice is more sharply ironized, more clearly ridiculed for its typically Romantic responses to sublime nature and its Rous-seauesque tendency to believe in man's innate goodness. Once again, the narrator finds himself the object of a child's eyes, eyes that are 'hollow, wild, and, one might say, begging' (*creux, farouches et comme suppliants*), with the 'one might say' (*comme*) providing us with sufficient indication of the narrator's personality to know that mere need will not stimulate a response from him. Indeed, it is the child's linguistic slip, in designating as cake the narrator's 'almost white bread' (*pain presque blanc*), that prompts this Romantic but uncharitable soul to give alms. It is typical of Baudelaire's ironic twisting of cliché that it also sparks off, on the immediate arrival of a second child, the epic battle for possession of the bread. The self-ironizing narrative voice depicts this battle through a series of mini-parodies, moving from classical epic through realism to the pompous heaviness of bourgeois material-ism: 'the cake's legitimate owner attempted to sink his little claws into the usurper's eyes.' (*le légitime propriétaire du gâteau essaya d'enfoncer ses petites griffes dans les yeux de l'usurpateur.*)[98] His adult, middle-class response falls characteristically short of what might be expected, for just as in 'Les Yeux des pauvres' the narrator, instead of taking any positive steps to assist the poor to whose gaze he has been subjected, merely turns to his beloved for confirmation of his emotions, so here, far from attempting to separate the combatants or simply providing a second piece of

[98] Ibid., i. 298.

bread, he merely remarks to his adult reader that 'this spectacle spoiled [his] pleasure in the landscape' (*ce spectacle [l]'avait embruni le paysage*).[99]

The reader will also have noticed the subtext underpinning the description of the bread disintegrating into crumbs, for this is one of the classic themes of the fairy tale, translated into adult form by Balzac in *La Peau de chagrin*. The gift one most wanted becomes that which is most destructive, the object one longed to touch disintegrates in one's hands, the classic invitation to make three wishes is invariably subverted, and there can be, to use Douglas Hofstadter's term, no 'metawishes',[100] no wish that the three wishes become an infinite number. In the context of 'Les Dons des fées', the narrator of 'Le Gâteau' is transmuted into a fairy godmother whose gift is not merely useless, as was the case with the godmother who presented 'the gift of pleasing' (*le don de plaire*),[101] but destructive, while the child's gift of an inappropriate signifier leads to the negation of the signified. Unpleasant characters, in both senses of the word. For all its irony, the poem appears to deconstruct into an assertion of the impossibility of sharing, and the folly of reaching for a cake when your class condemns you to black bread. The complexity of Baudelaire's response to the social conditions of his age thus finds, in his depiction of the theme of children and food, a further sardonic twist, as sardonic indeed as that of 'Assommons les pauvres', with its narrator beating the beggar 'with the obstinate energy of cooks trying to tenderize a steak' (*avec l'énergie obstinée des cuisiniers qui veulent attendrir un beefteack*).[102]

The extent to which children perceive food as central to the bourgeois system of mercantile values is also a theme explored by Balzac and Zola. In a patently tear-jerking picture of childhood estrangement and ostracization, Balzac's first-person narrator of *Le Lys dans la vallée*, Félix de Vandenesse, draws on the rich culinary heritage of Touraine, and particularly its *rillettes* and *rillons*, to delineate the vast difference between his ill-stocked lunch-box and the abundant provisions of his classmates, and thus indicates how poorly his mother provides for him in terms of maternal love:

---

[99] *Œuvres complètes*, i. 299.
[100] *Gödel, Escher, Bach*, 109–16.
[101] *Œuvres complètes*, i. 307.
[102] Ibid., i. 358.

In Tours that preparation [the famous potted pork-meats of Tours] rarely appeared on aristocratic tables; if I had heard people talk of it before I was sent to school, I had never experienced the happiness of seeing that brown jam spread for me on a piece of bread and butter; but even if it had not been in fashion at my school, my desire for it would have been none the less keen, for it had become an obsession, like the desire that possessed one of the most elegant duchesses of Paris for the stews cooked by her gatekeeper . . . Children can divine longing in other people's eyes just as you can read love in them: I therefore became a prime target for mockery.

cette préparation [les célèbres rillettes et rillons de Tours] paraît rarement à Tours sur les tables aristocratiques; si j'en entendis parler avant d'être mis en pension, je n'avais jamais eu le bonheur de voir étendre pour moi cette brune confiture sur une tartine de pain mais elle n'aurait pas été de mode à la pension, mon envie n'en eût pas été moins vive, car elle était devenue comme une idée fixe, semblable au désir qu'inspiraient à l'une des plus élégantes duchesses de Paris les ragoûts cuisinés par les portières . . . Les enfants devinent la convoitise dans les regards aussi bien que vous y lisez l'amour: je devins alors un excellent sujet de moquerie.[103]

It is the central and apparently humdrum theme of the *rillettes* that sets in train this complex network of metaphors and allows Balzac to play with class distinctions, with aspects of desire (longing is as easily decipherable for children as love is for adults), with ways in which children are as susceptible as adults to the sway of the obsession. Equally revealing of children's conceptions of the power base of adult society is Zola's depiction in *Germinal* of Jeanlin, whose sexual and intellectual precociousness allows him to ape adult modes of repression in his relationships with other children and thus to offer a particularly mordant comment on the patterns of dominance and subservience Zola portrays in the mining company. Étienne, discovering Jeanlin's well-stocked larder at a time when the miners are on the verge of starvation, finds his own half-baked revolutionary ideas rebounding back at him, from a mind that has instantly seized the elements of capitalism:

'Don't you know you're a pig to stuff yourself like that? . . . and what about the others?'
'Well, why are the others so stupid?'
'What's more, you're certainly right to hide, because if your Dad discovered you were stealing, he'd really fix you.'
'You're not going to tell me the bourgeois don't steal from us! You're the

103 *Le Lys dans la vallée,* 20.

one who's always saying so. When I filched this loaf from Maigrat, you can bet your life it was a loaf he owed us.'

Sais-tu que c'est cochon de t'empiffrer! . . . Et les autres, tu n'y songes pas?

—Tiens! pourquoi les autres sont-ils trop bêtes?

—D'ailleurs, tu as raison de te cacher, car si ton père apprenait que tu voles, il t'arrangerait.

—Avec ça que les bourgeois ne nous volent pas! C'est toi qui le dit toujours. Quand j'ai chipé ce pain chez Maigrat, c'était bien sûr un pain qu'il nous devait.[104]

Small wonder that Étienne, mouth full, falls silent before the child's cunning insight into social Darwinism. Juliette Adam, using sugar lumps to bribe her small friends into joining her Fourierist *phalanstères*, Richard-Lenoir finding the strength of will to save his walnuts to plant rather than eating them immediately, and Paul Adam, affirming in *Les Images sentimentales*, perhaps with the help of hindsight, that 'the bold luxury of sweet shops initiated me into inductive thinking. There I acquired faith in immeasurable riches' (*le luxe hardi des boutiques à gâteaux m'initia aux idées inductives. Là j'acquis la foi en des richesses incommensurables*)[105] are further examples of children reaching a sudden understanding of social forces through the medium of food.

Food can also be a vehicle for a moral message, as it is for the child Banville when his grandfather, convinced that adults should always strive to make children happy, urges him to remember that if ever he has both a piece of bread and a piece of cake, he should eat the cake first in case he should not live long enough to eat both.[106] Augustus Hare was less fortunate:

the most delicious puddings were talked of—*dilated* on—until I became, not greedy, but exceedingly curious about them. . . . They were put on the table before me, and then, just as I was going to eat some of them, they were snatched away, and I was told to get up and carry them off to some poor person in the village.[107]

Whether deprived of food it likes or forced to eat food it hates, the child frequently comes to associate the act of eating with an

[104] *Les Rougon-Macquart*, iii. 1370.
[105] *Les Images sentimentales*, 5.
[106] *Mes souvenirs*, 13.
[107] *The Story of my life*, 27.

invasion of individuality, brilliantly portrayed by Lewis Carroll, of course, when the cake with the words 'EAT ME' ('beautifully marked in currants') leads Alice to 'open out like the largest telescope that ever was'.[108] Predictably enough, perhaps, it is in the writing of the comtesse de Ségur that we find some of the richest examples of the associations such invasive food summons up in the child's mind, from horror to delight. The horror is rendered all the more forceful by the very flatness of Ségur's style when she describes an episode in which schoolboys watch their teachers prepare to eat:

Old Nick lifted the lid and really did see something black floating in the tureen; he drove in his fork and with great difficulty pulled out a cat, an enormous cat, the *surveillant*'s black cat. Everyone screamed in horror and terror.

Old Nick enleva le couvercle et vit flotter réellement quelque chose de noir dans la soupière; il piqua avec sa fourchette et retira avec grande peine un chat, un énorme chat, le chat noir du surveillant. Chacun poussa un cri d'horreur et de terreur.[109]

Horror can also be created by the contrast between expectation and fact, as when Sophie places her mother's goldfish on a plate and proceeds to cut them into pieces and salt them. Again the style remains resolutely matter-of-fact, over-explanatory:

at the first cut of the knife the unfortunate fish squirmed in despair but they soon became motionless, for they were dying. After the second fish, Sophie realized that she was killing them by cutting them into bits; she looked worriedly at the fish she had salted; not seeing them move, she examined them closely and saw that they were all dead.

au premier coup de couteau les malheureux poissons se tordaient en désespérés mais ils devenaient bientôt immobiles, parce qu'ils mouraient. Après le second poisson, Sophie s'aperçut qu'elle les tuait en les coupant en morceaux; elle regarda avec inquiétude les poissons salés; ne les voyant pas remuer, elle les examina attentivement et vit qu'ils étaient tous morts.[110]

Undercurrents of death, physical and spiritual, run throughout Ségur's writing, in which the passage from childhood to maturity is offered as an allegory for that from earth to heaven,[111] but this

---

[108] *The Annotated Alice*, 33–5.
[109] *Un bon petit diable*, 160. The *surveillant* is an adult employed as a monitor in the school.
[110] Ségur, *Les Malheurs de Sophie*, 27.
[111] See L. Kreyder, *L'Enfance des saints et des autres*, 201 ff.

specific linking of food and death suggests an unconscious and unspoken unease about the relationship between man and animal that points forward to Alice's position in regard to the oysters. Yet Mme de Ségur's ability to create and occupy common ground with children also allows her to convey the child's simple delight both in food and in beautiful and appropriate utensils. Blondine, accompanied by the doe, Bonne-Biche, and the cat, Beau-Minon, is delighted both by the richness of her own table setting and by the presence of 'a bunch of carefully chosen grass, fresh and succulent' (*une botte d'herbes choisies, fraiches et succulentes*) for Bonne-Biche and, for Beau-Minon, 'a golden bowl, full of little fried fish and snipe drumsticks' (*une écuelle en or, pleine de petits poissons frits et de cuisses de bécassines*).[112] This freedom to enjoy a delight in food without being made to feel guilty and without being forced to register gratitude is granted to very few children in French literature of the time.

The consumption of certain types of food is also associated in the child's mind with adult privilege and, therefore, with certain social patterns: Kay, in Masefield's *The Midnight Folk*, told that pork pie for breakfast will make him billious and unable to do his French; the child in 'Les Yeux des pauvres', knowing that the delights of the café are not for such as him; Vallès's Jacques, obliged to consume mutton day in day out to finish up the roast his parents taste only twice, are all made aware, through food, of incomprehensible and apparently unquestionable inequalities. Hence, no doubt, the delight in illicit feasts, particularly at midnight, which allow the child to appropriate not only adult behavioural patterns but also a space and a time normally the preserve of the grown-up. Jacques and his father, each equally stripped of individuality through the destructive moral code by which Mme Vingtras attempts to prove her social worth, celebrate a brief moment's escape from her tutelage with a meal associated with linguistic forms that also mark a short-lived revolt:

'Why don't we have a bite to eat? Those pig's trotters are whispering sweet nothings to me and I wouldn't mind answering them back.'
That's pretty bold language for a grade seven teacher but the Headmaster of Saint-Étienne is far away, the Headmaster of Nantes isn't here yet, and the pig's trotters offer their odorous toes. Oh! I can still taste

[112] *Histoire de Blondine*, 34.

that Sainte-Menehould sauce, with its scent of oil and vinegar and the bouquet of the white wine that washed it down! . . .
The light of my youth fades, my mother has woken up!

'Si nous cassions une croûte? Ces pieds de cochon me disent quelque chose; j'ai envie de leur répondre deux mots.'

C'est un langage hardi pour un professeur de septième; mais le proviseur de Saint-Étienne est loin; le proviseur de Nantes n'est pas encore là, et les pieds de cochon tendent leurs orteils odorants. Oh! j'ai encore le goût de la sauce Sainte-Menehould, avec son parfum de ravigote, et le fumet du vin blanc qui l'arrosa! . . . ma jeunesse s'éteint, ma mère est éveillée![113]

The father, temporarily freed because he is between posts, and Jacques, briefly eluding his mother's eye, express their fleeting defiance in terms of food, a ceremonial proclamation. Gilberte Swann, however, in mirroring with her young friends the behavioural patterns of her parents, loses her identity to become absorbed in her family name, as the cake and its trappings become a statement partly of social status, partly of the idiosyncrasies of the Swann family: 'the majestic nature of the chocolate cake, surrounded by a circle of cake-plates and small grey damask napkins, with designs printed on them, demanded by good breeding and particular to the Swann family' (*la majesté du gâteau au chocolat, entouré d'un cercle d'assiettes à petits fours et de petites serviettes damassées grises à dessins, exigées par l'étiquette et particulières aux Swann*).[114] Here, the children simply define themselves in terms of their parents and their class.

But, if there is one area in a nineteenth-century child's experience where the general unhappiness of its situation is made even worse by having to eat in public, it is certainly the boarding-school. Rémusat's angry indictment speaks for countless others here:

I considered that our dining hall, although it was a former chapel with a lofty ogival vault, smacked of bars and cabarets, that the pupils' manners were poor and somewhat crude, and that the cooking was detestable.

Je trouvais que notre réfectoire, qui était pourtant une ancienne chappelle à voûte ogivale très haute, sentait la gargotte et le cabaret, que les élèves avaient des manières rudes et un peu sales, et que la cuisine était détestable.[115]

---

[113] *L'Enfant*, 233–4.
[114] Proust, *A la recherche*, i. 506.
[115] *Mémoires de ma vie*, 71.

Indeed, however multifarious the responses to food, the image of the school that nineteenth-century representations of childhood provide is almost universally condemnatory.

SCHOOL

The nineteenth century in France saw itself as an age of education, the Third Republic in particular delighting in the sobriquet, 'the Teachers' Republic'.[116] In the course of the century the secondary syllabus was altered no fewer than fifteen times and the relative increase both in literacy and in the general availability and affordability of books was unprecedented. Influential teachers and enthusiastic theorists abounded. Yet the image of the school both in fiction and in autobiographies is almost always associated with boredom, humiliation, deep unhappiness, and, not infrequently, indignant anger. While the ability to read and the discovery of literature were, as we have seen, sources of vast delight for the majority of those who came to write about childhood, literacy for the masses was perceived by many educationalists and politicians less as a means of discovery and pleasure than, to quote H. J. Graff, as 'the most effective vehicle for the creation and maintenance of the moral economy and the moral society'.[117] Moreover, as Graff claims, 'reading and writing were seldom seen as ends in themselves or valued as individual attainments; indeed, undirected, they were thought to be dangerous and subversive'.[118] Furthermore, the kinds of works children were made to read at school were selected in such a way as to reinforce the élitist, bourgeois culture and to devalorize the myths, traditions, and patois of rural communities and of the working classes.[119] And, while the Third Republic in particular witnessed a wave of publications exemplifying new teaching methods and conveying the essence of the sciences in terms

---

[116] Education in France is of course a vast subject. As Furet and Ozouf claim, the passionate interest in the history of teaching and of schools goes back to the Restoration and continues throughout the century (*Lire et écrire*, 14). Useful introductions and bibliographical information can be found in Anderson, Arnold, Durkheim, Furet and Ozouf, Prost, and Zeldin, *Intellect and Pride*.

[117] *The Literacy Myth*, 33.

[118] Ibid., 48.

[119] See Furet and Ozouf, *Lire et écrire*, 48.

accessible to young children,[120] Anderson asserts that it remains the case that whereas 'a large section of the French upper classes received a scientific rather than a literary training throughout the nineteenth century, . . . the idea that science should be part of general education was slow to develop'.[121] Moreover, many college teachers were themselves only poorly educated and the profession as a whole, but particularly primary teaching, attracted little esteem and low wages.

There are, of course, depictions of children, in all social classes, for whom school was a source of great joy or a key to success. Arène, in his novel *Jean-des-figues*, manages to transform school-days into an image of freedom and beauty by making his first-person narrator exclaim: 'Let who will curse school! For me that hated name is associated only with long rambles in the fields and memories of flowering hedges.' (*Maudisse le collège qui voudra! ce nom exécré ne me rappelle que longues courses dans les champs et souvenirs de haies fleuries.*)[122] Yet the comparison with what is expected—'that hated name'—and the evocation of what he associates with school tends more to point to a grim reality deliberately thrust below a somewhat tinselly surface. More convincing are the assertions of a future primary-school teacher, Charles Brun, who describes a mountain community with such a long-standing love of education that each winter a teacher was hired to run what was called a 'little school' (*petite école*).[123] Here the sense of a tradition that welcomed education and a society where everyone took turns to provide for the teacher's bed and board, together with an educational programme that addressed itself specifically to what was useful—reading and writing for girls, with the addition of 'figuring' for boys—suggests a relatively happy relationship both between pupil and teacher and between learner and what was learnt, a relationship dependent on the needs and demands of a small community rather than on dictates emanating from Paris. The political implications of education can also transform the image it leaves behind. Thus, schooling, even at its

[120] See e.g. the publications of Biart, Pape-Carpentier, and especially Macé.
[121] *Education in France*, 59.
[122] *Jean-des-figues*, 19.
[123] *Trois plumes au chapeau*, 39. The title refers to the tradition of teachers wearing one feather in their hat if they could teach reading, two if they could also teach their pupils to write, and a third to indicate that they were capable of teaching all three basic skills.

most basic, is presented by the mason and trade-union activist, Nadaud, as a means of strengthening the power of the workers and enabling the establishment of literacy classes run for workers by workers, where once again control lies with the specific group rather than with the government.[124] Adults whose political tendencies were élitist and right-wing are, predictably, more likely to evoke school-days with approbation. The doughty literary critic Nisard has no time for those who find school less than congenial: 'How could I not like the school régime, and when I hear people attack it, how could I not defend it?' (*Comment n'aimerais-je pas le régime du collège, et quand je l'entends attaquer, comment n'en prendrais-je pas la défense?*),[125] yet even he has to admit that 'in those days, for a school graduate, there were, as people said, only two career openings, giving lessons or writing for the newspapers' (*à cette époque, pour un lauréat de collège, il n'y avait, comme on dit, que deux débouchés, donner des leçons ou écrire dans les journaux*).[126] Perhaps the most interesting of these affirmations of the value of contemporary schooling is Morillon's *Souvenirs de Saint-Nicolas*, with its almost hagiographic evocation of the changes wrought by the arrival of Dupanloup as the school's headteacher. Drawing on the Jesuit principles of competition and their belief that teachers should be concerned for all aspects of the child, from soul to shoe-laces as he put it,[127] Dupanloup, according to Morillon, transformed 'boredom, listlessness, suffering' (*l'ennui, l'atonie, la souffrance*) into 'ardour, emulation, hope' (*ardeur, émulation, espérance*).[128] The kind of adulation certain teachers undoubtedly both inspired and encouraged transformed them into substitute father-figures and forged their pupils into closely knit peer groups in which children found the ideal, or at least idealized, family that, according to Freud, forms the substance of the young child's 'family story'. Moreover, it encouraged that sense of belonging to a particular generation that is such a remarkable

[124] *Mémoires de Léonard*, 206.
[125] *Souvenirs*, 205.
[126] Ibid., 298. The question of the disparity between the large numbers of qualified young men and the small numbers of satisfying posts is examined in Spitzer, *The French Generation of 1820*, 206–24.
[127] *Souvenirs de Saint-Nicolas*, 23. On the influence of the Jesuits on French education see esp. Durkheim.
[128] Ibid., 3 and 31.

feature in the power structures that developed in France in the nineteenth century.[129]

Nevertheless, despite the occasional enthusiastic testimonials, the majority of writers exploring childhood, no matter at what stage in the century, emphasize a very different response, summed up by the prince de Joinville in the brief phrase 'Woe is me' (*Ay di mi*).[130] Even leaving aside those fictional works where the teacher is seized on as an easy target for somewhat facile ridicule,[131] the school provides many nineteenth-century writers with an archetypal symbol of restriction, humiliation, isolation, and despair, where, through a kind of perverse mirroring, such images as the happy enclosure provided by the garden, or the delightful escape offered by the book, are transformed into images of physical and intellectual imprisonment. Where reading opened new vistas of space and time, real or imaginary, and unfolded for the child an apparently boundless range of future possibilities and models, school was the vehicle whereby society imposed its will and its fetters on the child's mind and body. For most nineteenth-century writers dealing with children, the years at school are presented as being not only unhappy at the time but also exerting an ineradicable pernicious influence on the child's future personality. Not all such descriptions, moreover, are by adults looking back at their school-days after the passage of many years: Renan, as a very young man writing in notebooks not intended for publication, asserts, in vocabulary that further intensifies the image of corruption and imprisonment, that 'the public education given in schools is not tenable. No mid-course: either a frightening licentiousness, or a horrible hatred felt by the pupil for his tyrants.' (*l'éducation publique des collèges n'est pas tenable. Pas de milieu: ou une effroyable licence, ou une haine horrible de l'élève à ses tyrans.*)[132] Both autobiographies and fiction reinforce Renan's argument. Du Camp, for instance, insists that his protagonist's ten years at school were 'ten years of endless struggle' (*dix années de luttes incessantes*) and he adds: 'if I frequently look back to that period of my life, it is

---

[129] See for a study of one such group and the importance of the *lycée* in consolidating it, Spitzer, *The French Generation of 1820*.

[130] *Vieux Souvenirs*, 38.

[131] One thinks in particular of Champfleury's *Les Souffrances du professeur Delteil* and Daudet's *Le Petit Chose*.

[132] *Cahiers de jeunesse*, 321.

because it exerted over my character a disastrous influence.' (*si je reviens fréquemment sur cette époque de ma vie, c'est qu'elle a eu sur mon caractère une influence désastreuse.*)[133] Isaac, in his autobiography, is even more forceful in designating his five years at the *lycée* Lakanal as 'five years of internment, five years of seclusion—of imprisonment—and what more precious years, from 13 to 18' (*cinq ans d'internat, cinq ans de réclusion—d'emprisonnement—et quelles plus précieuses années, de 13 à 18 ans*),[134] while Lavisse finds a slightly different image to evoke his 'entry into school' (*entrée à l'école*) as a 'passage from light to shadow' (*passage de la lumière à l'ombre*).[135] The school's transformation of the child's space and time is, however, nowhere more virulently presented than in Lautréamont's *Les Chants de Maldoror*:

When a boarding pupil, in a high school, is governed for years, which are centuries, from morning to evening and from evening to the following day, by one of civilization's pariahs, who constantly has his eye on him, he feels tumultuous floods of tenacious hatred rise, like thick smoke, to his brain, which seems on the point of bursting open. From the moment when he is thrown into this prison to the moment when he leaves, a moment that is not far off, an intense fever turns his face yellow, thrusts his eyebrows together, and hollows his eyes. At night he reflects, because he does not want to sleep. During the day, his thoughts leap over the walls of this stultifying domain, until the moment when he escapes, or when he is thrown like a plague-bearer from this eternal cloister.

Quand un élève interne, dans un lycée, est gouverné, pendant des années, qui sont des siècles, du matin jusqu'au soir et du soir jusqu'au lendemain, par un paria de la civilisation, qui a constamment les yeux sur lui, il sent les flots tumultueux d'une haine vivace, monter, comme une épaisse fumée, à son cerveau, qui lui paraît près d'éclater. Depuis le moment où on l'a jeté dans la prison, jusqu'à celui, qui s'approche, où il en sortira, une fièvre intense lui jaunit la face, rapproche ses sourcils, et lui creuse les yeux. La nuit, il réfléchit, parce qu'il ne veut pas dormir. Le jour, sa pensée s'élance au-dessus des murailles de la demeure de l'abrutissement, jusqu'au moment où il s'échappe, ou qu'on le rejette, comme un pestiféré, de ce cloître éternel.[136]

In this powerful and remarkably concise passage, Lautréamont

---

[133] *Mémoires d'un suicidé*, 51.
[134] *Expériences de ma vie*, 51.
[135] *Souvenirs*, 3.
[136] *Œuvres complètes*, 70–1.

locks together images of time and space, power and repression, physical illness and intellectual and moral destruction, to provide a double model: first, of the political repression of one group by another and, second, of the ways in which the innocence and potential of the child are crushed by society's demands for conformity.

Despite the clues provided by Lautréamont, one might still ask why school should be represented through such dark images in the midst of childhoods marked by a delight in reading, in discovery, in knowledge. The constancy of the images, in novels, in autobiographies, in letters or diaries written by pupils, suggests that, while some element of infectious cliché may be at work here, the conflict between the interest in education professed by many adults in the course of the century and the remembered experience of children undergoing that education was very profound and cannot simply be dismissed as an expected and hackneyed trope, although it certainly functions to some extent in such a way.

Certainly the physical conditions in which the child found itself at school left a great deal to be desired during much of the nineteenth century. Dupont-Ferrier, in his history of daily life at Louis-le-Grand, tells us, for instance, that 'for a long time the classrooms had no desks. It was considered enough to fit them with tiers and to let the pupils use their knees as desks.' (*longtemps, les classes n'eurent pas de tables. On s'était contenté de leur donner des gradins et l'élève prenait ses genoux comme pupitre.*) He adds: 'under the tiers were . . . mysterious refuges. Crowds of rats had set up home there.' (*au dessous de ces gradins demeurèrent . . . des retraites mystérieuses. Un peuple de rats y élisait domicile.*)[137] Unheated dormitories and refectories, minimal sanitation, and large classes of sixty or seventy, together with the very long hours the pupils were meant to devote to their studies, make it less surprising that so many writers gave expression to what Du Camp calls 'the hatred felt by pupils for these great prisons in which their childhoods are locked away in the name of instruction' (*la haine des écoliers pour ces grandes prisons dans lesquelles on enferme leur enfance sous prétexte d'instruction*).[138] According to Marie d'Agoult, moreover, the situation for girls in convents, even those chosen by the aristocracy, was even worse:

[137] *La Vie quotidienne*, 136.
[138] *Mémoires d'un suicidé*, 52.

you could not imagine anything more insufficient, more neglected, than the food and other physical care provided in boarding-schools run by nuns. . . . At Sacré-Cœur you took a bath only on doctor's orders.

on ne saurait rien se figurer de plus insuffisant, de plus négligé, que la nourriture et les autres soins de corps dans les pensionnats tenus par des nonnes. . . . On ne prenait de bains au Sacré-Cœur que par ordonnance du médecin.[139]

Nevertheless, physical discomforts might have been passed over in silence, except in so far as they offer a symbol for mankind's existential sense of insertion into a physical context for which we are ill adapted.

What arouse more anger in these evocations are the infringements of the child's liberty and dignity, both physical and intellectual. Beatings might have been forbidden in the majority of *lycées*, but teachers in rural schools, private tutors, and, occasionally, the *pions* (or adult monitors) in state schools, certainly resorted to physical chastisement. The kind of barbarity recorded by Daudet in *Jack* no doubt owes much to the novelist's dominant desire for tear-jerking melodrama, but it finds a calmer reflection in works that are far more restrained in tone. Perdiguier, evoking a school in which many of the teaching texts were written in Latin, although French itself was problematic enough for children who spoke patois, consolidates this image of intellectual alienation and repression by depicting his teacher as possessing 'hard hands, sticks, straps . . . coshes' (*des mains dures, des férules, des courroies . . . des nerfs de bœuf.*)[140] Nevertheless, evocations of childhood suggest that what was resented even more than physical punishment was the teachers' recourse either to withering sarcasm or to inordinately long impositions. Dupont-Ferrier provides a historical context for these accounts when he affirms that

humiliating punishments, which were suspended for a time in 1849, existed only until 1854 but impositions and detentions, as well as withdrawal of the right to go out, and the use of the school prison, were retained until the reform of 1890.

les peines humiliantes, suspendues quelques temps, en 1849, ne subsistèrent qu'en 1854 mais les pensums, les retenues, les privations de sortie, la prison furent conservés jusqu'à la réforme de 1890.[141]

[139] *Mes souvenirs*, 158–9.
[140] *Mémoires d'un compagnon*, 5.
[141] *La Vie quotidienne*, 475.

Baudelaire's childhood letters, with their interminable confessions that he is yet again forbidden to leave the school for the weekend, contain a boyish, but good-natured, parody of a teacher doling out punishments:

Pupil: Hey, neighbour, lend me your homework so I can copy it.
Teacher: You sir, half an hour's detention.
Pupil: Oh, that's unfair!
Teacher: You can do twice as long for muttering.
Pupil: But wh . . .
Teacher: Three times as long.
Etc., etc., etc., etc., etc., sometimes that can go a long way.

L'élève: Eh, dis donc, voisin, prête-moi donc ton devoir afin que je copie.
Le maître: Monsieur, une demi-heure d'arrêt.
L'élève: Ah! vilain!
Le maître: Monsieur, pour murmurer, vous en ferez le double.
L'élève: Et pourqu . . .
Le maître: Triple.
Etc., etc., etc., etc., etc., ça mène bien loin quelquefois.[142]

Michelet suggests, in his autobiography, the kind of verbal lashings that were indulged in by certain teachers: 'in his exaggerated love of duty, he thought he could see all possible vices in a pupil who did not arrive on time. Anyone who had not finished his translation was told that he would suffer eternal damnation.' (*dans son amour exagéré du devoir, il croyait découvrir tous les vices dans un élève peu exact. Celui qui n'avait pas fini son thème, il lui prédisait qu'il serait perdu.*)[143] Yet, what seems to dominate in these depictions of school presented through the child's eyes is less the punishment as such than the constant threat: 'the atmosphere of terror did not leave us for a moment while the class lasted' (*l'atmosphère de terreur ne nous lâchait pas une minute, tant que durait la classe*), Sylvère recounts,[144] and Isaac, despite having been hardened by a soldier father convinced of the truth of the dictum that children should be seen and not heard, recalls with anger the intimidating military tradition of the *lycée* in which children moved to the roll of drums and, at least when he first went there, silence was obligatory even in the refectory.[145] Whether the school's discipline was

[142] *Correspondance*, i. 33.
[143] J. Michelet, *Ma jeunesse*, 67.
[144] *Toinou*, 36.
[145] *Expériences de ma vie*, 38.

structured like that of a monastery or like that of the army, in other words, it exposed the child to patterns of control far more rigorous than any it was likely to have encountered hitherto and provided writers with a metaphor for the kinds of surveillance and punishment the State itself was developing in response to the frequent political unrest. If Haussmann's Paris offers a physical correlative for the power structures of the Second Empire, writers can locate in the school a broader-based image of control, and one, moreover, with which the vast majority of readers would be only too familiar.

The image is all the more wide-ranging in that, if the punishments inflicted by teachers were a source of enduring resentment for some, the presence of other children was for others an equally intimidating and unhappy experience. While, in his *Vie de Henry Brulard*, Stendhal frequently regrets his isolation from children his own age, and while for the lonely Jack in Daudet's novel the awareness of the bleaker exile of many of his schoolmates at least mitigates his own, the school as microcosm of society is more frequently associated, not with the joys of friendship, but with the pain and humiliation inflicted by children on children. Balzac's evocation of Félix de Vandenesse's discovery that the scorn with which his family treats him guarantees that his schoolmates will in turn despise him, Flaubert's depiction of the mockery reserved for the newcomer who does not know what to do with his cap, and Maupassant's images of school-yard teasing provide a constant thread through the century, which also finds a reflection in the autobiographies. Michelet recalls the terrible teasing he underwent, but still recounts as delightfully funny the teasing inflicted on another child; Pierre Loti explores the way in which the sensitive child responds by creating a second persona reserved for school, and the future priest Gratry points to the more serious danger of sexual corruption, when he alludes to the 'terrible dangers of corruption when children are all together' (*les terribles dangers de la contagion des enfants entre eux*).[146]

Nevertheless, what is depicted as having aroused most resentment in schoolchildren, or at least in adults reconsidering childhood, is the crushing boredom provoked by the substance of what was taught and the methods employed to teach it. While few

[146] *Souvenirs*, 18.

children possessed or claimed anything like the power of Louis Lambert's intellect, Balzac none the less appears to speak for many in the following terse formula: 'full of scorn for the all but useless studies to which we were condemned, Louis strode along his aerial pathway.' (*plein de mépris pour les études presque inutiles auxquelles nous étions condamnés, Louis marchait dans sa route aërienne.*)[147] Indeed, the uselessness of what was taught, its inappropriateness for the careers the children would eventually pursue, the extent to which it was divorced from their daily experience, provide the basis for a litany of complaints. Michelet's terse indictment—'education in those days had little substance. History was not taught.' (*l'éducation avait alors peu de substance. Point d'enseignement de l'histoire*)[148]—might seem somewhat biased were it not supported and dilated on by so many others. Sylvère asserts that 'the notions that were taught were scrupulously stripped of everything that would have made them interesting' (*les notions enseignées étaient soigneusement débarrassées de ce qui en eût fait l'intérêt*);[149] Taine, in *Étienne Mayran*, insists that 'Our school education leads us to consider the works of the mind as the only tasks worth undertaking and every year quantities of geniuses leave school and, having dirtied much white paper, find themselves copyists, clerks, or salesmen' (*Notre éducation de collège nous conduit à considérer les œuvres d'esprit comme les seules qu'il vaille la peine d'entreprendre, et il en sort tous les ans quantité de génies qui, après avoir sali beaucoup de papier blanc, se trouvent à la fin expéditionnaires, clercs ou commis*);[150] Hermant affirms that all that children learnt was 'the teaching of competition' (*l'enseigne-ment de la concurrence*),[151] and the poet Maurice de Guérin insists: 'I spent ten years in school and I left bearing with me a few scraps of Latin and Greek, and a great weight of boredom. That, more or less, is the result of our entire education in French schools.' (*J'ai consumé dix ans dans les collèges et j'en suis sorti emportant avec quelques bribes de latin et de grec, une masse énorme d'ennui. Voilà à peu près le résultat de toute éducation de collège en France.*)[152]

[147] *Louis Lambert*, 378.
[148] J. Michelet, *Ma jeunesse*, 179.
[149] *Toinou*, 36: he also underlines the problems for children to whom no assistance was given with the comprehension of the vocabulary employed.
[150] *Étienne Mayran*, 142.
[151] *Confessions*, 15.
[152] *Journal*, 6. See also Quinet, *Histoire de mes idées*, pt. III, ch. 1.

There is also a sense, as Lautréamont's reference to a social pariah suggests, that the child felt that this boredom was inflicted by someone who was, either socially or intellectually, an inferior. Baudelaire's childhood letters, while bearing in mind an adult audience clearly perceived as being at least to some extent in cahoots with the system, nevertheless reveal that, like many other pupils, he was only too sharply aware of the limitations of some of his teachers, only too critical of a linguistic pomposity that failed to hide an intellectual poverty: 'the teacher even said to me in his characteristic style: "Work on your Latin verse: it's a future string you're breaking." That made me laugh.' (*le professeur n'a-t-il pas été jusqu'à me dire dans sons style: 'Travaillez donc les vers latins: c'est une corde d'avenir que vous cassez.' Ça m'a fait rire.*)[153] Renan, too, in notebooks written as a young man, snorts:

Never have I seen anything more stupid, more pedantic, more exasperatingly colourless than those teachers at Henri IV, and, I'm convinced, the entire teaching profession seen from the distance of the school boarding house. They have a mania for adopting scholarly pretensions when dealing with children.

Oncques ne vis rien de plus sot, de plus pédant, d'une fadeur plus exaspérante que ces professeurs du Collège Henri IV et, je crois, tout ce genre professeur vu à la distance de la pension du collège. Manie d'affecter le savant vis-à-vis de ces enfants.[154]

For the strongly conservative forces at work in nineteenth-century France, any desire for intellectual freedom was anathema, and what was to be trained was not the imagination but a respect for conformity. The bourgeois distrust of the Romantics, with their interest in the irrational, in madness, in the mystical, is closely bound in with this deeply reactionary and restrictive vision, and it is hardly surprising that the Romantics were among those who most forcefully denounced the current philosophy of education as an imprisonment of the mind. Hugo's virulent poem, 'A propos d'Horace', in *Les Contemplations*, may not be among his finest, but it gives expression to the sense of angry frustration that seems inevitably to be conjured up by memories or even merely the mention of school:

---

[153] *Correspondance*, i. 39.
[154] *Cahiers de jeunesse*, 337–8.

Merchants of Greek! Merchants of Latin! pedants! bulldogs!
Philistines! beaks! I hate you, pedagogues!
For, in your grave, infallible, dazed self-assurance
You deny the ideal, you deny grace and beauty!
For your texts, your laws, your rules are fossils!
For, despite your profound airs, you are imbeciles!
For you teach everything and you know nothing!
For you are nasty and wicked!—My blood boils
Whenever I so much as think of that time when, a dreamy blockhead,
I was 16 and in the rhetoric class!

Marchands de grec! marchands de latin! cuistres! dogues!
Philistins! magisters! je vous hais, pédagogues!
Car, dans votre aplomb grave, infaillible, hébété,
Vous niez l'idéal, la grâce et la beauté!
Car vos textes, vos lois, vos règles sont fossiles!
Car, avec l'air profond, vous êtes imbéciles!
Car vous enseignez tout, et vous ignorez tout!
Car vous êtes mauvais et méchants!—Mon sang bout
Rien qu'à songer au temps où, rêveuse bourrique,
J'avais seize ans et j'étais en rhétorique![155]

Even if Hugo's weighty ire strikes us as a little self-indulgent, that sense of the blood boiling as the adult recalls the restrictions of school-days typifies much of childhood experience, at least in so far as it is encapsulated within literature, and it finds yet more violent expression in Rimbaud's poem 'Les Assis'. Here, the child's request for the intellectual freedom to explore those books not included in the school programme meets with a refusal that in turn prompts an extraordinarily intense outpouring of imaginative metamorphoses:

These old men have always been one with their seats,
Feeling the strong sun percalize their skin,
Or, eyes to the window where snows are fading,
Trembling with the painful tremble of a toad.

Ces vieillards ont toujours fait tresse avec leurs sièges,
Sentant les soleils vifs percaliser leur peau,
Ou, les yeux à la vitre où se fanent les neiges,
Tremblant du tremblement douloureux du crapaud.[156]

---

[155] *Les Contemplations*, bk. 1, poem XIII.
[156] *Œuvres complètes*, 37.

For girls either sent to be educated in a convent or taught privately, the situation is often presented as being even worse. Marie d'Agoult evokes the abysmal ignorance that resulted from a system more concerned with preventing girls gaining certain kinds of information than with conveying any knowledge, while the narrative voice in Prévost's *Mademoiselle Jauffre* notes ironically that

for the development of the mind, elementary instruction sufficed: for the essential principle of all education is that it should be proportionate to the power of the pupil's faculties and the use to which such knowledge is to be put . . .

pour le développement de l'esprit, un enseignement élémentaire suffisait: car c'est le principe essentiel de toute éducation qu'elle doit se mesurer à la puissance des facultés du sujet et à l'usage qu'il doit faire de ses connaissances . . . [157]

And Gautier's Madeleine de Maupin, it will be recalled, is constrained to resort to transvestism in order to discover what her education kept so scrupulously hidden from her. An interesting sidelight is cast by the letter in which Mlle Leroyer de Chantepie recounts for Flaubert's benefit the paucity of her own schooling:

I received a hopeless education from nuns, I was taught to read, to write a little French, and that was the limit of my entire teaching. The care of my health was entrusted to an ignorant doctor, that of my soul to a fanatical priest, helped by a yet more fanatical spinster.

je reçus une éducation nulle chez des religieuses, on m'apprit à lire, à écrire un peu de français, là s'est bornée toute mon instruction. On confia le soin de ma santé à un médécin ignorant, celui de mon âme à un prêtre fanatique, aidé d'une vieille fille plus fanatique encore. [158]

The restrictions contemporary society imposed on women, therefore, are encapsulated and foreshadowed in these texts by the image of schooling. It matters little for our purposes whether this is an accurate description or an imaginative reconstruction of the truth: the point here is that the image of education crystallized around it a remarkably limited and clearly defined series of responses, almost all of which were negative.

A deeper awareness of the adult's attitude to the child is provided

---

[157] *Mademoiselle Jauffre*, 33. Original ellipses.
[158] Flaubert, *Correspondance*, ii. 694.

both by Judith Gautier's account of being taken to the convent school and left there without having been told in advance what her parents had decided to do, and by the memoirs of a former teacher, who announces, without any apparent awareness of fatuity, that 'If I am to guide a child, he must give me his heart with his hand, as a son gives his heart to his father' (*Pour que je puisse conduire un enfant, il faut qu'il me donne son cœur avec sa main, comme un fils le donne à son père*).[159] Between the mindless cruelty of the former instance and the sentimental silliness of the second, the child must frequently have felt itself adrift in a world of hostile and designing aliens.

What arises from these evocations of school and of education more generally is the overwhelming sense of a small element within society attempting to shape children's minds according to its needs and convictions rather than according to the needs of the child, or, indeed, of the future adult. Running through all this bleak picture is a corresponding awareness of the adults' distrust of the child, a deeply ingrained sense of the child both as a potentially disruptive force and as the voice of the irrational in a society that sought to depict itself as supremely rational. And, finally, Lautréamont's violent rhetoric provides us with a further reason behind his conviction that the child contracts at school a form of plague that will for ever mark him, for the time at school corresponds to the years in which childhood becomes adolescence, its intellectual and physical purity is sullied, and its individuality is crushed under the pressures to conform to a debased and debasing norm.

What school seems to evoke for the majority of those concerned with depicting childhood in the nineteenth century, therefore, is a sudden and unjustified restriction of the child's space, its time, its mind, and its uniqueness, which coincides with a period of profound and largely incomprehensible physical changes. Of all the common themes in nineteenth-century evocations of the child's world it remains the bleakest, but also the most open to the charge of merely reproducing an established and expected cliché. What makes such a charge at least questionable is the joy and pleasure in learning frequently expressed by those who were educated privately or whose main sources of information were not members of the teaching profession: Juliette Adam's pleasure in discovering

---

[159] Fontanel, *Nos lycéens*, 17.

literature through the (often conflicting) opinions of her father and her great-aunts, or Pierre Loti's passion for informing himself about butterflies, indicate the other side of the coin, the satisfaction of the child's boundless curiosity. While this, too, is not free from a certain, somewhat smug, element of cliché, it nevertheless sheds further light on the image of childhood, adding yet more layers to the increasingly complex series of myths the topic created.

5
Embodying Childhood

A child is born in me who is not of today
A child of forever through a unique kiss
More carefree than a first butterfly .
At dawn the spring gives him a second
And death is conquered a child leaves the ruins
Behind him the ruins and the night fade away

Un enfant naît en moi qui n'est pas d'aujourd'hui
Un enfant de toujours par un baiser unique
Plus insouciant qu'un premier papillon
A l'aube le printemps lui donne une seconde
Et la mort est vaincue un enfant sort des ruines
Derrière lui les ruines et la nuit s'effacent

P. Élvard, 'Le Dur désir de durer'

THE association of particular themes with the general motif of the child in nineteenth-century French literature suggests a degree of stereotyping, if not necessarily in the presentation of individual child-figures, at least in the way in which childhood was envisaged. One of the consequences of this can be seen in the frequency with which the child appears both as a unique entity and as metonymical for such generalized notions as the artist, the rebel, the criminal, and so forth. Of course, to some extent, all reading depends on an expectation of metonymy, and it may be that the child-figure, either because its personality is less clearly formed than that of the adult, or because the problems of allowing it a personal voice are, as we have seen, greater than they are for an adult, lends itself particularly easily to such an interpretation.

Romanticism's interest in the imagination and the oneiric, together with its privileging of the mind unshackled by the conventions of civilization, leads to the association of the child and the artist, the mind as yet unshaped by custom and the mind that rejects custom in order to create and discover. Baudelaire's affirmation of the parallelism between childhood and genius merely states with particular cogency a belief shared by many contemporary writers and thinkers. Michelet, for instance, insists in *Le Peuple*, first published in 1846, that the genius is 'he who, while acquiring the gifts of the critic, has retained the gifts of the simple man' (*celui qui, tout en acquérant les dons du critique, a gardé les dons du simple*), a statement he clarifies by adding: 'genius has the gift of childhood, as the child never has.' (*le génie a le don de l'enfance, comme ne l'a jamais l'enfant.*)[1] Like Baudelaire, therefore, Michelet uses the terms 'child' and 'childhood' to evoke less a natural stage in the individual's development than a network of associations and concepts that imply spontaneity, intensity, freedom. While this does not mean that childhood is reduced to a mere label, having little connection with any external reality, it does suggest that for such writers the central interest tends to lie with the adult's recovery of the childlike rather than with the child's discovery of art or ambition.

The novelists for whom the link between childhood and artistic talent is most obviously not of *post facto* interest are Balzac, in *Louis Lambert*, and George Sand, who in *Les Maîtres Sonneurs* reveals herself fascinated by the disparity between the child's gifts and its inability to perform those tasks other children find simple. For both writers, the genius as child is misunderstood, his gifts unsuspected by almost all. While both present their protagonists from the viewpoint of a first-person narrator of the same age who watches him, without necessarily understanding him, Balzac chooses to explore Louis through a narrator who admires him, whereas George Sand's narrator is frequently hostile. *Louis Lambert* begins with an extremely brief evocation of Louis's early childhood before moving on to a detailed evocation of the college and its regulations, stressing the closed nature of the institution, which pupils left only once their education was complete and in which corporal punishment was still employed, but also emphasizing the sources of pleasure—the pigeons and the gardens the children were permitted as substitutes for the presence of their families, the games played in the courtyard, and the little shop that opened each Sunday. The main purpose of this description, presented entirely through the eyes of the narrator, is to establish him, for all that he has the nickname 'the poet', as an ordinary child, sharing the delights and boredom of childhood: 'who among us does not remember with delight,' he asks, 'despite the bitterness of learning, the bizarreness of the cloistered life?' (*qui de nous ne se*

[1] J. Michelet, *Le Peuple*, 185 and 187.

rappelle encore avec délices, malgré les amertumes de la science, les bizarreries de cette vie claustrale?),[2] and again: 'who among us is so unfortunate as to have forgotten how his heart beat at the thought of that shop periodically opened during the Sunday breaks?' (*qui de nous est assez malheureux pour avoir oublié ses battements de cœur à l'aspect de ce magasin périodiquement ouvert pendant les récréations du dimanche?*)[3] The answer, no doubt, is Louis himself. This budding philosopher, having attracted the interest of Mme de Staël, who pays for him to attend the college, finds himself in a repressive environment which is both physically and intellectually inimical. The genius he has been announced as possessing can find no means of revealing itself in the limited and unimaginative exercises of traditional schooling, his moments of meditation on the great philosophical questions are interpreted by the masters as day-dreaming and laziness, his *Traité de la volonté*, which, Balzac insists, might be the work of a child but contains ideas that are wholly adult, is confiscated and mocked. The school becomes, therefore, metonymical for society, with all its petty restrictions and its self-satisfied materialism, as Louis himself figures the genius mocked by the philistinism and lack of intelligence of his contemporaries. Nevertheless, in summing up the stages in his protagonist's development, Balzac suggests the necessity both of a happy early childhood, spent in fresh air and supported by a loving family, and of a subsequent period of unhappiness when the older child, no longer free to wander at will, turns to meditation as the only means of escape from an intolerable situation. That period of unhappiness becomes, therefore, the seed-time of an inner know-ledge far more important to the future philosopher than the all but useless studies that school offers. For all the maturity of Louis's thinking, Balzac is eager to stress that he is still a child: as the narrator insists, 'we were indeed children, both of us.' (*nous étions bien enfants l'un et l'autre.*)[4] However brief the passages evoking Louis's childhood and boyhood, there can be no doubt, therefore, that Balzac is concerned not merely to explore and intensify the Romantic belief in the child's innate genius but also to reveal how extreme intelligence condemns the child, exactly as it does the adult, to the incomprehension and hostility of most of those he meets.

[2] *Louis Lambert*, 362–3.
[3] Ibid., 363.   [4] Ibid., 384.

George Sand's portrayal of the genius as child, for all its apparent dependence on that same belief, is at once more subtle, less self-indulgent, and psychologically more perceptive than Balzac's. Thus, in *Les Maîtres Sonneurs*, Joset, the future master piper, is perceived by most of his peers, and by many of the adults of the village, as an '*ébervigé*', a backward child, the slowest of the boys in the catechism class, self-absorbed, preferring to sit at a distance from the other children, gazing at nothing, apparently hearing and seeing things inaudible and invisible to others and thus considered as being 'one of those who *see the wind*' (*de ceux qui* voient le vent).⁵ The dichotomy between this apparent lack of intelligence and the latent genius he possesses is conveyed all the more forcefully in that the narrative is presented through the limited first-person voice of Tiennet, who as a child grew up with Joset and, to a large extent, shared the general judgement of him, but realized that Brulette, the little girl they both admired, saw more in the apparent simpleton than did the others. While Michelet and Baudelaire offer an affirmation of the links between childhood and genius, therefore, George Sand is more concerned with an analysis that depends on Tiennet's gradual and reluctant discovery that his prejudices concerning Joset are false. This realization is prepared for by the throwing into doubt of Tiennet's superstitions concerning the strange music that seems to come from the great elm tree and the mysterious man who is spotted there. Joset's total lack of fear, together with his amusement at Tiennet's alarm, suggest to the reader a mind of a different order from the normal, and lead Tiennet to see his friend with other eyes: 'it seemed to me that Joset had changed both in stature and in expression. He appeared taller, carrying his head higher, walking more swiftly, and speaking more boldly.' (*il me sembla que Joset n'avait ni sa taille ni sa figure des autres fois. Il me paraissait plus grand, portant plus haut la tête, marchant d'un pas plus vif, et parlant avec plus de hardiesse.*)⁶ This in itself is not, of course, sufficient to bring about a complete alteration in Tiennet's judgement of Joset, for the narrator, as a boy, is shown to be steeped in the prejudices that demanded conformity and distrust individuality: 'I had heard tell that people with pale faces and green eyes, people whose temperaments are melancholy and whose speech is hard to understand, tend to enter

⁵ *Les Maîtres Sonneurs*, 67.
⁶ Ibid., 101.

into pacts with evil spirits.' (*je m'étais laissé conter que les gens qui ont la figure blanche, l'œil vert, l'humeur triste et la parole difficile à comprendre, sont portés à s'accointer avec les mauvais esprits.*)[7] The truth is revealed through Brulette, who, for all her vanity and frivolity, is less trammelled by convention than Tiennet, and who guesses the real cause of Joset's strangeness. She, moreover, is able to put into words ideas of which his own linguistic control is incapable. Joset, loving music and demanding of it more than the local piper can offer, needs an instrument to give expression to his deepest convictions and emotions. As Brulette expresses it: 'it's because he never had this borrowed voice that our lad always appeared sad, or dreamy, or lost in a world of his own.' (*c'est pour avoir toujours manqué de cette voix d'emprunt, que notre gars a toujours été triste, ou songeur, ou comme ravi en lui-même.*)[8]

In this novel of initiation, in which all five major characters go through a period of education and self-discovery, Joset is in no way idealized and his is the most difficult and in some ways the least rewarding of apprenticeships. The self-absorbed nature of the child becomes egotism in the adult; the man who, as a boy, chose not to play with the other children, cannot accept that Brulette might not choose to accept him as a lover. The common Romantic dichotomies between muse and mistress, between domestic bliss and artistic creativity, dominate and determine Joset's future, offering him Brulette's friendship but denying him her love, while the envy felt by the merely competent when faced with genius ensures his isolation and, perhaps, his mysterious death. Only at the end of his childhood, when the orphan Joset at last discovers the substitute father who can teach him how to play first the flute, then the bagpipes, does he achieve a brief moment of happiness. This happiness is the result of at last discovering a means of expressing the complexity of his emotions and the beauty of his memories. Again it is Tiennet who gives the philistine's response to Joset's flute-playing—'what's the use of that, what do you mean by that' (*à quoi ça peut servir, et qu'est-ce que tu veux signifier par là*)[9]—and Brulette who teaches him how to listen, by revealing that through his music Joset spoke to her directly of the time when they were very young children:

7 Ibid., 102. Cf. Baudelaire's poem 'Les Bienfaits de la lune'.
8 *Les Maîtres Sonneurs*, 109.
9 Ibid., 116.

I felt I was being carried with you by a strong wind that took us now over ripe wheat fields, now over wild grasses, now over flowing water; . . . in short, I had so many dreams that it's already all growing blurred and muddled; and if that made me want to cry, it's not because I was unhappy, but because it gave me such an emotional shock.

je me sentais portée avec toi par un grand vent qui nous promenait tantôt sur les blés mûrs, tantôt sur des herbes folles, tantôt sur les eaux courantes; . . . enfin, j'ai vu tant de rêves que c'est déjà embrouillé dans ma tête; et si ça m'a donné l'envie de pleurer, ce n'est point par chagrin, mais par une secousse de mes esprits.[10]

This judgement is all Joset needs to affirm his triumph: 'and now, Joset the madman, Joset the innocent, Joset the simpleton, you can go back to being an imbecile; you are as strong, as knowledgeable, as happy as anyone else.' (*à présent, Joset le fou, Joset l'innocent, Joset l'ébervigé, tu peux bien retomber dans ton imbécillité; tu es aussi fort, aussi savant, aussi heureux qu'un autre!*)[11]

From this moment in the novel, the analysis switches from childhood to adolescence, and widens its focus to explore in more detail the other characters, leaving Joset as an enigmatic figure never entirely understood by the narrator and never again so clearly explained by Brulette. From our point of view, however, his early development and the dual focus George Sand employs to present it—Tiennet's pragmatism contrasting with Brulette's sensitivity— make of him a symbol of the child as Romantic artist, at once misunderstood and strangely compelling, the vehicle through which music can find expression.

The image of the child as creative spirit is also present in Rimbaud's writing, particularly in the poem 'Les Poètes de sept ans', with its virulent contrasts between appearance and reality, between the child's apparent acceptance of adult demands and his secret revolt, and above all between what everyday experience offers and what he longs to find. Lying in the clay at the bottom of the garden with the worm-eaten espalier beside him, he escapes into a vertiginous world of visions, just as he can replace the bare bedroom and its closed shutters with images conjured up by a favourite novel, or tell himself stories inspired by illustrated newspapers. What Rimbaud provides in the sixty-five lines of his poem is a series of brief vignettes creating a complex image of the

---

[10] *Les Maîtres Sonneurs*, 117–18.   [11] Ibid., 118.

child and his surroundings rather than the analytical and descriptive modes adopted by Balzac and Sand, yet the basic conviction is the same: the intensity of childhood experience lies at the base of the adult artist's ability to create, and the child's experience is therefore metonymic of that of the artist.

Nevertheless, in an age which saw a proliferation of novels about artists, successful or not—one thinks, for instance, of Balzac's *Illusions perdues*, or his *Le Chef-d'œuvre inconnu*, and of Zola's *L'Œuvre*, among others—it is remarkable how few give more than a passing reference to the protagonist's childhood. And while Balzac and George Sand are clearly using their heroes for metonymical purposes, these purposes are not spelled out but left for the reader to discover. With Hugo, however, part of the pleasure of describing children obviously derives from the opportunity afforded to analyse the ways in which modern life abounds in symbols which it is part of the artist's task to decipher for the profane. Hugo, moreover, is far less concerned to show the relationships between the child and the artist (as distinct from those between artistic genius and the intensity of childhood) than with using the child as a symbol both of fragility and of resilience. Thus, Cosette, as the child at the mercy of the Thénardier couple, surfaces first as a network of similes. Between the husband and wife, themselves allegories of ruse and rage, she is 'like a creature simultaneously crushed by a millstone and shredded by pincers' (*comme une créature qui serait à la fois broyée par une meule et déchiquetée par une tenaille*),[12] a physical symbol of oppression, a fly in servitude to spiders, a mouse obeying an elephant. She then becomes the universal little girl, lost in admiration of a doll she sees as a 'dame', as a vision, in a toyshop she perceives as a palace. From this network of similes, Cosette arises both as a symbol of what Hugo perceives as woman's destiny, and as individual subject. In describing her playing with the doll that she has created by wrapping up a sabre, the novelist reveals some of his most distinctive traits: the powerful lexical imagination, the desire to capture the eternal in the ephemeral, the tendency to reduce the complexity of the other, particularly the female other, to the level of icon. Following so close on the depiction of Eponine's idiosyncratic story about the cat as little girl, the passage explaining Cosette's

---

[12] *Les Misérables*, i. 494.

imperious need for a doll to play with is also disturbingly generalizing, as if the relationships between Cosette and Hugo's doubly lost daughter have continually to be kept at bay through a constant effort to make both participate in Hugo's personal image of womanhood and daughterhood:

Dolls are at the same time one of the most imperious needs and one of the most charming instincts of female childhood. Healing, clothing, adorning, dressing, undressing, dressing again, teaching, scolding a little, rocking, cuddling, sending to sleep, imagining that something is someone, therein lies all woman's future.

La poupée est un des plus impérieux besoins et en même temps un des plus charmants instincts de l'enfance féminine. Soigner, vêtir, parer, habiller, déshabiller, rhabiller, enseigner, un peu gronder, bercer, dorloter, endormir, se figurer que quelque chose est quelqu'un, tout l'avenir de la femme est là.[13]

One could of course equally argue that in 'imagining that something is someone' (*se figurer que quelque chose est quelqu'un*) lies the future of the poet, for Hugo's desire to reduce the complexity of his highly imaginative images to a simple, compelling message frequently ensnares him into making associations whose ambiguity he seems unwilling to acknowledge, but in which the text's logic deconstructs to reveal a masculinity shoring itself up rather desperately against what it perceives as the powerful feminine impulses working within it.

Similar rhetorical tendencies are at work in Hugo's description of Paris. In *Les Misérables* in particular, Hugo, always more interested in the narration than in the narrative, seizes with obvious and irresistible delight on the opportunity to analyse the links between the city and its population, moving easily into a metaphorical presentation of Paris as vast and fertile mother, and the street urchin as natural product of modern urban existence.

What dominates, in his presentation of Gavroche, is a desire to expand the belief in childhood innocence to incorporate the image of a joyous and innocent street child, in what might well appear to modern sensibilities a wilful and callous blindness, but which might merely be a combination of living in exile, linguistic exuberance, and the desire to find a means of epitomizing Paris through a symbol that will allow Hugo to expand yet again on that favourite antithesis of the very great and the very small:

---

[13] *Les Misérables*, i. 521–2.

this little being is full of joy. He does not eat every day and he goes to a show, if he wants to, every evening. He hasn't a shirt on his back, no shoes on his feet, nothing to cover his head; he is like the flies of the air which possess none of those things. He is between 7 and 13 years old, lives in gangs, walks the pavement, sleeps in the open, wears a pair of his father's old trousers . . . he runs, watches, searches, wastes time, cleans out his pipe, swears like a soul in hell, haunts cabarets, knows thieves, is on familiar terms with prostitutes, talks in slang, sings obscene songs, and has not an ounce of evil in his heart. That is because he has a pearl in his soul, the pearl of innocence, and pearls are not dissolved by mud.

ce petit être est joyeux. Il ne mange pas tous les jours et il va au spectacle, si bon lui semble, tous les soirs. Il n'a pas de chemise sur le corps, pas de souliers aux pieds, pas de toit sur la tête; il est comme les mouches du ciel qui n'ont rien de tout cela. Il a de sept à treize ans, vit par bandes, bat le pavé, loge en plein air, porte un vieux pantalon de son père . . . court, guette, quête, perd le temps, culotte des pipes, jure comme un damné, hante le cabaret, connaît des voleurs, tutoie des filles, parle argot, chante des chansons obscènes, et n'a rien de mauvais dans le cœur. C'est qu'il a dans l'âme une perle, l'innocence, et les perles ne se dissolvent pas dans la boue.[14]

Unless one is content merely to read this as a linguistic exercise, there is something deeply disturbing about Hugo's metaphorical games, which allow him to slip so easily from the specific to the general, from the real to the fanciful, from the sharply etched portrait of the child's appearance and behaviour to the apparently wilful blindness of his affirmation of the child's essential and incorruptible innocence. The assertion that there exists an exact equivalence between innocence and a pearl on the one hand, and vice and mud on the other, is part of Hugo's overriding optimism about the human species, an optimism untouched by the violence of the revolutions or the squalor of much of contemporary Parisian life. Writing, for Hugo, becomes a means of creating a reality parallel to that of daily life, a reality constructed, precisely, of such unquestioned metonymies and metaphors as that which presents Gavroche as archetype, and innocence as a pearl. Nevertheless, rhetoric is such a slippery monster that even Hugo finds himself on the point of being thrown by it. Thus, referring to the statistics concerning abandoned children in Paris, he writes: 'That, moreover is the most disastrous of social symptoms. All adult crimes begin with the child's vagabondage.' (*C'est là, du reste, le plus désastreux des symptômes sociaux. Tous les crimes de l'homme commencent*

[14] *Les Misérables*, ii. 151.

au vagabondage de l'enfant.) But he adds quickly: 'But we should make an exception for Paris. . . . The air of Paris preserves the soul.' (*Exceptons Paris pourtant.* . . . *Respirer Paris, cela conserve l'âme.*)[15]

Living in exile and yet possessed of a driving desire to reform both the political and the social conditions of contemporary France, Hugo finds a further purpose for the gamin, one that follows the technique already tested in the case of Cosette, that of revealing the nation's future encapsulated in the behaviour and experience of the child. The gamin's inexhaustible resourcefulness combines with both a refusal to be overwhelmed by situations or individuals, and a total disregard for rules and regulations, to create the archetype of anarchism. Here Hugo acknowledges that the gamin's gaiety and carelessness are only skin-deep, covering a growing awareness of the realities of modern existence, realities that it will soon be within his power to alter. It is at this point that the myth changes shape to join, however briefly, the vision of the child presented in the *Orientale* entitled 'L'Enfant':

He [the gamin] thinks he hasn't a care; that's not true. He looks on, ready to laugh; ready for other things, too. Whoever you are, you whose name is Prejudice, Abuse, Ignominy, Oppression, Iniquity, Despotism, Injustice, Fanaticism, Tyranny, watch out for the gawking gamin. This little child will grow.

Il se croit lui-même insouciant; il ne l'est pas. Il regarde, prêt à rire; prêt à autre chose aussi. Qui que vous soyez qui vous nommez Préjugé, Abus, Ignominie, Oppression, Iniquité, Despotisme, Injustice, Fanatisme, Tyrannie, prenez garde au gamin béant. Ce petit grandira.[16]

However much this passage might suggest the complexity of Hugo's image of the child, what controls Hugo's writing here is not the desire to explore the gamin as individual, but the need to incorporate him into the battery of allegorical figures that flesh out—or more precisely create—the poet's vision of present realities and future possibilities. Indeed, whatever the delight we may detect in the rounding out of Gavroche's personality (even if he always remains within the general framework of the gamin), the overwhelming need for icon and symbol subsumes the individual child in the scene on the barricade, in which the boy's identity is demolished in the welter of allegories long before the bullets

---

[15] *Les Misérables*, ii. 158.   [16] Ibid., ii. 154.

destroy the flesh-and-bone creature. Gavroche, dodging the bullets in a gruesome game of hide-and-seek, is a sparrow pecking at hunters, a strange fairy-like creature, the invulnerable dwarf of the battle, a pocket-sized Antaeus, whose slang is transformed into a song we are left to complete for ourselves:

> I fell from the air,
> Blame Voltaire,
> In the gutter's my nose,
> The blame's . . .

> Je suis tombé par terre,
> C'est la faute à Voltaire,
> Le nez dans le ruisseau,
> C'est la faute à . . . [17]

Moreover, because of the very delight Hugo reveals in his manipulation of rhetorical devices, he paves the way for writers later in the nineteenth century to present the child as metonym of the working classes or of the downtrodden more generally. In the passage entitled 'L'Avenir latent dans le peuple', for example, Hugo is at pains to demonstrate with absolute clarity the workings of such transpositions: 'to paint the child is to paint the city; and it is for that reason that we have studied that eagle through this sparrow' (*peindre l'enfant, c'est peindre la ville; et c'est pour cela que nous avons étudié cet aigle dans ce moineau franc*),[18] and in a further cluster of images he insists on the way in which such devices become means of vision:

Look through the people and you will see truth. The vile sand you trample underfoot, the sand that is thrown into furnaces, just let it melt and boil there, and it will become a splendid crystal; it is thanks to that crystal that Galileo and Newton were to discover the planets.

Regardez à travers le peuple et vous apercevrez la vérité. Ce vil sable que vous foulez aux pieds, qu'on le jette dans la fournaise, qu'il y fonde et qu'il y bouillonne, il deviendra cristal splendide, et c'est grâce à lui que Galilée et Newton découvriront les astres.[19]

Writers before Hugo had indeed suggested the parallelism between child and proletariat, although they may not have done so with

---

[17] Ibid., iii. 273: the logic of the song's previous verses suggests that the missing word is Rousseau, but the logic of the novel itself suggests a much more universal guilt, although one might equally well note the rhyme with Hugo.

[18] Ibid., ii. 169.   [19] Ibid., ii. 170.

such imaginative flourishes. Michelet, in particular, affirms that 'the child is the interpreter of the working class' (*l'enfant est l'interprète du peuple*) and justifies his equation with the following assertion:

Sharing with the working class a happy ignorance of the accepted language, of the formulae and set phrases that dispense with the need for invention, the child shows you through its example how the working class is obliged constantly to seek and to discover its language: both the child and the worker often discover a language possessing a felicitous energy.

L'enfant étant, comme le peuple, dans une heureuse ignorance du langage convenu, des formules et des phrases faites qui dispensent d'invention, vous montre, par son exemple, comment le peuple est obligé de chercher son langage et de le trouver sans cesse: l'un et l'autre le trouvent souvent avec une heureuse énergie.[20]

Michelet's point here is that freedom from the shackles of a conventional usage of language allows both the child and the populace a vision of existence that has a freshness and energy inaccessible to the cultured, except by an effort of imaginative recovery of the state of childhood. For the historian, therefore, the child acts as spokesman for the uneducated.

Certainly, the image of the child as revolutionary had been present from an early stage in nineteenth-century literature. The Romantics' image—and perhaps above all the image conveyed by the German and English Romantics—of a new vision based on freshness, the imaginative, and the refusal of convention did, as we have seen, privilege a certain archetype of the child. While few of the French Romantics succeeded in making the child-figure more than a symbol, by the time that Baudelaire was writing the link between the child and revolution had been firmly and memorably established by such paintings as Delacroix's *La Liberté sur les barricades*. Baudelaire's clearest statement of childhood rebellion against parental authority comes, as we have seen, in his study of Pierre Dupont, but *Le Spleen de Paris* is rich in vignettes of children rejecting or at least questioning what society provides for them: the rich child preferring the live rat to his own carefully made toys, the little boy gazing at the sumptuous café with intimations that he is excluded from it by his very nature, the child in 'Les Vocations' for whom the strolling players offer an image of an ideally untram-

[20] J. Michelet, *Le Peuple*, 158.

melled existence. For other writers, the child as rebel is a more intensely individual, indeed idiosyncratic image. Rimbaud's depiction in 'Après le déluge' of the child's arm-wheeling rejection of the re-establishment of bourgeois values combines with the virulence of his vocabulary and imagery when he gives the young adolescent's view of female beauty or accepted modes of behaviour to suggest a more personal revolt, just as Lautréamont's sado-masochistic representations of sexuality and of the enclosed family group, although they can be read as political satire, have far more to do with a profound metaphysical revolt.

Although both Hugo and Zola depict children involved in what can be seen as political revolt, neither suggests that their interest is anything other than merely playful. Gavroche's taunting of the soldiers on the barricade is simply an extension of his habitual jeering at representatives of authority, while his joy in the uprising is presented as a natural part of his pleasure in 'a certain state of violence' (*un certain état violent*).[21] In a careful juggling act, Hugo delights in conveying the gamin's potential as future revolutionary while insisting on his present insouciance: 'there are two things that tantalize him and that he constantly wants but never obtains: to overthrow the government and to repair his trousers.' (*il y a deux choses dont il est le Tantale et qu'il désire toujours sans y atteindre jamais: renverser le gouvernement et faire recoudre son pantalon.*)[22] Similarly, although Zola shows the effect on children of violent revolt in *Germinal*, where Lydie and Bébert die of gunshot wounds when soldiers fire into the rioting mob, their presence in the crowd is fortuitous, a result of curiosity and chance. This reluctance to attribute true political convictions to children would not, perhaps, be surprising were it not that two women writers reflect in their autobiographies an early awareness of national and political realities, however simplistic may be their conception of them. George Sand, who asserts that 'in those days we sucked the pride of victory with our mother's milk' (*on suçait avec le lait, à cette époque, l'orgueil de la victoire*),[23] refers to the intensity of her response to Napoleon's campaign in Russia in the following terms:

in the midst of our games and golden dreams, the news from Russia that autumn struck terrifying and painful chords. We began to listen when

[21] *Les Miserables*, ii. 162.   [22] Ibid., ii. 162.
[23] *Histoire de ma vie*, 736.

newspapers were read to us and the burning of Moscow struck me as a great act of patriotism.

au milieu de nos jeux et de nos songes dorés, les nouvelles de Russie vinrent, à l'automne, jeter des notes effrayantes et douloureuses. Nous commencions à écouter la lecture des journaux, et l'incendie de Moscou me frappa comme un grand acte de patriotisme.[24]

And she adds of the defeat in Russia:

children are excited in their own way by general facts and public misfortunes. No one around us spoke of anything other than the Russian campaign and for us it was as immense and fabulous as Alexander's expeditions to India.

les enfants s'impressionnent à leur manière des faits généraux et des malheurs publics. On ne parlait d'autre chose autour de nous que de la campagne de Russie, et pour nous c'était quelque chose d'immense et de fabuleux, comme les expéditions d'Alexandre dans l'Inde.[25]

Similarly, Juliette Adam explores at length the battle for her political allegiance waged by her grandparents and her father from the time when she was only 4, and although she suggests that much of her delight in Fourierism stemmed from its applicability to the school playground, she nevertheless conveys a sense of the child's awareness of the central issues. Quinet, too, refers to being deeply affected by the collapse of the Empire in his childhood and claims to have been irrevocably shaped by it.[26] Obviously much of this may be a form of retrospective illusion, but it nevertheless suggests that for certain writers the child's capacity for political understanding was considerably greater than that implied by Hugo or Zola.

It is almost certainly Jules Vallès, however, who seizes most forcefully on the relationship btween the child and the downtrodden and uses that relationship as the enabling factor of his trilogy, *Jacques Vingtras*. Through the multiple focus he adopts in the first part of the trilogy, *L'Enfant*, he reveals the pressures brought to bear on the child's father by his employers, on Jacques's mother by society, and on the boy himself not only by his parents but also by his teachers and schoolmates. The child thus becomes a figure through which Vallès can explore the ways in which those in power seek to maintain and consolidate their position, and the

[24] *Histoire de ma vie*, 734.   [25] Ibid., 737.
[26] *Histoire de mes idées*, 200–1.

experiences that nevertheless allow Jacques to break through this *'cordon sanitaire'*, to use Donzelot's term,[27] and become the subsequent revolutionary. Part of Vallès's purpose in this metonymical use of the child-figure is to give particularly forceful voice to an attack on the powers society grants the father, who in turn images the controlling forces in society itself. By adopting a child's-eye view, Vallès is able to give special intensity to his questioning of the father's absolute control over his progeny, at least until they reach the age of 21. Two images are chosen to enforce this attack. First, that of the little girl, Louisette, beaten to death by a father whom the law does not punish. Vallès's indignation at this point is so intense as to render him all but incoherent, conveying his impotent rage in a series of ejaculations:

They hurt her so much! She begged for forgiveness but it was in vain.

As soon as her father came near her, the ounce of reason she possessed in her angelic head would start trembling . . .

And he was not sent to the guillotine, that father! The law of an eye for an eye was not inflicted on the man who had assassinated his own child, that coward was not tortured, he was not buried alive beside his dead daughter!

On lui faisait si mal! et elle demandait grâce en vain.

Dès que son père s'approchait d'elle, son brin de raison tremblait dans sa tête d'ange . . .

Et on ne l'a pas guillotiné, ce père-là! On ne lui a pas appliqué la peine du talion à cet assassin de son enfant, on n'a pas supplicié ce lâche, on ne l'a pas enterré vivant à côté de la morte![28]

Melodramatic this may be, but its sincerity is unmistakable, and it is at least free from that distasteful undertone of sadistic half-complicity detectable in Zola's *L'Assommoir*, when he presents the image of the child Lalie beaten by her father. If Vallès has chosen to depict the suffering child as female, it is to intensify the gap between the father's strength and the child's weakness, whereas in *L'Assommoir* the child stands for suffering womanhood in general, as Zola makes clear in the text, and the description, for all its indignation, carries with it a sexual charge that makes it disturbing in quite different ways from Vallès's outburst. As Vallès insists in a letter to his friend Arnould:

---

[27] *La Police des familles*, 48.   [28] *L'Enfant*, 287. Original ellipses.

Embodying Childhood

It is . . . the State that creates ferocious fathers by sanctifying their authority, by placing above the heads of children, as it places above insurgents' heads, a providential law, an unquestioned religion—the respect passed down from father to child for the law!

C'est . . . l'Etat qui fait les pères féroces en sanctifiant l'autorité en mettant au-dessus des têtes d'enfants comme des têtes d'insurgés un droit providentiel, une religion indiscutée,—le respect de père en fils du respect de la loi![29]

The physical aggressions perpetrated against the child are only part of the general image of a controlling group that seeks to limit the physical and intellectual liberty of its subjects. Vallès, having shown in a variety of ways the physical infringements of the child's freedom and dignity, uses the final sections of *L'Enfant* to reveal the attempts to limit freedom of thought in the older child. Jacques as adolescent, indeed on the verge of manhood, finds that his determination to abandon any ambition to become a teacher and to work in a factory instead is rendered impotent, first by his mother's emotional blackmail—'You want to throw your father into despair, you wretched boy!!' (*Tu veux désespérer ton père, malheureux*!!)[30]—and then by his father's yet more powerful invocation of the law:

He has therefore the right to have me seized, he has the right to treat me as a thief, he is my master just as if I were a dog . . .
'Until you have reached the age of majority, my lad!'
He says this angrily, tapping a book called *The Code*; that evening I find this old book in a corner. I read it in secret, in the light of the street light that shines into my bedroom.
'*Can be locked up on the order of his parents*, etc.'

Il a donc le droit de me faire prendre, il a le droit de me traiter comme un voleur, il est maître de moi comme d'un chien . . .
'Jusqu'à ta majorité, mon garçon!'
Il a dit cela avec emportement, en tapant sur un livre qui s'appelle le Code; je le retrouve le soir dans un coin, ce vieux livre. Je le lis à la lumière du réverbère qui éclaire ma chambre.
'*Peut être enfermé, sur l'ordre de ses parents*, etc.'[31]

Nor should we consider this merely as a histrionic device used to increase Jacques's sense of revolt against the paternalistic power

Le Proscrit, 184.   *L'Enfant*, 385.
L'Enfant, 385–6. Original ellipses.

structures of mid-nineteenth-century France: Vallès himself was indeed imprisoned, on the order of his parents, in a mental asylum, where a doctor confirmed he was suffering from a brain disorder, although, when he succeeded in informing his friends, the fear of an inquiry led to his being released, miraculously cured. Indeed it was not until the Third Republic that the father's power over his child was severely curtailed.

For Vallès, therefore, the child, both in the sense of the small human being and in the legal sense of the individual who has not yet attained the age of majority, becomes a means of figuring in literature the numerous ways in which the forces in power control those subservient to them. Although other writers were also beginning to use the child in this way—Daudet in *Jack* and, somewhat later, Jules Renard in *Poil de carotte*, for instance—none equals the power of Vallès and he himself cannot maintain that blend of intensity, humour, psychological insight, and verbal inventiveness in his later novels.

While Zola may not share Vallès's interest in the child as political rebel, he is particularly interested in the child as criminal. In his notes for *Germinal* he indicates that through the character Jeanlin he intends to explore the formation of the criminal from his earliest years, drawing, as always, on heredity and environment to explain the development of personality and showing how intelligent observation of the workings of society lead the boy to reproduce around him the conditions of manipulation and repression that he believes lie at the heart of contemporary existence. Moreover, by using a device he frequently exploits, that of focusing the narrative through an outsider, in this case Étienne, Zola is able to depict Jeanlin both as an individual and as an archetype. Throughout the novel, Jeanlin is shown as a victim of society: small for his age, with thin limbs and scrofulous joints, poverty and the accident in the pit make of him a physical cripple just as the amorality and promiscuity of life in the mining community make of him a moral cripple. Cunning enough to perceive that survival depends on exploiting others and sufficiently imaginative to discover numerous ways of doing so, he is depicted by Zola as being precocious in a sickly way and as possessing the dark intelligence and lively skill of a human runt returning to its animal origins.[32] Realizing that the

---

[32] *Les Rougon-Macquart*, iii. 1249–5.

bourgeois benefit by getting others to work for them, Jeanlin forces
Bébert and Lydie to work for him; observing the sexual behaviour
of adults around him, he indulges with Lydie in 'the sorts of games
played by lecherous little dogs' (*des jeux de petits chiens vicieux*);
and noting the brutality with which the men frequently treat their
wives, he takes to beating her 'as you beat your legal wife' (*comme
on bat une femme légitime*).[33] His final act takes him even further
into crime, when he murders a soldier on guard, in cold blood and
for no reason other than that he wants to do it. Zola stresses at this
point the fact that for all his precocity Jeanlin is still a child, by
referring to 'that silent growth of crime in the depths of the child's
skull' (*cette végétation sourde du crime au fond de ce crâne
d'enfant*).[34] Significantly, he is one of the few members of the
family to survive in this singularly pessimistic novel.

   Although one can thus find a range of child-figures presented in
such a way as to invite and indeed demand metonymical readings, it
is none the less surprising, given the growing fascination with the
idea that in the development of the individual can be read that of
the race, as well as Taine's affirmation of the intrinsic interest of the
child's use of language and Michelet's study of the child as
representative of the working classes, that more writers did not
choose to exploit the figure of the child for metonymical purposes.
Indeed, I would argue that except, perhaps, in the works of certain
minor poets, nineteenth-century French literature saw relatively
little reduction of the child to mere stereotype.

---

[33] *Les Rougon-Macquart*, iii. 1239 and 1365.   [34] Ibid., iii. 1492.

Conclusion

> Only the child is alive, because childhood is expectation and desire. The adult runs the disappointing risk of achieving those desires.
>
> L'enfance seule vit parce qu'elle est l'attente et le désir. La virilité encourt le risque décevant de réaliser.
>
> (P. Adam, *Les Images sentimentales*)

ALTHOUGH it is widely believed, not least by the French themselves, that the figure of the child is far less common in French than in English literature, this study has revealed that the facts are rather different. Indeed, in the course of an artistic age marked by attempts to find aesthetic responses to the rapidly changing conditions of existence, and by increasingly intense and public self-analysis, the figure of the child, that *tabula rasa*, gradually becomes a dominant image of mankind's search for identity as French writers depict it. Above all, the orphan, the foundling, the child separated from its parents, or the child rejected by family or peers, comes to represent the sense of alienation in a world whose parameters seem to have altered, when such traditional frameworks as class and trade no longer hold firm and when even the concepts of space and time have shifted. That the nineteenth century should be one that not only attempts to create a literature accessible to children but also sees more consistent and widespread attempts than before to give children a role and a voice in adult literature is not merely, I would argue, an indication of changing attitudes towards both the self and that self as child, but also a reflection of a much broader degree of literary investigation, a questioning of the boundaries of literary genres and an exploration of the possibilities of narrative voice. Flaubert's experiments with *style indirect libre*, the attempts by Aloysius Bertrand, Baudelaire, Rimbaud, and Mallarmé, among others, to create prose poetry, the wider use of colloquialisms and slang in literary language, the provocative clashes of register, are all part of a general mood of discovery, a testing of muscles and sinews, in which the challenge to convey the experience, the thought, and the images of childhood plays a role that is far from unimportant.

Certainly the challenge of evoking children and childhood acts as a means of encouraging and refining not only certain themes and images but also narrative devices that then feed back into other areas of literature. R. Pascal's insistence that those nineteenth-century English novels that delve into childhood would be unthinkable without the great autobiographies can, of course, be extended to the novels and poetry of France, and given the rider that this is a two-way relationship, with the novelists and poets taking advantage of technical and thematic possibilities explored in autobiography, and autobiographers opening their range of references to include areas that had become acceptable in fiction, notably sexual drives in children and the difficulty of relations with parents and siblings. The three central areas in which such mutual stimulation can be perceived are those of the evocation of time, the creation of a space that externalizes mood and character, and the problems of narrative focus. The child-figure offers challenging ways of depicting phenomenological space and time, not only because its boredom threshold is normally lower than that of an adult, making it more aware of the treacle-like slowness or torrent-like swiftness with which time can pass, but also because it is more frequently obliged to accept the space and the use of time that others impose upon it. The most evident and most frequently repeated device used to explore this aspect of experience is that of the school, but both writers and artists also experiment with the space and time created by the child's imagination, particularly when it is absorbed in a book or in play. Both because of the child's freshness of vision and because of its limited linguistic range, the challenge of giving the child a voice set creative writers throughout the century a series of prickly problems to which they only gradually responded, exploring *style indirect libre*, a broader literary vocabulary than might otherwise have been employed, and polyphonic techniques that exploit the possibilities of intermingling the thought of adult and child, protagonist and observer. Taine's insistence that 'children's language is as instructive for the psychologist as the embryonic states of the body are for the naturalist. That language is mobile, constantly transformed, different from our own' (*le langage des enfants est aussi instructif pour le psychologue que les états embryonnaires du corps organisé pour le naturaliste. Ce langage est mouvant, incessamment transformé, autre que le nôtre*)[1] provoked, however, surprisingly little response in literature, perhaps because those closest to the child learning to speak—mothers and nurses—rarely had the time, experience, or encouragement to record their observations.

In terms of the boredom, the pain, or the pleasure it can experience, or the ways in which it reveals patterns of power or manipulation that the greater complexity of adult society obscures, the child is often a more sharply defined image of the adult, merely by dint of being simplified. It is, I believe, none the less misleading to argue that the use of the child-figure as a symbol necessarily reduces it to a stereotype. Hugo's transformation of Cosette to icon of the downtrodden and of Gavroche to archetype of the gamin can operate with such power only because both children also exist as individuals in their own right. Moreover, the range of character-istics attributed to child figures throughout the century is undeni-ably wide, even in works where they appear only briefly. What is more likely to be presented stereotypically is the fictional adult's response to the child, whose individuality he or she may well overlook in the dominant desire to find in the child confirmation of certain hopes or prejudices. These hopes and prejudices then fuse to form what can be termed a personal mythology of childhood.

It is the interplay of these two focal points, that of the experiencing child and that of the observing or reminiscing adult, that determines the various central images of childhood provided in the course of the century. The insistence on the child's purity, happiness, and insouciance that shapes the fictional works of the first half of the century depends, by and large, on an adult focus and, as historical records and autobiographical recollections reveal, it reflects more the adult's need to believe in such characteristics than any external reality. By the middle of the century the mood of cynicism and despair, the *mal du siècle* variously experienced as *ennui* or *spleen*, comes in turn both to colour the depictions of children and to encourage a deeper exploration of the writer's own childhood in search of the seeds of such discontent. As a result, a wider range of emotions is attributed to the child, who is now more frequently presented from a dual perspective, where child's-eye view and adult view intermingle. Since the optimistic association of

[1] *De l'intelligence*, I. 41–2.

the innate goodness of the noble savage and that of the unspoiled child could no longer be maintained in the face of the evidence, the belief in evil existing in children, which is of course in any case a basic tenet of Calvinist and Jansenist convictions, becomes an increasingly common literary theme. Towards the end of the century, while the child is frequently depicted as a prey to both physical and metaphysical suffering, there is nevertheless the beginning of that urge to happiness that marks the early memories of *A la recherche du temps perdu* and *Le Grand Meaulnes* and that is to become so dominant a theme in later, twentieth-century accounts of childhood. There is, moreover, a significant change of tone as the gushing and patronizing view of children is gradually replaced by an increasing awareness of the role of childhood traumas in forming the adult personality. And, finally, the century is marked by a growing interest in adolescence as a state separate both from childhood and from adulthood. Although I have deliberately excluded from this book any study of adolescence as such, it is abundantly clear that both thematically and narratologically it would provide the basis for further explorations.

The desire for political change, as well as fear of such change, meant that people both to the right and to the left of the political spectrum took an increasing interest in the education of a broader cross-section of the population than had hitherto been the case. While in Protestant countries, as is often argued,[2] the ability to read was seen as an essential means of salvation, the influence of the Catholic Church in France had, until the nineteenth century, presented the ability to read fluently and widely as the prerogative of the powerful. This religious difference, together with the associated fact that in Britain a network of lending libraries made it possible for children to read a far larger number of books than they could have afforded to buy, is often presented as one of the main reasons behind the relative rarity of good children's books originally written in French. Equally, the value placed on rationality and on clarity, or so the French like to aver, discouraged the creation in French of works similar to those of Lewis Carroll or Edward Lear. Whatever the reasons behind the choice of books written for, and offered to, children in nineteenth-century France,

---

[2] See e.g. J. Bratton: 'Protestantism is based on Bible study and therefore on literacy; to save one's soul one needs to be able to read' (*The Impact of Victorian Children's Fiction*, 14).

there can be no doubt, as our study of the autobiographical record reveals, and as references in fiction suggest, that what was read and experienced both in and out of school played an important role in shaping the imaginations of the writers and artists of the future. To my knowledge there is as yet no equivalent for nineteenth-century French writers and artists of Juliette Dusinberre's compelling exploration of the relationship between childhood reading and the creations of the Bloomsbury group, *Alice to the Lighthouse*, yet such a work would undoubtedly illuminate central nineteenth-century images and preoccupations that have hitherto been associated with the experience of adulthood or at best late adolescence.

Whatever the saccharine nostalgia and self-indulgent condescension of the presentation of children and childhood at certain moments in the nineteenth century, they nevertheless reveal themselves not only as central images of a rapidly changing society but also as the *locus* of considerable narrative and stylistic experimentation. For many nineteenth-century writers, the attempt to recover the lost content of childhood placed them in Alice's dilemma, for they were either small enough to go through the locked door to the magic garden or tall enough to reach the key, but never simultaneously both sufficiently small and in possession of the key. And for them there was no easy solution, no cake with the words 'EAT ME', beautifully marked out in currants. Nevertheless, the artistic exploration of the child's kaleidoscopic vision, of its freedom from the shackles of rationality, and of its imaginative linguistic transformations still appears as a major enabling factor in that joyous acceptance of change and the irrational that lies at the heart of modernism.

References

This bibliography contains only those works referred to in the text or footnotes, or works which, while they may not have been mentioned explicitly, nevertheless exerted an influence on my findings too significant for them not to be acknowledged. Critical works concerned with autobiography as a mode are indicated with an asterisk. Particularly useful bibliographies can be found in Chambart de Lauwe, Coe, Dupuy, Heywood, Lejeune (1975), Pollock, Spengemann, and Stearns. A selection of works read for comparative purposes is appended at the end of this bibliography.

ACKERMANN, L., *Œuvres* (Paris: Lemerre, 1885; repr. Farnborough: Gregg International, 1971).

ADAM, J., *Le Roman de mon enfance et de ma jeunesse* (Paris: Lemerre, 1902).

ADAM, P., *Les Images sentimentales* (Paris: Ollendorff, 1893).

AGOULT, MARIE D' (*pseud.* Daniel Stern), *Mes souvenirs* (Paris: Calmann-Lévy, 1877).

AMPÈRE, A.-M. and J.-J., *Correspondance et souvenirs* (Paris: Hetzel, 1875).

ANDERSON, R. D., *Education in France 1848–1870* (Oxford: Clarendon Press, 1975).

ANDRÉ, R., *L'Enfant miroir* (Paris: Gallimard, 1978).

ANTHOINE, E., *A travers nos écoles* (Paris: Hachette, 1887).

ARÈNE, P., *Jean-des-figues* (1868; repr. Paris: Lemerre, 1884).

ARIÈS, P., *L'Enfant et la vie familiale sous l'Ancien Régime* (1960; repr. Paris: Seuil, 1973).

——*L'Homme devant la mort* (Paris: Seuil, 1977).

ARMENGAUD, A., 'L'Attitude de la société à l'égard de l'enfant au XIXe siècle', *Annales de démographie historique*, 1973, pp. 303–12.

——'Eléments de bibliographie', *Annales de démographie historique*, 1973, pp. 345–52.

——*La Population française au dix-neuvième siècle* (Paris: Presses universitaires de la France, 1971).

ARNOLD, M., *Schools and Universities on the Continent* (Ann Arbor, Mich.: University of Michigan Press, 1964).

AUDOUX, M., *Marie-Claire* (1910; repr. Paris: Club français du livre, 1950).

AULNOY, MME D', *Contes de fées* (Paris: Chez Tiger, n.d.).

BADINTER, E., *L'Amour en plus* (Paris: Flammarion, 1980).

BAILLET, A., *Des enfants devenus célèbres par leurs études ou par leurs écrits* (Paris: Dezallier, 1858).

BALSEN, A., *Les Illustrés pour enfants* (Tourcoing: Duvier, 1920).

BALZAC, H. DE, 'L'Enfant maudit', in *Œuvres complètes*, ix (Paris: Pléiade, 1950).

——*Louis Lambert*, in *Œuvres complètes*, x (Paris: Pléiade, 1950).

——*Le Lys dans la vallée*, in *Œuvres complètes*, viii (Paris: Pléiade, 1937).

——*Pierrette*, in *Œuvres complètes*, iii (Paris: Pléiade, 1935).

BANCQUART, M., *Jules Vallès* (Paris: Seghers, 1971).

BANVILLE, T. DE, *Mes souvenirs* (Paris: Charpentier, 1882).

BARBIER, A., *Souvenirs personnels et silhouettes contemporaines* (Geneva: Slatkine, 1973).

BARDIN, A., *Angélina, une fille des champs* (Paris: Bonne, 1956).

BATANY, J., 'Regards sur l'enfance dans la littérature moralisante', *Annales de démographie historique*, 1973, pp. 123–8.

BAUDELAIRE, C., *Correspondance* (Paris: Pléiade, 1973).

——*Œuvres complètes* (Paris: Pléiade, 1975–6).

——*Un mangeur d'opium*, ed. M. Stäuble (Neuchatel: Baconnière, 1976).

BAZIN, H., *Vipère au poing* (Paris: Grasset, 1948).

BELLENGER, C. (ed.), *Histoire générale de la presse française*, ii (Paris: Presses universitaires de la France, 1969).

BELLET, R., *Jules Vallès journaliste du Second Empire, de la Commune de Paris et de la Troisième République* (Paris: Les Éditeurs français réunis, 1977).

BENDA, J., *La Jeunesse d'un clerc* (Paris: Gallimard, 1968).

BÉRANGER, P. J., *Ma biographie* (Paris: Perrotin, 1857).

BERLIOZ, H., *Mémoires* (Paris: Garnier-Flammarion, 1969).

BERNARDIN DE SAINT-PIERRE, J. H., *Paul et Virginie* (Paris: Folio, 1984).

BERQUIN, ARNAUD, J., *Ami de l'adolescence*, 3 vols. (Paris: Pissot & Barrois, 1786).

——*Ami des enfants* (1792: Paris: Didier, 1831).

BETHLENFALVAY, M., *Les Visages de l'enfant dans la littérature française du XIXe siècle: Esquisse d'un typologie* (Geneva: Droz, 1979).

BETTELHEIM, B., and ZELAN, K., *On Learning to Read: The Child's Fascination with Reading* (London: Thames & Hudson, 1982).

BIART, L., *Entre frères et sœurs* (Paris: Hetzel, n.d.).

BLAIS, M. C., *Pierre* (Montreal, Que.: Primeur, 1984).

BOAS, G., *The Cult of Childhood* (London: Warburg Institute, 1966).

BOER, J. P. DE, *Victor Hugo et l'enfant* (Paris: Champollion, 1934).

BOIGNE, COMTESSE DE, *Mémoires*, vol. i: 1781–1814 (Paris: Plon, 1907).

BOLLÈME, G., *La Bibliothèque bleue* (Paris: Juillard, 1971).

BONEY. E., 'The Influence of E. T. A. Hoffmann on George Sand', in Glasgow, *George Sand*, pp. 42–52.

BONJEAN, G., *Enfants révoltés et parents coupables: Étude sur la désorganisation de la famille et ses conséquences sociales* (Paris: Colin, 1895).

BONJEAN, G., *La Protection de l'enfance abandonnée ou coupable* (Paris: Sociéte de la protection de l'enfance abandonnée ou coupable, 1896).

BONNET, B., *Vie d'enfant*, trans. from Provençal by A. Daudet (Paris: Dentu, 1895).

BORDEAUX, H., 'Le Règne de l'enfant', *Le Correspondant*, 214 (1904), pp. 354–73.

BOSCO, H., *Un oubli moins profond* (Paris: Gallimard, 1961).

BOUCHER, H., *Souvenirs d'un parisien: 1830–1852* (Paris: Perrin, 1908).

BOURGET, P., *André Cornélis* (Paris: Lemerre, 1887).

——*Le Disciple* (Paris: Plon, 1901).

BOUVIER, J., *Mes mémoires: Une syndicaliste féministe 1876–1935*, ed. D. Armogathe and M. Albistun (Paris: La Découverte, Maspéro, 1983).

BOYLESVE, R., *L'Enfant à la balustrade* (1903; repr. Lausanne: Société coopérative éditions Rencontre, 1961).

BRATTON, J. S., *The Impact of Victorian Children's Fiction* (London: Croom Helm, 1981).

BRAUNSCHVIG, M., 'L'Enfant au XIXᵉ siècle', *Pages libres*, 22 Aug. 1903.

BRAVO-VILLASANTE, C., 'Le Vice et la vertu: L'Enfant bon et l'enfant méchant dans l'œuvre de Berquin', in Escarpit, *The Portrayal of the Child*, pp. 335–44.

BRÉHAT, A. DE, *Les Aventures d'un petit parisien* (Paris: Hetzel, 1871).

BROMBERT, V., *The Intellectual Hero* (London: Faber & Faber, 1960–1).

BRÜGGEMANN, T., 'L'Enfant lecteur et sa représentation par l'image: Un exposé historique', in Escarpit, *The Portrayal of the Child*, 147–56.

BRUN, C., *Trois plumes au chapeau: Ou l'instituteur d'autrefois* (Paris: Arthaud, 1950).

BRUN, R., *Le Livre français* (Paris: Presses universitaires de la France, 1969).

BRUNEAU, J., *Les Débuts littéraires de Gustave Flaubert 1831–1845* (Paris: Colin, 1962).

BRUNO, G. (Augustine Fouillée), *Le Tour de France par deux enfants* (Paris: Librairie classique d'Eugène Belin, 1977; facsimile of 1877 ed.).

*BRUSS, E. W., *Autobiographical Acts: The Changing Situation of a Literary Genre* (Baltimore: Johns Hopkins University Press, 1978).

BUGNIOT, L'ABBÉ, *Les Petits Savoyards: Ou l'exploitation de l'enfant par l'homme* (Châlon-sur-Saone: Mulcey, 1863).

BUGUET, H., *L'Esprit des enfants* (Paris: Librairie française Alphonse Piaget, 1886).

BUISINE, A., *Tombeau de Loti* (Paris: Aux amateurs de livres, 1988).

*BUTLER, R., *The Difficult Art of Autobiography* (Oxford: Clarendon Press, 1968).

CACÉRÈS, B., *Histoire de l'éducation populaire* (Paris: Seuil, 1964).

CAHUN, M., *Une jeunesse quai Conti*, manuscript: Bibliothèque nationale NAF 14880.

CALVET, J., *L'Enfant dans la littérature française*, 2 vols. (Paris: Lanore, 1930).

CANLER, F., *Mémoires*, i (Paris: Le Bien public, 1874); ii (Paris: Roy, 1882).

CARCO, F., *Mémoires d'une autre vie: Souvenirs d'enfance* (Paris: Albin Michel, 1934).

CARDINAL, M., *Les Mots pour le dire* (Paris: Grasset, 1975).

CARPENTER, H., and PRITCHARD, M., *The Oxford Companion to Children's Literature* (Oxford: Oxford University Press, 1984).

CARROLL, L., *The Annotated Alice* (Harmondsworth: Penguin, 1971).

CARY, J., *A House of Children* (London: Michael Joseph, 1951).

CAVE, T., *Recognitions* (Oxford: Oxford University Press, 1989).

CELLINI, B., *Autobiography*, trans. W. Gaunt (London: Dent, 1967).

CHABREUL, MME DE, *Jeux et exercices des jeunes filles* (Paris: Hachette, 1856).

CHAMBART DE LAUWE, M. J., 'La Représentation de l'enfant dans la littérature d'enfance et de jeunesse', in Escarpit, *The Portrayal of the Child*, pp. 5–22.

——*Un monde autre: L'Enfance* (Paris: Payot, 1971).

CHAMPFLEURY, J., *Les Souffrances du professeur Delteil* (Paris: Lévy, 1857).

——*Souvenirs et portraits de jeunesse* (1872; repr. Geneva: Slatkine, 1970).

CHARPENTIER, A., *L'Enfance d'un homme* (Paris: Lemerre, 1890).

CHASLES, P., *Mémoires*, 2 vols. (Paris: Charpentier, 1876–7).

CHASTENAY, MME DE, *Mémoires*, i (Paris: Plon, 1896).

CHATEAUBRIAND, C. R. DE, *Atala: René* (Paris: Roches, 1930).

——*Mémoires d'outre-tombe*, 6 vols., (Paris: Garnier, 1947).

CHEVALIER, L., *Classes laborieuses et classes dangereuses à Paris pendant la première moitié du dix-neuvième siècle* (Paris: Plon, 1958).

CHOPPIN, A., et al., *Les Manuels scolaires en France de 1879 à nos jours* (Paris: Université de la Sorbonne, service de l'histoire de l'éducation, 1981).

CHRISTIE, A., *An Autobiography* (London: Collins, 1977).

CLARE, J., *Poetry* (Oxford: Oxford University Press, 1984).

CLARÉTIE, J., *Les Jouets de France, leur histoire, leur avenir* (Paris: Delagrave, 1920).

*COE, R. N., 'Reminiscences of Childhood', in *Proceedings of the Leeds Philosophical Society*, 19/6 (1984), pp. 221–321.

——'Stendhal, Rousseau and the Search for Self', *Australian Journal of French Studies*, 16 (1979), pp. 27–47.

*——*When the Grass was Taller* (New Haven, Conn.: Yale University Press, 1984).

COLET, L., *Enfances célèbres* (Paris: Hachette, 1858).

CONSTANT, A., *Œuvres* (Paris: Pléiade, 1957).

COULMANN, J. J., *Réminiscences*, i (1862; repr. Geneva: Slatkine, 1973).

COURNOT, A., *Souvenirs 1760–1860* (Paris: Hachette, 1913).

COVENEY, P., *The Image of Childhood: The Individual and Society: A Study of a Theme in English Literature* (Harmondsworth: Penguin, 1967).

CRUBELLIER, M., *L'Enfance et la jeunesse dans la société française 1800–1950* (Paris: Colin, 1979).

CUSTINE, *Aloys* (Paris: Vézard, 1829).

DABOT, HENRI, *Lettres d'un lycéen et d'un étudiant de 1847 à 1854* (Paris: Peronne, n.d. but preface dated 1909).

DAINVILLE, F. DE, *L'Éducation des jésuites* (XVIe–XVIIIe *siècles*) (Paris: Minuit, 1978).

DÄLLENBACH, L., *Le Récit spéculaire: Contribution à l'étude de la mise en abyme* (Paris: Seuil, 1977).

——'Réflexivité et Lecture', *Revue des sciences humaines*, 49/173 (Jan.–Mar. 1980), pp. 23–37.

DAUDET, A., *Jack* (1876; repr. Paris: Dentu, 1889).

——*Le Petit Chose*, ed. J. H. Bornecque (1868; rep. Paris: Fasquelle, 1947).

DAUMARD, A., *Les Bourgeois de Paris au* XIXe *siècle* (Paris: Flammarion, 1970).

DE MAUSE, L. (ed.), *The History of Childhood* (New York: Psychohistory Press, 1974).

DELÉCLUZE, E., *Souvenirs de soixante années* (Paris: Lévy, 1862).

DELZONS, L., *La Famille française et son évolution* (Paris: Colin, 1913).

DESBORDES-VALMORE, M., *Œuvres poétiques*, 2 vols., ed. M. Bertrand (Grenoble: Presses universitaires de Grenoble, 1973).

——*Poésies*, ed. Y. Bonnefoy (Paris: Gallimard, 1983).

DESCHANEL, E., *Le Bien et le mal qu'on a dits des enfants* (Paris: Lévy, 1857).

DESNOYERS, L., *Les Mésaventures de J. P. Choppart* (Paris: Allardin, 1834).

DICKENS, C., *Great Expectations* (1861; London: Dent, 1971).

——*Hard Times* (1854; New York: Signet, 1961).

*DIDIER, B., *Le Journal intime* (Paris: Presses universitaires de la France, 1976).

DONZELOT, J., *La Police des familles*, postface by Gilles Deleuze (Paris: Minuit, 1977).

DROZ, G., *Monsieur, Madame et Bébé* (Paris: Hetzel, 1866).

DU CAMP, M., *Mémoires d'un suicidé* (Paris: Librarie nouvelle, 1855).

DUCRAY-DUMINIL, F. G., *Les Fêtes des enfants, ou, recueil de petits contes moraux*, 2 vols. (Paris: Haut-Cœur & Gayet Jeune, 1822).

DUMAS, A. (père), *La Bouillie de la comtesse Berthe* (Paris: Hetzel, 1845).

——*Mes mémoires*, i (Paris: Le Vasseur, n.d.).

DUPANLOUP, F. A. P., *L'Enfant* (Paris: Douniol, 1874).

DUPONT-FERRIER, G., *La Vie quotidienne d'un collège parisien*, 3 vols. (Paris: Boccard, 1921–5).

DUPUY, A., *Un personnage nouveau du roman français: L'Enfant* (Paris: Hachette, 1931).

DURAND, E., *Le Règne de l'enfant* (Paris: Lecône & Oduin, 1889).

DURKHEIM, E., *L'Évolution pédagogique en France*, 2 vols. (Paris: Alcan, 1938).

DUSINBERRE, J., *Alice to the Lighthouse* (London: Macmillan, 1987).

*EARLE, W., *The Autobiographical Consciousness* (Chicago: Quadrangle Books, 1972).

*ELBAZ, R., *The Changing Nature of the Self: A Critical Study of the Autobiographical Discourse* (London: Croom Helm, 1988).

ERIKSON, E. H., *Childhood and Society* (New York: Norton, 1963).

ESCARPIT, D. (ed.), *The Portrayal of the Child in Children's Literature* (Munich: Saur, 1985).

ESQUIROS, ADÈLE, 'Souvenirs d'enfance', BN cat. no. Ye676 (1849?).

Europe, special number on Hetzel, Nov.–Dec. 1980.

FAUCHER, N., *Mon histoire* (Lille: Imprimerie L. Danel, 1886).

FÉBVRE, L., and MARTIN, H. J., *L'Apparition du livre* (Paris: Albin Michel, 1958).

FÉNELON, F., *Les Aventures de Télémaque* (1699; Paris: Garnier, 1987).

——*L'Éducation des filles*, in *Œuvres*, i (Paris: Pléiade, 1983).

FEUILLET, OCTAVE MME, *Quelques années de ma vie* (Paris: Calmann-Lévy, 1894).

FISCHER, U., *Premiers maîtres:Collège de Saint-Claude (1864–73)* (Paris: private publication, 1931).

FLANDRIN, J. L., 'L'Attitude à l'égard du petit enfant et les conduites sexuelles dans la civilisation occidentale', *Annales de démographie historique*, 1973, pp. 143–210.

FLAUBERT, G., *Bouvard et Pécuchet* (Paris: Garnier-Flammarion, 1966).

——*Correspondance*, i and ii (Paris: Pléiade, 1973 and 1980).

——*L'Éducation sentimentale* (Paris: Livre de poche, 1972).

——*Madame Bovary* (Paris: Garnicr, 1971).

——*Œuvres de jeunesse*, i (Paris: Conard, 1902).

FLORIAN, J. P. CLARIS DE, *Choix des plus jolies fables* (Paris: Delarue, 1868).

——*La Jeunesse de Florian* (Paris: Briand, 1810).

FONTANEL, J., *Nos lycéens* (Paris: Plon, 1913).

FOUCAULT, M., *Surveiller et punir: Naissance de la prison* (Paris: Gallimard, 1975).

FRANCE, A., *Jean Servien* (Paris: Calmann-Lévy, 1882).
——*Le Livre de mon ami* (Paris: Calmann-Lévy, 1924).
——*Pierre Nozière* (Paris: Lemerre, 1899).
FRANKLIN, A., *La Vie privée d'autrefois*, vol. xvii: *L'Enfant* (Paris: Plon, 1895).
FRANKLIN, MILES, *Childhood at Brindabilla* (Sydney: Angus & Robertson, 1963).
FREUD, S., *An Autobiographical Study*, trans. J. Strachey (New York: Brentano's, 1928).
——*Gesammelte Werke, II–III* (London: Imago, 1942).
——*Gesammelte Werke, V* (London: Imago, 1942).
FRIEDMANN, J., *Alexandre Weill, écrivain constestaire et historien engagé, 1811–1899* (Strasbourg: Istra, 1980).
FROMENT, TH., *Rêves et devoirs* (Paris: Lemerre, 1873).
FROMENTIN, E., *Lettres de jeunesse*, ed. P. Blanchon (Paris: Plon, 1909).
FURET, F., and OZOUF, J., *Lire et écrire: l'alphabétisation des Français de Calvin à Jules Ferry* (Paris: Minuit, 1977).
GALLAND, A. (trans.), *Les Mille et une nuits* (Paris: Classiques Garnier, 1988).
GARDE, REINE, *Marie-Rose, histoire de deux jeunes orphelins* (Paris: Garnier, 1855).
GAUTIER, J., *Le Collier des jours* (Paris: Juven, 1904).
GAUTIER, T., *Souvenirs de théâtre, d'art et de critique* (Paris: Charpentier, 1882).
GENETTE, G., *Figures III* (Paris: Seuil, 1972).
GENLIS, MME DE, *Mémoires* (Paris: Didot, 1857).
——*Le Théâtre de l'éducation* (Paris: Didier, 1846).
GERBOD, P., *La Condition universitaire en France au dix-neuvième siècle* (Paris: Presses universitaires de la France, 1965).
——*La Vie quotidienne dans les lycées et collèges au dix-neuvième siècle* (Paris: Hachette, 1968).
GIDE, A., *Si le grain ne meurt* (Paris: Gallimard, 1928).
GLASGOW, J. (ed.), *George Sand: Collected Essays* (Troy, NY: Whitston, 1985).
GOFFMAN, E., *The Presentation of the Self* (Harmondsworth: Penguin, 1969).
*GOLDBERG, J., 'Cellini's Vita and the Conventions of Early Autobiography', *Modern Language Notes*, 89/1 (1974), pp. 71–83.
GONCOURT, E. DE, *Chérie* (Paris: Charpentier, 1884).
GOSSE, E., *Father and Son* (London: Folio Society, 1972).
GRAFF, H. J., *Literacy in History: An Interdisciplinary Research Bibliography* (Chicago: Newberry Library, 1976).
——*The Literacy Myth: Literacy and Social Structure in the Nineteenth Century* (New York: Academic Press, 1979).

GRAHAME, K., *The Wind in the Willows* (1908; London: Methuen, 1970).

GRATRY, A., *Souvenirs de jeunesse* (Paris: Douniol, 1874).

GREEN, J., *Partir avant le jour* (Paris: Grasset, 1963).

GUÉRIN, EUGÉNIE DE, *Journal et lettres* (Paris: Didier, 1863).

GUÉRIN, MAURICE DE, *Journal, lettres et poèmes* (Paris: Didier, 1862).

GUILLAUMIN, E., *La Vie d'un simple*, préface de Daniel Halévy (Paris: Stock, 1934).

GUIZOT, F., *Mémoires pour servir à l'histoire de mon temps*, 2 vols. (Paris: Lévy, 1858–9).

HARE, A., *The Story of my Life*, ed. M. Barnes (1896; repr. London: Allen & Unwin, 1952).

HAUSSMANN, BARON D', *Mémoires* (Paris: Harvard, 1890–3).

HAUSSONVILLE, COMTE D', *Ma jeunesse* (Paris: Calmann-Lévy, 1885).

HAUSSONVILLE, O., VICOMTE D', 'L'Enfance à Paris', *Revue des deux mondes*, 17 (1 Oct. 1876).

HAZARD, P., *Les Livres, les enfants et les hommes* (Paris: Bouvin, 1949).

HERMANT, A., *Confessions* (Paris: Flammarion, 1922).

HÉROARD, J., *Journal* (Paris: Fayard, 1989).

HEYWOOD, C., *Childhood in Nineteenth-Century France* (Cambridge: Cambridge University Press, 1988).

HOFSTADTER, D., *Gödel, Escher, Bach* (Harmondsworth: Penguin, 1979).

HOUSSAYE, A., *Les Confessions: Souvenirs d'un demi-siècle 1830–1880*, 6 vols. (Paris: Dentu, 1885–91).

HOUSTON, J. P., *The Demonic Imagination* (Baton Rouge, La.: Louisiana State University Press, 1969).

HOWE, P., 'The Child as Metaphor in the Novels of Fontane', *Oxford German Studies*, 10 (1979), pp. 121–38.

HUGO, V., *L'Art d'être grand-père* (1877; Paris: Ollendorff, 1914).

——*Les Contemplations* (1856; Paris: Garnier, 1969).

——*Les Misérables*, 3 vols. (1862; Paris: Folio, 1973).

——*Œuvres poétiques*, i (Paris: Pléiade, 1964).

HUIZINGA, J., *Homo ludens: A Study of the Play Element in Culture* (London: Temple Smith, 1970).

HUNT, D., *Parents and Children in History: The Psychology of Family Life in Early Modern France* (New York: Basic Books, 1973).

HÜRLIMANN, B., *Three Centuries of Children's Books in Europe*, trans. and ed. B. W. Alderson (Cleveland: World Publishing, 1968).

ISAAC, J., *Expériences de ma vie* (Paris: Calmann-Lévy, 1960).

JAMES, H., *What Maisie Knew* (1897: Harmondsworth: Penguin, 1966).

JAMMES, F., *De l'âge divin à l'âge ingrat* (Paris: Plon Nourrit, 1921).

JAN, I., *On Children's Literature*, trans. C. Storr (London: Allen Lane, 1973).

JANET, P., *La Famille* (Paris: Ladrange Cotillon, 1855).

JASENAS, E., *Marceline Desbordes-Valmore* (Geneva: Droz, 1962).

References

*JAUSS, H. R., 'Literary History', *New Literary History*, 11/1 (Autumn 1970), pp. 7–37.

JOINVILLE, PRINCE DE, *Vieux Souvenirs*, ed. D. Meyer (Paris: Mercure de France, 1970).

JOLLÈS, A., *Formes simples*, trans. A. M. Buguet (1930; repr. Paris: Seuil, 1972).

JOYCE, J., *A Portrait of the Artist as a Young Man* (1916; repr. London: Cape, 1945).

JUNG, C. G., *Analytical Psychology* (New York: Pantheon, 1968).

——*Memories, Dreams, Reflections*, trans. R. and C. Winston, ed. A. Jaffé (London: Fontana, 1983).

KERMODE, F., *The Sense of an Ending* (New York: Oxford University Press, 1967).

KEY, E., *The Century of the Child* (New York: Knickerbocker Press, 1909).

KIPLING, R., *Stalky & Co.* (1899; Oxford: Oxford University Press, 1987).

KNIBIELHER, Y., and FOUQUET, C., *Histoire des mères* (Paris: Montalba, 1977).

KOCK, P. DE, *Mémoires* (Paris: Dentu, 1873).

KREYDER, L., *L'Enfance des saints et des autres* (Fasano: Schena-Nizet, 1987).

KROLL, J., 'The Concept of Childhood in the Middle Ages', *Journal of the History of Behavioural Sciences*, 13/4 (1977), 384–93.

KUHN, R., *Corruption in Paradise: The Child in Western Literature* (Hanover, NH: University Press of New England, 1982).

LACAN, J., *Écrits* (Paris: Seuil, 1966).

LACENAIRE, PIERRE-FRANÇOIS, *Mémoires*, ed. M. Lebailly (Paris: Albin Michel, 1968).

LACOMBLE, E. E. B., *Perles de la poésie française contemporaine* (Brussels: Lebègue, n.d.).

LAMARTINE, A. DE, *Confidences* (Paris: Hachette, 1862).

——*Jocelyn* (Paris: Garnier, 1954).

——*Méditations poétiques: Nouvelles méditations poétiques* (Paris: Gallimard, 1981).

——*Œuvres poétiques* (Paris: Pléiade, 1973).

*LANDOW, G. (ed.), *Approaches to Victorian Autobiography* (Athens, Oh; Ohio University Press, 1979).

LAPRADE, V. DE, *L'Éducation homicide: Plaidoyer pour l'enfance* (Paris: Didier, 1868).

——*Le Livre d'un père* (Paris: Hetzel, n.d.).

LASLETT, P., 'The Wrong Way through the Telescope', *British Journal of Sociology*, 27 (1976), pp. 319–42.

LATZARUS, M. T., *La Littérature enfantine en France dans la seconde moitié du* XIXe *siècle* (Paris: Presses universitaires de la France, 1923).

LAUTRÉAMONT, *Œuvres complètes* (Paris: Pléiade, 1970).

LAVISSE, ERNEST, *Souvenirs* (Paris: Calmann-Lévy, 1988).

LE MEN, S., *Les Abécédaires illustrés du dix-neuvième siècle* (Paris: Promodis, 1984).

LE ROY LADURIE, E., *Montaillou: Village occitan de 1294 à 1324* (Paris: Gallimard, 1978).

LEGOUVÉ, E., *Soixante ans de souvenirs: I; Ma jeunesse* (Paris; Hetzel, 1886).

*LEJEUNE, P., *L'Autobiographie en France* (Paris: Colin, 1971).

——*Je est un autre: L'Autobiographie de la littérature aux médias* (Paris: Seuil, 1980).

——*Moi aussi* (Paris: Seuil, 1986).

——*Le Pacte autobiographique* (Paris: Seuil, 1975).

LEPAGE (*pseud.* Egapel X.), *Soixante ans de la vie d'un prolétaire* (Paris: Vanier, 1900).

LEWIS, C. S., 'On Three Ways of Writing for Children', in *Of Other Worlds* (New York: Harcourt, 1967).

——*Surprised by Joy* (London: Bles, 1955).

LLOYD, R., *Baudelaire's Literary Criticism* (Cambridge: Cambridge University Press, 1981).

LOTI, P., *Prime jeunesse* (Paris: Calmann-Lévy, 1919).

——*Le Roman d'un enfant* (1890; repr. Paris: Flammarion, 1988).

MACÉ, J., *L'Arithmétique de grand-papa: Histoire de deux petits marchands de pommes* (Paris: Hetzel, 1872).

——*Contes du petit château* (Paris: Hetzel, 1895).

——*Les Soirées de ma tante Rosy* (Paris: Hetzel, 1895).

MALOT, H., *Sans famille*, 2 vols. (1878; repr. Paris: Livre de poche, 1987).

MALRAUX, A., *Antimémoires* (Paris: Folio, 1972).

*MAN, P. DE, 'Autobiography as De-facement', *Modern Language Notes*, 96/5 (Dec. 1979), pp. 919–30.

*——*The Rhetoric of Romanticism* (New York: Columbia University Press, 1984).

MARMONTEL, J. F., *Mémoires*, ed. John Renwick, i (Clermont-Ferrand: G. de Bussac, 1972).

MAROUZEAU, J., *Une enfance* (Paris: Denoël, 1937).

MARTIN, H. J., and CHARTIER, R., *Histoire de l'édition française*, ii and iii (Paris: Promodis, 1984–5).

MASEFIELD, J., *The Midnight Folk* (1927; London: Pan, 1957).

MAUPASSANT, G. DE, *Contes et nouvelles*, 2 vols. (Paris: Pléiade, 1974–79).

——*Œuvres complètes* (Paris: Conard, 1919–30).

*MAY, G., *L'Autobiographie* (Paris: Presses universitaires de la France, 1979).

MAYEUR, F., *L'Éducation des jeunes filles en France au dix-neuvième siècle* (Paris: Hachette, 1979).

——*L'Enseignement secondaire des jeunes filles* (Paris: Presses de la fondation nationale des sciences politiques, 1977).

*MEHLMAN, J., *A Structural Study of Autobiography* (Ithaca, NY: Cornell University Press, 1974).

MERCIER, R., *L'Enfant au* XVIIIe *siècle*, thesis for the University of Paris (Dakar, 1961).

MÉRIMÉE, P., *Romans et nouvelles* (Paris: Pléiade, 1934).

MERLIN, COMTESSE DE, *Mes douze premières années* (Paris, 1837).

MICHELET, A., *Mémoires d'une enfant* (Paris: Hachette, 1867).

MICHELET, J., *Ma jeunesse* (Paris: Calmann-Lévy, 1884).

——*Le Peuple* (Paris: Didier, 1946).

——*Nos fils* (Paris: Librairie internationale, 1870).

MISTLER, J., *La Librairie Hachette* (Paris: Hachette, 1964).

MISTRAL, F., *Mes origines: Mémoires et récits* (Paris: Plon, 1906).

MOORES, P. M., *Vallès: L'Enfant* (London: Grant & Cutler, 1987).

MORILLON, A., *Souvenirs de Saint-Nicolas* (Paris: Lecoffre, 1869).

MOULIN, J., *Marceline Desbordes-Valmore* (Paris: Seghers, 1955).

MÜLLER, G., *Morphologische Poetik* (Darmstadt: Wissenschaftliche Buchgesellschaft, 1968).

MÜLSCH, ELISABETH-CHRISTINE, *Zwischen Assimilation und Selbstverständnis: David Léon Cahun (1841–1900) ein Journalist und Jugendbuchautor im Umfeld der Dreyfüs-Affäre* (Bonn: Romanistischer Verlag, 1987).

MUSSET, A. DE, *Confession d'un enfant du siècle* (Paris: Gallimard, 1973).

NADAUD, M., *Mémoires de Léonard*, ed. M. Agulhon (Paris: Hachette, 1976).

NERVAL, G. DE, *Œuvres complètes* (Paris: Classiques Garnier, 1958).

NISARD, D., *Souvenirs et notes biographiques* (Paris: Calmann-Lévy, 1888).

NODIER, C., *Contes fantastiques* (Paris: Charpentier, 1861).

——*Souvenirs de jeunesse: Extrait des mémoires de Maxime Odin* (Brussels: Société belge de librairie, Hauman, 1842).

NORA, P. (ed.), *Les Lieux de mémoire* (Paris: Gallimard, 1984).

*OAKESHOTT, E., *Childhood in Autobiography* (Cambridge: Cambridge University Press, 1960).

O'BRIEN, J., *The Novel of Adolescence in France: The Study of a Literary Theme* (New York: Columbia University Press, 1937).

*OLNEY, J. (ed.), *Autobiography: Essays Theoretical and Critical* (Princeton, NJ: Princeton University Press, 1980).

*——*Metaphors of Self: The Meaning of Autobiography* (Princeton, NJ: Princeton University Press, 1972).

ORDINAIRE, D., *Les Régents de collège* (Paris: Armand le Chevalier, 1873).

*ORLANDO, F., *Infanzia, memoria e storia da Rousseau ai Romantici* (Padua: Liviana Editrice, 1966).

OZOUF, J. and M., 'Le Tour de la France', in Nora, *Les Lieux de mémoire*, pp. 291–321.

PAPE-CARPENTIER, M., *Le Secret des grains de sable: Géométrie de la nature* (Paris: Hetzel, 1862).

PARKER, C. S., *The Defense of the Child by French Novelists* (New York: G. Banta, 1925).

*PASCAL, R., *Design and Truth in Autobiography* (Cambridge, Mass.: Harvard University Press, 1960).

PERDIGUIER, AGRICOL, *Mémoires d'un compagnon* (Paris; Denoël, 1943).

PEREC, G., *W: Ou souvenirs d'enfance* (Paris: Denoël, 1975).

PERRAULT, C., *Contes de ma mère l'oye* (Paris: Folio, 1977).

PERSE, SAINT-JOHN, 'Pour fêter une enfance', in *Œuvres complètes* (Paris: Pléiade, 1972).

PICHOIS, C., *Philarète Chasles* (Paris: Corti, 1965).

——'Les Vrais Mémoires de Philarète Chasles', *Revue des sciences humaines*, 81 (Jan.–Mar. 1956), pp. 71–97.

POLLOCK, L., *Forgotten Children* (Cambridge: Cambridge University Press, 1983).

PONSON DU TERRAIL, *L'Héritage mystérieux* (Paris: Garnier, 1977).

PONTMARTIN, *Mes mémoires: Enfance et jeunesse*, 2 vols. (Paris: Calmann-Lévy, 1885–6).

PORTER, D., 'Stendhal and the Impossibility of Autobiography', *French Studies* 32/2 (Apr. 1978), pp. 158–69.

PORTER, H., *The Watcher on the Cast-Iron Balcony* (London: Faber & Faber, 1963).

POUILLON, J., *Temps et roman* (Paris: Gallimard, 1946).

PRÉVOST, *Mademoiselle Jauffre* (Paris: Lemerre, 1889).

PROST, A., *Histoire de l'enseignement en France* (Paris: Flammarion, 1968).

PROUST, M., *A la recherche du temps perdu*, 3 vols. (Paris: Pléiade, 1954).

QUINET, E., *L'Enseignement du peuple*, xi (Paris: Librairie Germer-Baillière, 1876).

——*Histoire de mes idées* (Paris: Flammarion, 1972).

RAHN, S., *Children's Literature: An Annotated Bibliography* (New York: Garland, 1981).

*RAOUL, V., *The French Fictional Journal* (Toronto: University of Toronto Press, 1980).

RÉMUSAT, C. DE, *Mémoires de ma vie: Enfance et jeunesse; la restauration libérale*, ed. C. H. Pouthas (Paris: Plon, 1958).

RENAN, E., *Cahiers de jeunesse 1845–46* (Paris: Calmann-Lévy, 1906).

——*Souvenirs d'enfance et de jeunesse* (Paris: Calmann-Lévy, 1883).

RENARD, J., *Journal 1887–1910* (Paris: Pléiade, 1965).

——*Œuvres*, i (Paris: Pléiade, 1970).

——*Poil de carotte* (Paris: Imprimerie nationale, 1988).

RICHARD, C., *Edgar Allan Poe, journaliste et critique* (Paris: Klincksieck, 1974).

RICHARD-LENOIR, F., *Mémoires* (Paris: Delaunay, 1837).
RICHARDSON, H. H., *The Getting of Wisdom* (1910: London: Virago, 1981).
——*Myself when Young* (London: Heinemann, 1964).
RICHTER, A., 'L'Enfant dans la littérature fantastique moderne', *Revue générale* (Dec. 1983), pp. 61–70.
RIMBAUD, A., *Œuvres* (Paris: Classiques Garnier, 1987).
——*Œuvres complètes* (Paris: Gallimard, Pléiade, 1972).
ROBERT, M., *Roman des origines, origines du roman* (Paris: Gallimard, 1972).
ROUSSEAU, J. J., *Émile* (1762; Paris: Pléiade, 1969).
——*Œuvres complètes, I: Confessions* (Paris: Gallimard, Pléiade, 1959).
*ROUSSET, J., *Narcisse romancier* (Paris: Corti, 1973).
RUSKIN, J., *Praeterita I* (London: George Allen, 1905).
RUSSELL, B., *Autobiography* (1967; repr. London: Unwin, 1978).
SAID, E. W., *Beginnings, Intention and Method* (Baltimore: Johns Hopkins University Press, 1975).
SAND, GEORGE, *François le champi* (Paris: Livre de poche, 1976).
——*Histoire de ma vie* (Paris: Pléiade, 1970).
——*Histoire du véritable Gribouille* (Paris: Hetzel, 1851).
——*Les Maîtres Sonneurs* (Paris: Folio, 1979).
——*La Mare au diable* (Paris: Garnier-Flammarion, 1964).
——*La Petite Fadette* (Paris: Garnier-Flammarion, 1967).
The George Sand Papers: 1 (New York: AMS, 1980).
The George Sand Papers: 2 (New York: AMS, 1980).
SANDEAU, J., *La Roche aux mouettes* (Paris: Hachette, 1932).
SANDRIN, J., *Enfants trouvés* (Paris: Aubier Montaigne, 1982).
SARCEY, F., *Journal de jeunesse* (Paris: Bibliothèque des annales, n.d.).
——*Souvenirs de jeunesse* (Paris: Ollendorff, 1885).
SARRAUTE, N., *Enfance* (Paris: Gallimard, 1983).
SARTRE, J. P., *L'Idiot de la famille*, 3 vols. (Paris: Gallimard, 1971–2).
SCHLUMBERGER, J., 'Eveils', in *Œuvres*, vi (Paris: Gallimard, 1960).
——'La France sévère à l'enfance', *Les Nouvelles littéraires*, 8 Sept. 1934.
SCHWEITZER, A., *Aus meiner Kindheit und Jugendzeit* (Munich: Becksche Verlag, 1924).
SEGALEN, M., *Love and Power in the Peasant Family: Rural France in the Nineteenth Century*, trans. S. Mathews (Oxford: Blackwell, and Chicago: Chicago University Press, 1983).
SÉGUIN, J. P., *Nouvelles à sensation: Canards du XIXe siècle* (Paris: Colin, 1959).
SÉGUR, COMTESSE DE, *Histoire de Blondine* (Paris: Livre de poche, 1982).
——*Les Malheurs de Sophie* (Paris: Hachette, 1886).
——*Quel amour d'enfant!* (Paris: Hachette, 1875).
——*Un bon petit diable* (Paris: Hachette, 1901).

SERS, BARON DE, *Mémoires: Souvenirs d'un préfet de la monarchie 1786–1862* (Paris: Fontemoing, 1906).

*SHAPIRO, S., 'The Dark Continent of Literature: Autobiography', *Comparative Literature Studies*, 5 (1968), pp. 421–54.

SHORTER, E., *The Making of the Modern Family* (London: Collins, 1976).

SIMON, J., *L'École* (Paris: Lacroix, Verboekhoven, 1865).

——*L'Ouvrier de 8 ans* (Paris: Librairie internationale, 1867).

——*Premières années* (Paris: Flammarion, c. 1924).

SKINNER, Q., *Foundations of Modern Political Thought* (Cambridge: Cambridge University Press, 1978).

SOLIDAY, G. L., HAREVEN, T. K., VANN, R.T., and WHEATON, R., (eds.), *History of the Family and Kinship* (Millwood, NY: Knaus International, 1980).

SOMMERVILLE, C. J., *The Rise and Fall of Childhood* (Beverley Hills, Calif.: Sage, 1982).

*SPENGEMANN, W., *Forms of Autobiography* (New Haven, Conn: Yale University Press, 1980).

SPITZER, A. B., *The French Generation of 1820* (Princeton, NJ: Princeton University Press, 1987).

STAROBINSKI, J., *Jean-Jacques Rousseau: La Transparence et l'obstacle* (Paris: Gallimard, 1971).

——'Le Style de l'autobiographie', *La Relation critique* (Paris: Gallimard, 1971), 83–98.

STEARNS, P., *Paths to Authority: The Middle Class and the Industrial Labor Force in France 1820–1848* (Urbana, Ill.: University of Illinois Press, 1978).

STELLA, J., and BOUZONNET-STELLA, CLAUDINE, *Les Jeux et plaisirs de l'enfance* (Paris, 1667; repr. Geneva: Slatkine, 1981).

STENDHAL (Henri Beyle), *Œuvres intimes* (Paris: Pléiade, 1955).

——*Souvenirs d'égotisme* (Paris: Folio, 1983).

——*Vie de Henry Brulard*, 2 vols. (Paris: Le Divan, 1949).

STONE, L., *The Family, Sex and Marriage in England 1500–1800* (London: Weidenfeld & Nicolson, 1977).

SYLVÈRE, A., *Toinou: Le cri d'un enfant auvergnat* (Paris: Plon, Terre Humaine, 1980).

TAINE, H., *De l'intelligence*, 2 vols. (Paris: Hachette, 1870).

——*Étienne Mayran* (Paris: Hachette, 1910).

TERME, J. F., and MAUFALCON, J. B., *Histoire statistique et morale des enfants trouvés* (Paris: Baillière, 1837).

——*Nouvelles considérations sur les enfants trouvés* (Lyon: La Guillotière, 1838).

TOLÉDANO, A. D., *La Vie de famille sous la restauration et la Monarchie de Juillet* (Paris: Albin Michel, 1943).

TOLSTOY, L., *On Education*, trans. L. Wiener (Chicago: Chicago University Press, 1967).

TÖPFFER, R., *La Bibliothèque de mon oncle* (Paris: Nillson, n.d.).

——*Monsieur Crépin* (Geneva: Kessmann, 1846).

TOUCHARD-LAFOSSE, G., *Souvenirs d'un demi-siècle* (Paris: Librairie de Dumont, 1836).

TOURNIER, M., *Les Météores* (Paris: Folio, 1975).

TOURSCH, V., *L'Enfant français à la fin du* XIXe *siècle d'après ses principaux romanciers* (Paris: Presses modernes, 1939).

TURIN, Y., 'Enfants trouvés, colonisation et utopie: Étude d'un comportement social au XIXe siècle', *Revue historique*, 496 (Oct.–Dec. 1970), pp. 329–56.

VALLÈS, J., *L'Enfant* (Paris: Livre de poche, 1972).

——*Littérature et révolution, recueil de textes littéraires*, ed. R. Bellet (Paris: Éditeurs français réunis, 1969).

——*Œuvres complètes*, 15 vols. (Paris: Éditeurs français réunis, 1950–73).

——*Œuvres I (1857–1870)* (Paris: Pléiade, 1975).

——*Le Proscrit: Correspondance avec Arthur Arnould*, ed. L. Scheler (Paris: Éditeurs français réunis, 1973).

VAN DE WALLE, E., *The Female Population of France in the Nineteenth Century* (Princeton, NJ: Princeton University Press, 1974).

*VERCIER, B., 'Le Mythe du premier souvenir: Pierre Loti, Michel Leiris', *Revue d'histoire littéraire de la France*, 75/6 (Nov.–Dec. 1975), pp. 1029–40).

VERLAINE, P., *Mes prisons et autres écrits autobiographiques* (Paris: Livre de poche, 1973).

VÉRON, L., *Mémoires d'un bourgeois de Paris* (Paris: Gonet, 1853).

VIGÉE-LEBRUN, E., *Mémoires d'une portraitiste* (Paris: Scala, 1989).

——*Souvenirs de Mme Louise-Elisabeth Vigée-Lebrun: Notes et portraits: 1755–1789* (Paris: Fayard, n.d.).

VIGNY, A., *Mémoires inédits* (Paris: Gallimard, 1958).

VINET, A., *Chrestomathie française: Littérature de l'enfance* (Lausanne: Bridel, 1874).

VOILQUIN, S., *Souvenirs d'une fille du peuple ou la Saint-Simonienne en Egypte 1834 à 1836* (Paris: Sauzet, 1866).

WALVIN, J., *A Child's World: A Social History of Childhood 1800–1914* (Harmondsworth: Penguin, 1982).

WEILL, A., *Ma jeunesse*, 3 vols. (Paris: Dentu, 1870).

WHEATON, R., and HAREVA, T. K., *Family and Sexuality in French History* (Philadelphia: University of Philadelphia Press, 1980).

WILDER, LAURA INGALLS, *Little House Books* (1932–43; Harmondsworth: Penguin, 1963).

*WILLIAMS, H., *Rousseau and Romantic Autobiography* (Oxford: Oxford University Press, 1983).

WORDSWORTH, W., *The Prelude* (begun 1798; Oxford: Oxford University Press, 1950).

YALOM, M., 'Towards a History of Female Adolescence: The Contribution of George Sand', in Glasgow, *George Sand*, pp. 204–15.

ZELDIN, T., 'Biographie et psychologie sous le Second Empire', *Revue d'histoire moderne et contemporaine*, 21 (Jan.–Mar. 1974), pp. 58–74.

——*France 1848–1945: Ambition and Love* (Oxford: Oxford University Press, 1979).

——*France 1848–1945: Intellect and Pride* (Oxford: Oxford University Press, 1980).

——*France 1848–1945: Taste and Corruption* (Oxford: Oxford University Press, 1980).

ZOLA, E., *Les Rougon-Macquart*, 5 vols. (1871–93; Paris: Pléiade, 1960–7).

Further Reading

AKSAKOFF, S., *Years of Childhood*, trans. from Russian by J. D. Duff (1856; repr. Oxford: Oxford University Press, 1983).

ARON, M., *Le Journal d'une sévrienne* (Paris: Alcan, 1912).

AVERY, G., and BULL, A., *Nineteenth-Century Children* (London: Hodder & Stoughton, 1965).

BARTHES, R., *Roland Barthes par Roland Barthes* (Paris: Seuil, 1975).

BÉALU, M., *Le Chapeau magique*, vol. i: *Enfances et aprentissages* (Paris: Pierre Belfond, 1980).

BEAUVOIR, S. DE, *Mémoires d'une jeune fille rangée* (Paris: Gallimard, 1958).

BÉLY, A., *Kotik Letaev*, trans. G. Janacek (Ann Arbor, Mich.: Ardis, 1971).

BERTHAUD, ABBÉ, *Quadrille des enfans ou système nouveau de l'écriture* (Paris: Chez Couturier, 1777).

BÉZIERS, S., *La Protection de l'enfance ouvrière* (Montpellier: Mari-Lavit, 1935).

BRATTON, J. S., *The Impact of Victorian Children's Fiction* (London: Croom Helm, 1981).

BRONTË, C., *Jane Eyre* (1847; Harmondsworth: Penguin, 1962).

——*Villette* (1853; Harmondsworth: Penguin, 1979).

CACÉRÈS, B., *Histoire de l'éducation populaire* (Paris: Seuil, 1964).

CADOGAN, M., and CRAIG, P., *You're a brick, Angela! A New Look at Girls' Fiction from 1839 to 1975* (London: Gollancz, 1976).

CANETTI, E., *Histoire d'une jeunesse: la langue sauvée*, trans. B. Kreiss (Paris: Albin Michel, 1980).

CAROSSA, H., *Eine Kindheit* (Oxford: Blackwell, 1942).

COLMER, J. and D. (eds.), *Australian Autobiography* (Harmondsworth: Penguin, 1987).

DARTON, F. J. HARVEY, *Children's Books in England: Five Centuries of Social Life* (1932; Cambridge: Cambridge University Press, 1982).

DELARUE, P., et TENÈZE, MARIE-LOUISE, *Le Conte populaire français*, i (Paris: Erasme, 1957); ii (Paris: Maisonneuve & Larule, 1964); iii (Paris: Maisonneuve & Larule, 1976).

DOUGLAS, N., *London Street Games* (1916; repr. London: Chatto & Windus, 1931).

EEDEN, F. VAN, *The Deeps of Deliverance*, trans. M. Robinson (New York: Twayne, 1974).

EGOFF, SHEILA A., *Children's Periodicals of the Nineteenth Century* (London: Library Association, 1951).

——(ed.), *Only Connect: Readings on Children's Literature* (Toronto: Oxford University Press, 1969).

——*The Republic of Childhood* (Toronto: Oxford University Press, 1967).

FEN, E., *A Russian Childhood* (London: Methuen, 1961).

FROEBEL, F., *Autobiography*, trans. E. Michaelis and K. Moore (London: Swan Sonnenschein, 1903).

GORKY, M., *My Childhood* (Harmondsworth: Penguin, 1966).

HANRAHAN, B., *The Scent of Eucalyptus* (London: Chatto & Windus, 1973).

HARDY, THOMAS, *Our Exploits at West Poley* (London: Oxford University Press, 1952; written 1882).

HAYDON, B., *Autobiography and Memoires (1786–1846)*, ed. T. Taylor (London: Peter Davies, 1926).

HERZFELD, M. VON, 'Goethe's Images of Children', *German Life and Letters*, 25 (1971–2), pp. 219–31.

HORNE, D., *The Education of Young Donald* (Sydney: Angus & Robertson, 1967).

HUDSON, W. H., *Far Away and Long Ago* (1939; repr. London: Dent, 1985).

HUGHES, M. V., *A London Childhood of the 1870s* (Oxford: Oxford University Press, 1934).

KEMPTON, A. P. L., 'The Theme of Childhood in the French Eighteenth-Century Novel', *Studies on Voltaire and the Eighteenth Century*, 132 (1975), pp. 205–25.

LE GOFF, J., 'Petits enfants dans la littérature des xiiᵉ–xiiiᵉ siècles', *Annales de démographie historique*, 1973, pp. 129–32.

LEIRIS, M., *L'Âge d'homme* (1922; repr. Paris: Gallimard, 1972).

MARTINEAU, H., *Autobiography*, i (1877; repr. London: Virago, 1983).

McINNES, G., *The Road to Gundagai* (London: Hamish Hamilton, 1965).

MEAD, M., *Blackberry Winter: My Earlier Years* (New York: William Morrow, 1972).

MILNE, A. A., *It's Too Late Now* (London, 1939).

MORITZ, K. P., *Anton Reiser* in *Werke*, ii (Berlin: Aufbau Verlag, 1973).

OPIE, I. AND P., *The Lore and Language of Schoolchildren* (Oxford: Oxford University Press, 1959).

——*The Singing Game* (Oxford: Oxford University Press, 1984).

OZMENT, S., *When Fathers Ruled: Family Life in Reformation Europe* (Cambridge, Mass.: Harvard University Press, 1983).

PAGNOL, M., *La Gloire de mon père* (1957; repr. Paris: Éditions de Fallois, 1988).

PERGAUD, L., *La Guerre des boutons* (1912; repr. Paris: Folio Junior, 1987).

PICKERING, SAMUEL F. JUN., *John Locke and Children's Books in Eighteenth-Century England* (Knoxville, Tenn.: University of Tennessee Press, 1981).

PONTALIS, J. B., *L'Amour des commencements* (Paris: Gallimard, 1986).

RICHTER, JEAN-PAUL, *Levana and Autobiography* (London: George Ball, 1897).

SAXBY, H. M., *A History of Australian Children's Literature 1841–1941* (Sydney: Wentworth Books, 1969).

——*A History of Australian Children's Literature 1941–1970* (Sydney: Wentworth Books, 1971).

STEEDMAN, C., *The Tidy House* (London: Virago, 1983).

SULLY, J., *Studies of Childhood* (London: Longmans, Green, 1903).

TOLSTOY, L., *Childhood, Boyhood, Youth*, trans. R. Edmonds (Harmondsworth: Penguin, 1964).

TÖPFFER, R., *Un bouquet de lettres*, ed. L. Gautier (Lausanne: Payot, 1974).

VICO, G., *Autobiography*, trans. M. H. Frisch and T. G. Bergin (Ithaca, NY: Cornell University Press, 1944).

VODOVOSOVA, E. N., *A Russian Childhood*, trans. A. Brode and O. Lane (London: Faber & Faber, 1960).

YEATS, W. B., *Autobiographies* (London: Macmillan, 1927).

Index

Index